DISCARD

DISCARD

Chaste Liberation

THE BROOM

To and fro moves the broom
Across the room.
    With active grace,
     It seeks each place,
   While the guiding hand,
With a firm and forceful motion,
   Seems to understand,
And pay a true devotion
    To the sacred art of neatness,
    To the purity and sweetness
    That should reign in every room,
    Through the service of the broom.
Earnestly the patient broom
Seeks the shreds throughout the room . . .
    Many feet maybe have met,
    And their impress there have set.
But the broom in circling round
Makes of all one common ground.
Gathered in a centered heap,
Each with all communion keep,
Like the thoughts of men that come and go; . . .
Sweep from out the soul its selfish aiming!
Sweep away the greed of foolish gaming! . . .
    Loose the shutters, let God's sunlight enter;
Crowning conscience with her trusty broom
As she purifies the worker's room.

— Anon. *The Manifesto*
16 (May 1886): 118-19.

Chaste Liberation

CELIBACY AND
FEMALE CULTURAL STATUS

Sally L. Kitch

UNIVERSITY OF ILLINOIS PRESS
Urbana and Chicago

*Winner of the Illinois-National Women's Studies Association
Book Award*

© 1989 by the Board of Trustees of the University of Illinois
Manufactured in the United States of America
C 5 4 3 2 1

This book is printed on acid-free paper.

Library of Congress Cataloging-in-Publication Data

Kitch, Sally.
   Chaste liberation.

   Includes bibliographies and index.
   1. Celibacy.   2. Shakers—United States—History.
3. Koreshan Unity—History.   4. Woman's Commonwealth
(Belton, Tex.)—History.   I. Title.
HQ800.15.K58   1989   306.7′32   88-27928
ISBN 0-252-01608-4 (alk. paper)

To three men whose lives are exceptions to the rule analyzed herein: Tom, whose forbearance during the book's birth and rebirth sustained and anchored me, and Aaron and Justin, who kept growing in spite of everything.

CONTENTS

ACKNOWLEDGMENTS

I am indebted to many people: Professor Robert Paul of Emory University for recognizing value in the premise of this endeavor; the Woodrow Wilson Foundation for a very helpful research grant in women's studies; Professor Catharine Stimpson for encouraging the initial revision of the original work; Shaker Sisters Bertha and Gertrude (now deceased) of Canterbury and all the Shakers at Sabbathday Lake for their kind interviews and hospitality; Marlene Macracken and J. Ray Tardif for leading me to the modern home of the Woman's Commonwealth; Commonwealth Sister Martha Scheble for sharing her memories; the staff of the Winterthur Museum and Library for their supportive and efficient approach to scholarship; the jurors of the 1987 National Women's Studies Association Book Award for honoring this manuscript; and the University of Illinois Press and Carole Appel for promoting women's studies scholarship. I am especially grateful to my sisters and colleagues—especially Carol Konek, Gayle Davis, and Ginette Adamson—who commiserated and celebrated with me, and to the Women's Studies office staff at Wichita State University, especially Diane Oakes, who proofread and entered corrections into the computer—again and again. I would also like to thank the College of Liberal Arts and Sciences at W.S.U. for financial assistance with editorial costs.

INTRODUCTION

Shakerism, as seen in connection with the incoming cycle, is all rainbowed with promise, and aflame with the light and the love of God. Power does not consist in numbers. The gulf stream, in comparison with the ocean, is small; it sometimes seems as though the ocean would swallow it up; yet there it remains in the ocean, but not *of* the ocean; there it remains an everlasting river flowing steadily, bearing the choice treasures of the tropics to colder climes—changing temperatures, modifying the swift-footed winds, spreading the greater blessings of summer warmth .... So with believers, *in* the world, but not *of* the world—so with truth victorious in the end.[1]

"Truth victorious in the end . . .": those words reflect not only the sentiments of an ardent Shaker believer, but also my approach to the study of female celibacy in three utopian communities of the nineteenth century. J. M. Peebles, author of the preceding statement, was a Shaker who saw enduring truth in Shakerism, even though he realized that it would never overtake the course of mainstream American culture in which it quietly flowed. Like Peebles, I have learned to value the ideas and dreams of the Shakers and also the two other groups discussed in this work—the Koreshans and the Sanctificationists—even though the groups cannot be seen as successful or influential in mainstream American life. The cultural structures envisioned by believers in the three groups have value as theoretical rather than practical truths, and I approach those structures with less concern for their success or for their overall cultural influence than for their power as ideas.

My interest in these three groups reflects my perception that a form of feminism can be seen in Shaker, Koreshan, and Sanctificationist beliefs. The use of the term *feminism* is somewhat anachronistic when discussing these groups because believers never used it. Yet the term applies because each group, in its own way, advocated sexual equality and female economic and personal independence, as well as various forms of female power. Their support of such values, however, accompanied their acceptance of celibacy. The reliance of feminist values on celibacy may or may not have application to contemporary American life; I will consider that question later on. Yet the connection of feminist values to celibacy is of interest in today's society because of the questions it raises. The variety of forms of that connection in the documents of the three groups can also inform modern feminist debate.

In elucidating Shaker, Koreshan, and Sanctificationist beliefs, I will suspend judgment about the groups' successes in, and influences upon, mainstream society and focus instead upon their ideals for a celibate society. Even if imperfectly realized, such utopian visions can challenge familiar cultural constructs and suggest new logic and new theoretical premises on which to base new visions of cultural change. Therefore, whether influential or not, the principles of celibate feminism evident in these groups may become catalysts for a new understanding of women's place in human culture. I leave to others the task of explicating in depth each group's failures and condemning their hidden hypocrisies.[2] My specific concern will be to analyze the alternative cultural designs envisioned by each group rather than to describe or criticize specific practices or behaviors.

THE GROUPS COMPARED

The three communities can be compared because of common threads of belief that connect them. Within varied frameworks, Shaker, Koreshan, and Sanctificationist believers shared several insights, including the identification of celibacy as the key symbol of their societies. They also shared a religious motivation for their beliefs in celibacy and in female spiritual power. The groups are further linked by their extensions of celibate symbolism to economic and familial domains.

As a premise for human society, celibacy acquires meaning because it contrasts so markedly with the centrality in most societies of heterosexual intercourse and reproduction. As it does today, heterosexual intercourse had associations in nineteenth-century mainstream America with the nuclear family, with the private ownership of property and the means of production, with capitalism and the class system, as well as with the separation of the sexes, female subordination to males, and a lack of female political, social, and economic power. The substitution of celibacy for sex in a pivotal symbolic position promoted alternatives to each of those associations for Shaker, Koreshan, and Sanctificationist believers. For them, celibacy implied communal familial and economic systems, unified social classes, and, most important to this discussion, equality along with genuine, spiritual (rather than false, physical) unity of males and females. The female celibate was also given a privileged spiritual status in each of the cultural systems. Because of her new symbolic identity, which contrasted dramatically with the identity and role prescriptions for sexually active women in mainstream culture, the celibate female can be seen to embody certain values considered feminist by today's standards.

Having merged the theoretical perspectives of the three groups to compare them with mainstream culture, it is also necessary to recognize their differences. One difference is the composition of the groups: the Shakers and Koreshans were mixed-sex groups, whereas the Sanctification membership was predominantly female. That distinction alters the meaning of celibacy, particularly in female-female relationships, in the achievement of a specifically female form of social power. Other differences include the relative seriousness and longevity of the groups, as well as the relative volume of material available from which to extract the groups' cultural ideals. The disparity in number of sources for the three groups results in their disparate treatment in this book. The Shakers almost inevitably become a kind of standard by which the other groups are understood. These differences also require the bracketing of some historical concerns such as the "importance" of the groups, and the varied amounts of interpretation required for understanding the less-documented communities. Although these are concerns, they are not necessarily obstacles to an interesting and useful comparison of ideas and ideals in the three groups.

Selecting a specific time period, 1870-1910, within which to compare the groups has ensured a consistent temporal context for this analysis. The selection also presents some difficulties, however.[3] Although all groups were active during the period, those decades represent a period of decline in membership for the Shakers, whereas they represent peak levels of membership for the other two groups. That difference would be a greater obstacle if my intent were to characterize the essence of Shakerism (a futile goal in any case) or to discuss Shaker belief during a particularly characteristic period of their history. Although the temporal framework does distort Shakerism by focusing on a period of struggle for the group, that very struggle for survival drove Shaker believers to explain themselves to the outside world. Such explanations provide systematic articulations of the very arguments I seek — the theoretical linkage between celibacy and female status.

Differences in the size of the three groups also present a problem of interpretation. Among other things, the large size of the Shaker membership makes problematic any assumption of unanimity among believers on any issue or ideal. In fact, dissent has been documented for all periods of Shaker history. Because the writers I use as references were allowed to represent the community to the public, however, their views can be assumed to be at least representative of those of other believers. Because of their smaller sizes and the public's more limited knowledge of the Sanctificationists and Koreshans, greater consensus among believers can be more safely assumed (although there may well have been undocumented disagreements among Koreshan and Sanctificationist believers). Because I focus on publicly stated beliefs, however, this discussion is confined to expressed and published ideals; I leave it to others to ferret out dissent.

I will not resist the temptation to judge the relevance to modern feminism of the ideas of the three groups. Some goals in the groups' beliefs can certainly be regarded as feminist in modern terms. Believers in all groups shared a contempt for notions of female inferiority and argued for equality, at the very least, in the economic and social rights of men and women.[4] By supporting those ideals, they actually surpassed some of their mainstream feminist contemporaries. The last chapter will discuss whether the believers' visions surpass, reflect, or contradict those of modern feminism.

METHODOLOGY AND TERMINOLOGY

I have approached these three utopian groups as subcultures that were both independent of and interdependent with the mainstream

4

culture of their day. My identification of the Shakers, Koreshans, and Sanctificationists as subcultures reflects the observation of Claude Lévi-Strauss that a "culture can be considered as a complex of symbolic systems, in which language, the rules of matrimony, economic relations, art, science, and religion rank foremost. All these systems aim at expressing certain aspects of both physical reality and social reality, as well as the relations which these two types of reality maintain between them and that the symbolic systems themselves maintain with one another."[5] Even though the Shakers, Koreshans, and Sanctificationists were dependent in many ways upon the mainstream, each does represent a discreet cultural entity with distinct approaches to the items on Lévi-Strauss's list of symbolic concerns, including matrimonial rules (family), economic relations (work), and religion.

In Lévi-Strauss's view, beliefs and ideas within a particular culture can be interpreted as parts of an overall system of symbolic representation, often discernible in language, that forms a web of significance in that culture. He refers to that web of significance as a "symbolic system." The interrelationships of meaning that contribute to a symbolic system in a given culture are rarely explicit; order and systematic meaning must be inferred from words and behavior. In this process, the observed reality—the facts—are not necessarily the cultural reality—the meaning—at all.

I have extrapolated the symbolic systems of each of the groups primarily from documents written and published by believers or from recorded testimonies. Such documents—articles, broadsides, pamphlets, periodicals, books, and interview transcripts—provide the linguistic evidence of the symbolic level of the three cultures. I have found in such documents that celibacy is discussed as a variation on the themes of family and matrimonial rules in the groups' symbolic structures. Celibacy also appears as a key symbol for the conceptualization of social and cultural organization and purpose for each group. Further, celibacy stands in important symbolic relationship to ideals of sexual equality, sexual unity, and female spiritual power envisioned by the groups.

The identification of celibacy as a key symbol refers to an anthropological term, defined by scholars as an image, object, or figure of speech crucial to the distinctive organization of a given culture. The "keyness" of particular symbols—such as the sword and the chrysanthemum, which Ruth Benedict selected as key symbols of Japanese culture — can be determined by the extent to which cultural ideas are predicated upon, and make sense only in the context of, the meanings of those symbols.[6]

Most relevant to the symbolic analysis of the three groups in this work is the category of key symbol defined by scholars as the "key conceptual, elaborating symbol," which expresses a culture's conceptual framework for bringing order to the universe. Contributing to the elaborating key symbol are "root metaphors" and "key scenarios" that serve, respectively, as the "basic mechanism" of the symbol and "formulate the culture's basic means-ends relationships in actable forms." Among primitive peoples, the color patterns of particular animals or of the natural surroundings can serve as root metaphors for the perception of all color and light. In the United States, the stories of Horatio Alger encapsulate a key scenario of the kind of success allegedly possible in capitalist society.[7]

As a key symbol of the Shaker, Koreshan, and Sanctificationist cultural systems, celibacy contrasts with heterosexual intercourse, which can be identified as a key symbol of mainstream American culture. In each system, the key symbol stands at the summit of a veritable mountain of other symbolism involving the major cultural areas or domains of family, work, and religion. Also implicated in each system is the symbolism of gender — the cultural meanings given to biological sex. Celibacy within the systems of these groups has symbolic associations with communal economic and familial structures, whereas heterosexual intercourse in American culture promotes privacy in family and economic matters. The symbolism of heterosexual intercourse in American culture also associates special responsibilities for childcare and domestic work with woman's role in reproduction. Celibacy, on the other hand, alters woman's relationship to reproduction, thereby associating her with production and leadership rather than with consumption and submission.

HISTORICAL MEANINGS OF FEMALE CELIBACY

An association of celibacy with female freedom and sexual equality by the Shakers, Koreshans, and Sanctificationists is not unique in history. Some Shaker writers apparently knew of this historical association in the Judeo-Christian tradition. They recognized that long before the nineteenth century, celibate women escaped marriage and motherhood and thereby achieved independence, heightened status in spiritual matters relative to men, and even social or familial power.

At least as early as the Roman Empire, women embraced celibacy as the only alternative, other than prostitution, to the authority of fathers and husbands. Like Paul and other male leaders, Christian women became or remained celibate primarily to achieve spiritual purity and to free themselves for a spiritual life, but their decision also elevated them to a status within the church that was unavailable to sexually active and reproductive women.

Even in the earliest centuries of Christianity, female celibacy challenged the premises of male dominance by eroding the sexual and reproductive bases of gender difference. Some church fathers found virginal celibates particularly threatening. Clement, for example, warned men to avoid contact with unmarried (virgin) women because they might prove to be a special temptation. Tertullian preferred celibate women who had been married—and had, therefore, " 'travelled down the whole course of probation whereby a female can be tested' "—to virgins. The latters' lifelong independence weakened the grounds for classifying them as females. In fact, uncertainty about whether or not unmarried, virgin women could be considered female led to the fear that such women might have to be treated as men and, therefore, as equals to men in the church hierarchy. As late as the second century, marriage and a sexual identity were the keys to establishing a Christian woman's inferiority to men.[8]

Celibacy has not automatically or always ensured the improvement of female status or independence, however. It is debatable whether Catholic nuns have ever been the equals of celibate monks or priests. In the Protestant experience, experiments with celibacy have also been only occasionally related to feminist goals. American celibate utopians, such as those at Ephrata, New Jerusalem, Amana, Zoar, and Harmony, did not necessarily combine the ideal of celibacy with feminist or egalitarian goals in any domain—family, work, or religion. Few offered leadership or decision-making authority to women. But it is worthy of note that none of these groups considered celibacy as important to group organization as did the Shakers, Koreshans, and Sanctificationists. The Inspirationists of Amana are a good example of this difference. Organized in 1843 at Ebenezer, New York, by Christian Metz and transported to Iowa in the 1850s, Amanans were well known for their celibate doctrine. They diluted the importance of celibacy in their system, however, by tolerating marriage for those members who did not wish to enter into the highest ranks of their social structure.[9] Amanan doctrine also disparaged women and warned male believers to "fly from the society of women-kind as much as possible, as a very highly dangerous magnet and magical fire."[10] After the move to Iowa, even celibate members lived in nuclear family settings.[11]

The failure of such groups to combine their commitment to celibacy with ideas of sexual equality or with designs for alternative family forms that might reduce female subordination does not diminish the importance of the three celibate groups examined here, however. Nor does this failure by other groups detract from the cultural models represented by the cultural systems of the three groups.

The Three Groups Described

I selected the Shakers, the Koreshans, and the Sanctificationists precisely because texts by and about them reveal a connection of celibacy with sexual equality and with enhanced female cultural status. Documents from the groups outline new visions of female gender identity and redefine male-female relationships through celibacy. In short, the ideals of these groups suggest that celibacy can revise what it means to be female. Although celibacy also inevitably recasts male gender identity, I shall focus on that change only tangentially; women and female roles will be my primary subjects. (The quotations that begin chapters 1-5 are taken from the poem "The Broom.")

The Shakers

The most familiar and largest group of the three under study is the United Society of Believers in Christ's Second Appearing, known as the Shakers because of the vigorous dancing characteristic of their early religious rituals. The group was founded in England by Ann Lee, the illiterate daughter of working-class parents. Lee brought a small band of followers to the American colonies in 1774, following a divine revelation that the New World would be more receptive to her beliefs than had the Old. Unfortunately, tolerance was not always what believers encountered in the New York Colony, where they settled. The colonists accused the Shakers of treason because they would not take up arms, even in the Revolutionary War. People harassed them—sometimes violently—for their controversial beliefs, particularly their concept of a dual-gendered (or bisexual) God and their identification of Lee as the female Christ Spirit, as well as a temporal religious leader.

The communistic form of Shaker organization began at Watervliet (then called Niskeyuna) near Albany, New York, in 1776. Groups of believers at Watervliet and at nearby New Lebanon (then called Mt. Lebanon) formed official Shaker communities in 1787. New Lebanon later became the site of the Central Ministry, the governing umbrella organization for all Shaker communities that developed throughout the next century. The Shakers were (and are) proud that their Society is as old as the American nation itself. They have always seen theirs as a parallel culture to the American mainstream.

Ann Lee died in 1784, and her death initially inspired the expansion of Shakerism. A total of nineteen communities in a half-dozen states were established between 1776 and 1826, and another ten branches, "out-families," and short-lived communities rose and fell between the 1780s and the mid-1900s.[12] By 1891, however, only fifteen communities remained, following a decline in membership after the Civil War. There were 3,608 Shakers in 1840; 3,489 in 1860; 1,849 in 1880; but only 855 in 1900.[13] Scholars speculate that changes in the spiritual and economic atmosphere of the United States after the Civil War contributed to the reduction in Shaker membership. Urbanization and new technology rendered Shaker forms of manufacturing obsolete. Other reasons for the decline include the weakening of discipline and leadership and the merging of temporal and spiritual offices in Shaker communities.[14] There is no evidence that the weakening of discipline included laxity in the commitment to celibacy, however. Worldliness seems to have been a greater threat to Shaker doctrine than sex.

At present, two populated communities still function, one at Canterbury, New Hampshire, and one at Sabbathday Lake, Maine.[15] Today, the number of legitimate Shakers is a matter of some debate; at best, only a dozen or so remain. But a few Shakers do still remain, and following a pattern established by 1840, the women continue to outnumber the men.[16]

By the late nineteenth century, many Shaker writers advocated sexual equality at almost every level of the Shaker social structure. The ideal of an egalitarian society was reflected in their organizational design. Men and women shared the large communal houses, in groups known as "families," within each community. They ate at separate tables in common rooms, and they slept apart at different ends of the houses in order to avoid sexual temptation. The sharing of the houses and communities was an important part of their mixed-sex social ideal, however. To that same end, families and communities were governed by elders and eldresses, deacons and deaconesses, and other sex-balanced pairs of leaders. Men and women were instructed to play different but equally valued roles in work and worship. Interaction of the sexes in these roles was permissible but restricted in order to avoid all risk of sexuality.

After 1870, progressive leaders such as Frederick Evans reinterpreted the Shaker theory of celibacy as a premise for an even more aggressive commitment to the equal status of the sexes and the assignment of greater responsibility to women, particularly in economic matters. In fact, the period under study — 1870-1900 — can be regarded as a kind of renaissance in Shaker thought on the question of female social and religious status, even if it was not a renaissance in terms of membership.[17]

The Koreshans

The Koreshans, whose official organizational title was the Koreshan Unity, shared the Shaker belief in the dual sex of God (although there were differences) and supported female political and economic rights, both within the community and without. Although men and women probably played somewhat different roles in the community, Koreshan ideals promoted the obliteration of sexual differences, even physical ones, and envisioned the ultimate fusion of male and female characteristics in an androgynous being. Such views coexisted with a number of pseudoscientific claims about the nature of the universe that stretch credulity. But Koreshan texts do provide theoretical support for a connection of celibacy to ideals of sexual unity and equality, as well as for a temporary form of female spiritual power on the road to the elimination of sexual difference. Therefore, the Koreshan symbolic system deserves attention.

The Koreshan Unity was founded in the mid-1880s in Chicago by a physician, Cyrus R. Teed (who renamed himself "Koresh"), although Teed's inspiration for the group had occurred some years earlier. In 1894, Teed acquired land from William T. Dodd in Lee County, Florida, near Estero and Fort Myers, and he began to plan his ideal community.[18] By 1903, most of his Chicago followers had joined him in Florida, and they proceeded to build what they called "New Jerusalem, world capitol of the Koreshan system."[19] The city Koresh envisioned was to occupy multiple levels in order to accommodate varying kinds of traffic; the electromagnetic currents of earth and air would provide power; and the economy would function without money. Teed also predicted that the population would climb to eight or ten million. None of these elaborate visions materialized, however. The population of the community peaked in 1903 at a mere two hundred. For most of the community's existence—from incorporation in 1904 until Teed's death in 1908—membership averaged about forty people.[20]

The Koreshans were the only one of the three groups under discussion to be founded and led by a man, a fact that mitigates, but does not eliminate, theoretical benefits for the celibate female in the Koreshan system. Like the Shakers, Teed envisioned a bisexual God and prescribed a sex-balanced structure of governance. The organizational plan placed him in the role of male Pre-Eminent and called for a female Pre-Eminent as his counterpart. Annie Ordway (also known as Victoria Gratia), a Chicago follower, was selected by Teed for that position. The two Pre-Eminents were allegedly subject to the higher authority of a three-member Pre-Eminent Concilium. Other vaguely defined bodies, such as the Planetary Chamber, Stellar Chamber, and Signet Chamber, were also supposed to contribute to the group's governance. Some of the governance subgroups were designed to include equal numbers of men and women. The functions of other, all-female, groups were allegedly meant to balance those of the all-male groups.

Evidently Ordway did exert some power. She even tried to keep the community in St. Petersburg after Teed's death. The group's accumulated debts overwhelmed her efforts, however, and she was ultimately unsuccessful.[21] Some women probably did live in the city's all-female Planetary House. Overall, however, there is little evidence that any Koreshans other than Teed either wielded power or functioned in their designated roles.[22]

After 1909, when Ordway's efforts to save the community failed, most Koreshans either drifted away or aged and died in Estero. A few male Koreshans founded the Order of Theocracy and ran Fort Myers's largest laundry until the 1930s.[23] Hedwig Michel, a German-Jewish immigrant who joined the group in the 1940s, when there were still about thirty-five members, became president of the Unity in 1961. She was responsible for having the Florida property preserved as a state-run nature conservatory in the 1960s and as a historic site in 1976. She also revived a Koreshan paper, the *American Eagle*, first published in 1906, and published it for many years before her death, at age ninety, in 1982.[24] Although no Koreshans reside on the property, it is now run as a park. A board of directors still functions, overseeing the park, the library, and the publication of the *American Eagle*. Koresh's birthday is celebrated as a solar festival, and Ordway's as a lunar festival.

The Sanctificationists

The Sanctificationists, whose community was renamed the Woman's Commonwealth in 1898, became an official community in 1890 in Belton, Texas. The Commonwealth was essentially a single-sex community, as much by accident as by design, throughout its history. The group's original nickname, "The Sanctificationists," or sanctified sisters, was originally coined by critical townspeople as a derisive reference to the putatively sanctified bread sold by sisters in the early days.[25] The name also described the major feature of the religious conversion required for membership in the group. The women themselves referred to their community as the Sanctified Church or simply the church.

By the time the sisters gathered into an official community, they had already worshiped, worked, and lived together for many years. Their founder, Martha McWhirter, was a member of the Methodist church and believed in the Wesleyan doctrine of entire sanctification. Because of certain tragedies in her own life, however, she associated sanctification, bestowed on her by divine revelation, as a commitment to celibacy. Her unorthodox version of Methodism also included ecumenism. Neither celibacy nor ecumenism was popular in Belton. The former effectively terminated the marriages of McWhirter and her followers. The latter eventually alienated the group from the Methodist church that spawned their ideas. Both tenets caused the estrangement of the sisters from Belton townspeople for many years.

The transformation of the small group of believers into a community was precipitated by McWhirter's attempt, in about 1867, to establish an ecumenical Union Sunday School in the Methodist church. Other women who considered themselves similarly sanctified joined her crusade. By 1879, so many of the women had been either divorced or estranged from their husbands because of their beliefs that the formation of a commune became necessary for the women's economic survival. By 1880, the group had fifty members. By 1891, membership had dropped to thirty-two, and it continued to dwindle. The last member died in 1983.[26]

The 1902 incorporation of the Commonwealth followed the 1891 incorporation of the Central Hotel Company, the culmination of several boardinghouses, hotels, and other businesses owned and operated by the women in Belton and Waco, Texas, during the preceding twenty years. Their Central Hotel in Belton was still known as the "earliest and most successful venture of women into business activity in the state of Texas" in 1929, thirty-one years after the sisters had moved to Washington, D.C.[27] With their profits, the group purchased a large home in that city in 1898. They were reluctant to go back into the boardinghouse or hotel business there, but they were prepared to do so if necessary. Shortly thereafter, they also purchased land in Montgomery County, Maryland, which they farmed in a modest way and used as a retreat. Later they built a larger house on the property, which they planned to use as a retirement home.[28] The charismatic McWhirter died in 1904, but the surviving members continued their community until death claimed them. The last member, Martha Scheble, was living on the Maryland property when she died in 1983, at age 101. The house has since been sold.

The Sanctificationists left fewer public documents describing their views of celibate culture than did the Shakers or the Koreshans. Their understanding of celibacy as a catalyst for redefining female gender identity, as well as for establishing unity and equality between the sexes, can be extrapolated from the few documents that are available, however. Although they left no record of a belief in either a female God or a female Christ, court testimonies, interviews, and the group's constitution reveal a feminist approach not only to the economic and social independence of women from men, and to the personal autonomy of individual women, but also to a female-identified source of spiritual authority. As in the other groups, the women's understanding of celibacy as a key cultural symbol is basic to all of those ideals.

Although I did not realize it as I selected these groups for their views, all three interacted with one another. Cyrus Teed was made an honorary Shaker, although the Shakers found him rather strange. Martha McWhirter corresponded with Teed and actually went to Chicago in 1892. No formal alliance occurred between the groups, but there was interest in such a move between the Sanctificationists and the Koreshans for a short time. Two Koreshans stayed with the sanctified sisters for about nine months in 1891, but they failed to associate. In 1893, several other Koreshans came to Belton; one woman stayed four years. Two Shaker men from New Hampshire joined the sisters briefly in 1893. They soon decided they "could not come under a woman's rule," however, and left.[29] Two other Shaker men lived for a time in the Commonwealth in about 1903.

A NOTE ON SOURCES

To carry out this study, I endeavored to create comparable bodies of materials for the three groups that would yield sufficient evidence of their symbolic systems. As already indicated, the written records of the Shakers, Koreshans, and Sanctificationists are uneven in quantity. The Shakers produced an abundance of published and manuscript sources. The Koreshans were equally productive, at least of published work, but publications cover a much shorter period and were less sophisticated. The Sanctificationists, however, published nothing, with the exception of their constitution, which was printed in 1902.[30] Texts of interviews and McWhirter's testimony at her daughter's divorce proceedings, as well as an anonymous manuscript about McWhirter's "Life and Spiritual Experience," are available, however.

Because of the disparity in size and quality of the public sources, the Shakers dominate this analysis. In order to construct the cultural

14

systems of the groups, I have had to do more extrapolation for the Koreshans and the Sanctificationists than for the Shakers. The familiarity of most readers with the Shakers may also contribute to a Shaker bias. In spite of these factors, however, I have constructed as coherent a cultural system for each group as the sources would allow. I believe that conclusions about each community have separate, as well as comparative, validity.

In order to produce comparability in the analyses, I have followed three strategies. First, I have focused on public sources, which are available for all three groups. Such sources were designed to describe or argue group ideals for nonbelieving audiences. Thus, they are also most likely to contain the groups' ideals, which are my interest.

Second, I have restricted the analysis to the period from 1870 through 1900. (I have occasionally included earlier Shaker works when they are clear premises for later views.) All three groups flourished during these decades, and, although their selection eliminates many Shaker sources, they represent a period of high Shaker productivity. The years 1870-1900 also represent a time during which the Shakers were most articulate about the connection of celibacy with the ideals of sexual equality. Although earlier Shaker texts reveal less enthusiasm for feminist ideas, that fact does not diminish the later associations—consistent with later historical developments—that distinguish the texts on which I shall focus.[31]

Finally, the symbolic technique I have used in this study is itself a common denominator that produces comparability among the groups. The identification of celibacy as a commonly held key symbol provides a means for interpreting texts and actions in similar terms, including root metaphors, scenarios, and other forms of symbolic expression. Because none of the groups articulated explicit cultural theory, I used texts and testimonies concerning other topics—including general theology, female qualities in God and Christ, social and economic theory, gender roles and characteristics, female celibacy in particular, and, of course, celibacy in general—as the bases for my construction of each group's cultural symbolism.

Shaker Sources

The decades covered here are those in which Shaker publications, intended for "the world," proliferated. Their pages were filled with the writing of many prominent Shakers of the day, including Elder Frederick W. Evans, whose long life (1808-93) was devoted to many kinds of writing, including Jacksonian papers as well as Shaker works.[32] An emigrant from England in 1820, Evans joined the New Lebanon Shaker community in 1830. He and Eldress Antoinette Doolittle, also of New Lebanon, edited the *Shaker and Shakeress,* the Society's first periodical, published between 1873 and 1875. Both Evans and Doolittle were known as liberals because they advocated the inalienable right of citizens to land, equal rights for women both in Shaker communities and in the mainstream, equal education for both sexes, the abolition of capitalism, and a closer association of Shakers and outsiders.[33] Their views became more influential as more conservative leaders died.

Another important progressive writer of the period was Elder Henry Blinn of the Canterbury and Enfield communities in New Hampshire. Blinn joined the Shakers in 1832 at age fourteen, and he devoted the next sixty years to writing, editing, and typesetting Shaker texts.[34] Blinn edited another Shaker periodical, *The Manifesto,* toward the end of the century.

William Leonard, an elder of the Harvard, Massachusetts, community wrote all of his important works before the decades of this book's emphasis. He died before 1880, and his principal work, *A Disclosure on the Order and Propriety of Divine Inspiration and Revelation,* was published in 1853. Many of Leonard's works were reprinted in later years, however; one as recently as 1904. Therefore, his work can be seen as influential during the decades examined here.[35]

Anna White and Leila Taylor, two of the most influential women writers of any period in Shaker history, were both eldresses at New Lebanon during the decades of this study. Considered progressive and liberal as well, they wrote the last major Shaker public statement, *Shakerism: Its Meaning and Message,* in 1904. White, who also wrote frequently for Shaker periodicals, was a lifelong advocate of women's rights and one of Lucretia Mott's supporters.[36] Equally influential was Elder Daniel Fraser, an immigrant from Scotland, who joined the New Lebanon Shakers in the 1830s as an alternative to his original intention to found a workers' community of his own.

Bishop Harvey Eads, a member of the South Union, Kentucky,

community for eighty-four years, was another major writer. Eads, born to a recent Shaker convert in 1807, believed in the rigorous separation of the Shakers from the world. He was a conservative counterpart to the liberal Evans (although some of his views on equality and women resemble Evans's), and the two writers occasionally sparred in print. Several historians have considered him to be a spokesperson not only for the conservative view, but also for that of the Western Shaker societies.[37]

I have also utilized the works of Eldress Aurelia Mace of Sabbathday Lake, Elder Giles Avery of New Lebanon, Elder James Prescott of North Union, Kentucky, and Alonzo Hollister of New Lebanon. Mace wrote *The Aletheia* in 1899, and Hollister, who lived from 1830 to 1911, was a dedicated scribe of Shaker documents, as well as a scholar and writer himself.[38]

The work of Calvin Green and Seth Y. Wells survived through reprinting well into the late century. Their *Brief Exposition of the Established Principles of the United Society of Believers, Called Shakers* was originally published in 1830, but it was revised and reprinted until 1895. It can therefore be seen as significant in the period under discussion. The 1879 revision cited here is a reprint of a version originally completed before Green's death in 1869.

The 1870s through 1900 were also the prime decades of the Society's major periodicals. The *Shaker and Shakeress* became *The Shaker* in 1876. In 1877, the title was again changed, this time to *The Shaker Manifesto,* and its publication continued until 1882. The next year it became *The Manifesto.* That title was retained until the publication of all Shaker periodicals was suspended for the century in 1899. The elucidation of the relationship of celibacy to other aspects of Shaker culture is an important and recurring theme. In those periodicals, one can see some variations among the writers, but there is a surprising consensus on many of the key ideas. Perhaps the later writers, like those of earlier periods, strove to shape their experience according to dominant metaphors and symbolic expressions of their time.[39] Although no picture of Shaker theory at any particular period is completely consistent, research reveals that the views presented here were major and very likely dominated the thinking, if not the practice, of many Shakers during the late nineteenth century.

Koreshan Sources

The years from 1870 to 1900 were clearly critical in the formulation of Koreshan theory. Koresh's revelation led him to proselytize during the 1870s. *The Guiding Star,* the first Koreshan periodical, was published in the 1880s, and *The Flaming Sword* was published after 1889. Editions of *The Flaming Sword* published after Teed's death consist primarily of reprints of earlier material. Koresh, who was the major spokesperson for the group, produced his important printed works between 1896 and 1900. O. F. L'Amoreaux and several Koreshan women also wrote during those decades. As among the Shakers, most Koreshan followers were women. Several wrote for the group's publications, including Annie Ordway, A. M. Miller, and Lucie Page Borden. All of them came with Teed to Florida from Chicago. Although these writers made important contributions, it is clear from many of their texts that they considered Koresh to be the authority on Koreshanity and saw themselves primarily as translators of his beliefs rather than as espousers of their own theories.

Sanctificationist Sources

The period from the 1870s through 1900 was a particularly active one for the Woman's Commonwealth. The unofficial community was formed in 1879, and its incorporation took place in 1890. Important court records date from the 1880s. Newspaper and magazine coverage of the group in Belton, and later in Washington, D.C., spans from about 1882 to 1908. An unpublished, typewritten manuscript, probably written sometime after 1900 by one of the sisters, has recently been uncovered among Martha Scheble's papers and has been used in this book. The most scholarly and reliable secondary source from the group's active period is an article published in 1893 by the University of Texas historian George Garrison. Interviews with McWhirter were conducted and published by A. H. Mattox and by other magazine and newspaper reporters from 1901 to 1902. The group's constitution was printed in 1902. These public sources have made it possible to quote McWhirter and some of her followers directly and to extrapolate the group's ideas on various relevant topics.

NOTES

1. J. M. Peebles, "Nihilism—Socialism—Shakerism—Which?" *The Manifesto* 10 (April 1880): 89.

2. The revelation of such inconsistencies is one of the goals of Priscilla Brewer's *Shaker Communities, Shaker Lives* (Hanover, N.H.: University Press of New England, 1986).

3. The confinement to a limited time period presents some problems with Shaker theory if one is looking for a longitudinal study of Shaker attitudes toward celibacy and its relation to feminist ideals. That is not the purpose of the present study; it will not trace the development of Shaker ideas over the entire nineteenth century. Even within the time period selected, I can only discuss representative views because there was no single officially sanctioned Shaker doctrine or system of belief.

4. In her book about Shaker spiritual symbolism, Marjorie Proctor-Smith does not consider Shaker practice to be feminist, although she concedes both that Shaker theory had feminist intent and that Shaker women were more liberated than were most of their mainstream counterparts. The focus of Procter-Smith's work is the early nineteenth century, however, so her conclusions need not be seen as necessarily contradictory to those in this work. See *Women in Shaker Community and Worship: A Feminist Analysis of the Uses of Religious Symbolism,* vol. 16, Studies in Women and Religion (Lewiston, N.Y.: Edwin Mellen Press, 1985), pp. x, 66-67, 208, 223.

5. Claude Lévi-Strauss, "Introduction à l'oeuvre de Marcel Mauss," in Marcel Mauss, *Sociologie et Anthropologie* (1950; repr. Paris: Presses Universitaire de France, 1973), p. xix. The original French: "Toute culture peut-être considéré comme un ensemble de systèmes symbolique au premier rang desquels se placent le langage, les règles matrimoniales, les rapports économiques, l'art, la science, la réligion. Tous ces systèmes visent exprimer certains aspects de la réalité physique et de la réalité sociale, et plus encore les relations que ces deux types de réalité entretiennent entre eux et que les systèmes symboliques eux-mêmes entretiennent les uns avec les autres."

6. Sherry B. Ortner, "On Key Symbols," *American Anthropologist* 75 (1973): 1338-40.

7. Ortner, "On Key Symbols," pp. 1340-41.

8. JoAnn McNamara, *A New Song: Celibate Women in the First Three Christian Centuries* (New York: Haworth Press, 1983), pp. 53-55, 57, 109.

9. Raymond Muncy, *Sex and Marriage in Utopian Communities in Nineteenth-Century America* (Bloomington: Indiana University Press,

1973), p. 98; Charles Nordhoff, *The Communistic Societies of the United States: From Personal Visit and Observation* (1875; repr. New York: Dover Publications, 1966), p. 52. Koreshans did discuss limiting the ideal of celibacy to those in the inner circles, or Ecclesia. But Koreshan theory excluded noncelibates so completely that the Koreshans do not really belong in the same category as the Amanans. See Elliott J. Mackle, "The Koreshan Unity in Florida, 1894-1910" (master's thesis, University of Miami, 1971), p. 35.

    10. Nordhoff, *Communistic Societies of United States,* pp. 51, 53.

    11. Ibid., p. 30; Muncy, *Sex and Marriage,* p. 100.

    12. Edward D. Andrews, *The People Called Shakers* (New York: Dover Publications, 1963), pp. 57, 290-92.

    13. William Sims Bainbridge, "Shaker Demographics, 1840-1900," *Journal for the Scientific Study of Religion* 21 (1982): 355.

    14. Brewer, *Shaker Communities,* pp. 178-85.

    15. For a discussion of the controversy over membership that has arisen in the twentieth century, see Edward R. Horgan, *The Shaker Holy Land: A Community Portrait* (Harvard, Mass.: Harvard Common Press), pp. 181-86. In her study of the Shakers, D'Ann Campbell has discovered that women outnumbered men in all age groups. Adult women never comprised less than 56 percent of community member-ship. During the childbearing ages of twenty to forty-four, women outnumbered men two to one. See D'Ann Campbell, "Women's Life in Utopia: The Shaker Experiment in Sexual Equality Reappraised—1810-1860," *New England Quarterly* 51 (March 1978): 29n.

    16. Bainbridge, "Shaker Demographics," p. 360. Bainbridge points out that Shaker women comprised almost 58 percent of the Shaker population in 1840, whereas women comprised only 49 percent of the general white population of the United States. By 1900, Shaker women comprised 72 percent of the Shaker population, while the percentage of women in the general white population remained at 49.

    17. Brewer, *Shaker Communities,* pp. 189-93.

    18. Howard D. Fine, "The Koreshan Unity: The Chicago Years of a Utopian Community," *Illinois State Historical Society Journal* 48 (June 1975): 225.

    19. Mackle, "The Koreshan Unity in Florida," p. 35.

    20. For a detailed description of the political battles between Ko-reshans and other citizens of Lee County, see Elliott Mackle, "Cyrus Teed and the County Elections of 1906," *Florida Historical Quarterly* 52 (July 1978): 1-18; R. Lyn Rainard, "Conflict Inside the Earth: The Koreshan Unity in Lee County," *Tampa Bay History* 3 (1981): 5-16; and G. M. Herbert and I. S. K. Reeves, V, *Koreshan Unity Settlement:*

1894-1977, restoration study for Department of National Resources, Division of Recreation and Parks, 1977, p. 39. Ordway also used the name Victoria Gratia, which was her Koreshan name, just as Koresh was Teed's.

21. Mackle, "Koreshan Unity in Florida," p. 148.

22. Ibid., pp. 46-47, 58, 70-73, 98; Herbert and Reeves, *Koreshan Unity Settlement,* p. 33.

23. Mackle, "Koreshan Unity in Florida," p. 148.

24. Telephone interview with Elliott Mackle, July 31, 1984. See also Fine, "Koreshan Unity," p. 227; Jeff Leen, "New College Is Planned by Hollow World Order," *Miami Herald,* April 10, 1983; Kay Smith, "Koreshan Festival Focused on Women," Naples (Florida) *Daily News,* April 11, 1983.

25. "The Washington Capital," George Pierce Garrison Papers, Barker Texas History Center, the General Libraries, the University of Texas at Austin. Although the group was not called the Woman's Commonwealth until 1898, for convenience I will use that term to refer to them throughout their history.

26. George Pierce Garrison, "A Woman's Community in Texas," *The Charities Review* 3 (November 1893): 41-42.

27. John R. Lumsford, "Story of Women's Hotel One of Most Interesting in Life of Historic Belton," Temple (Texas) *Telegram,* November 24, 1929, George Pierce Garrison Papers.

28. "Married First Man She Met," Gatesville (Texas) *Star-Messenger,* April 24, 1908, George Pierce Garrison Papers.

29. "The Life and Spiritual Experience of Martha McWhirter Leader and Founder of the Woman's Commonwealth. Also a History of this People and Her Connection with them," n.p., n.d, pp. 16 and 20 (typewritten on U.S. Department of Interior stationery marked "confidential"). This paper was probably written by Margarita Gerry.

30. I was the first scholar to discover the existence of this constitution. Martha Scheble, the last member of the Sanctificationists, allowed me to reproduce her copy during an interview in 1983.

31. See Marjorie Procter-Smith, *Women in Shaker Community and Worship.* I would dispute Procter-Smith's overall judgment about early nineteenth-century Shakers as weak advocates of feminist ideals, however. I think she fails to distinguish Shaker attitudes about unredeemed men and women, still subject to the curse of Adam and Eve, and redeemed Shaker believers. Even she equivocates about that judgment on occasion and recognizes that Shaker women surpassed their mainstream sisters in rights and power (see especially pp. 61-62).

32. Although scholars consider Evans to be an exception among

Shaker believers, he was clearly influential in his role as spokesperson for Shaker beliefs. At any rate, his articulation of the relationship between celibacy and women's rights is reason enough for his repeated inclusion in this work.

33. Andrews, *People Called Shakers,* pp. 232-35.

34. Ibid., p. 109.

35. Diane Sasson, *The Shaker Spiritual Narrative* (Knoxville: University of Tennessee Press, 1983), p. 117.

36. Lelia S. Taylor, ed., *A Memorial to Eldress Anna White and Elder Daniel Offord* (Mt. Lebanon, N.Y.: North Family of Shakers, 1912), n.p.n. See also Brewer, *Shaker Communities,* p. 200.

37. Andrews, *People Called Shakers,* p. 109. In spite of his reputation as a conservative, however, Eads's work was often supportive of sexual equality, communism, and other theories advocated by Evans and other liberals. Perhaps the dividing lines are not as clear as they seem.

38. Sasson, *Shaker Spiritual Narrative,* pp. 84-89.

39. Ibid., pp. 19-20, 65.

· 1 ·

SEX AND SEPARATION:
THE AMERICAN WAY

"The thoughts of men that come and go"

In order to understand celibacy as a symbolic reversal of heterosexual intercourse, one must first understand the symbolic system of intercourse itself, for it is in light of heterosexual symbolism that theories of celibacy acquire much of their symbolic meaning. Without attempting an exhaustive survey of the historical and anthropological evidence, this chapter will establish the symbolic underpinnings of the American system of heterosexual intercourse and apply them to the nineteenth-century context in which Shaker, Koreshan, and Sanctificationist forms of celibacy were conceived and articulated. This process will make it possible to contrast the mainstream system with the celibate symbolic systems of the three groups.

The analysis will reveal that in the heterosexual American cultural context surrounding the three communities, gender identities of males and females were conceptualized in terms that reinforced fundamental and often irreconcilable distinctions, divisions, and hierarchies between the sexes, rather than in terms that united and equalized them. That is, heterosexual intercourse as a symbolic system depended upon gender theories in which males and females represented opposed and even warring subcultures that could be mediated by, but not truly blended in, sexual union. In addition, it can be observed that the principles and values of various domains of sexual culture, including family, work, and religion, reinforced such distinctions. Therefore, symbols of difference, opposition, and hierarchy between the sexes were woven into the systems of the major cultural institutions that conferred differential status and identity on men and women. Although the revelation of symbolic gender

23

difference in American culture contains no surprise, the connection of that symbolism to cultural structure via the symbolic system of heterosexual intercourse does yield some new insights.

In order to discuss and evaluate gender in symbolic terms, one must first be willing to generalize on theoretical grounds about the meaning of gender, specifically of female gender, even though such generalization will inevitably contradict the experience of certain women in the culture. This willingness builds upon the school of feminist anthropology that subordinates evidence of female and male behavioral variety in various cultures to the more compelling observation that, overall, cultures value male activities and male gender characteristics above those of females. This school maintains that examples of female power and of female cultural contributions do not, ultimately, obviate the evidence of a near-universal and firmly entrenched male symbolic and actual dominance over females.

Anthropologists of this persuasion explain that gender hierarchy has resulted because the "differences between men and women . . . [are conceptualized] in terms of sets of metaphorically associated binary oppositions," such as nature and culture, which imply unequal value. In short, according to this symbolic view, concepts of gender in most cultural systems are analogous to other conceptual categories that are characterized by difference, opposition, and hierarchy; therefore, male activities and symbolism appear superior to female activities and symbolism. As in other conceptual hierarchies, maleness even becomes the human standard that subsumes and encompasses femaleness.[1] Inevitably, such conceptual categories influence the experience of actual men and women as they conduct their lives in a given culture, if only to create guilt among the nonconformists and shame among those who cannot, for economic or other reasons, conform to cultural standards.

The contrasting view in anthropology, as well as in historical scholarship, holds that symbols or systems of gender are less important than the survival strategies used by particular individuals as they gain power or exert influence despite their membership in a devalued or disparaged group.[2] In this approach, women's informal or surreptitious power is counted as a victory over whatever system is attempting to oppress them.

The argument between the two positions is likely to persist for some time. Each approach has its uses, certainly, and the selection

24

of the symbolic approach for this study is not meant to suggest that an alternative approach might not yield interesting results. Although I will analyze women's status in symbolic and general terms, it is certainly true that exceptions to any generalization can be found. Furthermore, symbols and behavior are never completely congruent. Yet it is also true that behavior may appear victorious in a given cultural system because it violates and challenges cultural norms. Thus, the achievement of female power, unless it occurs in the odd matriarchy, is often best understood in light of the taboos or barriers that have been broken. Female power is often indirect or informal precisely because it must circumvent the limitations of sanctioned female gender identity. The limitations of the system remain the standard by which the exceptions are measured.

Contemporary American culture exemplifies the intransigence of certain traditional symbolic gender associations despite enormous social change. One might argue, for instance, that some symbolic systems of gender evident in nineteenth-century America are still valid in the 1980s, in spite of the women's movement, the increased participation of women (even married women and mothers) in the labor force, and the legislative changes of the 1960s and 1970s. Although some details or applications of gender symbolism may have changed, modern women are still more likely to appear as the appropriate coffee brewers, diaper changers, and caretakers of emotional needs (even in offices) than males are because of the continuing symbolic connection of women with a female nature suited to such tasks.

A focus on the symbolic systems, rather than the behavior, of the communards also serves as a valid basis of comparison among mainstream American culture and the three communities. Furthermore, comparison of symbolic systems reveals the deepest meanings of both heterosexuality and celibacy and provides pairs of related ideological elements — including male and female, earthly and spiritual, celibate and sexual — that can be followed and analyzed through both systems.

SEXUAL SYMBOLISM IN ANTHROPOLOGICAL THEORY

Before looking back to the nineteenth-century sex/gender symbolic system, it is necessary to turn to more recent interpretations of heterosexual intercourse as a key symbol in American culture. Although the terms of this analysis are not new, they are useful as a framework for evaluating the symbolic significance of sexual intercourse in the earlier period.

Nature versus Culture

According to recent theory, heterosexual intercourse functions as a key symbol of American culture because it signifies larger and more complex symbolic interactions throughout the culture. That is, heterosexual intercourse involves not only males and females, but also the conceptual categories of male and female and of nature and culture as defined by a particular social/cultural unit. In American culture, intercourse suggests nature through the biological substances involved in reproduction (represented by the symbol of blood), and it suggests culture because of the legal sanctions imposed upon sexual activity and reproduction in the forms of marriage and various sexual taboos.[3]

Although precise definitions of the realms of nature and culture vary from society to society, nature generally implies events or behaviors ostensibly related to biology or to material or bodily processes. Natural phenomena occur or endure without or in spite of human intervention. Culture, on the other hand, connotes events, institutions, and behaviors that reflect the civilizing influence, creativity, or intentionality of human beings.

On one level, intercourse succeeds in blending certain symbols of nature and culture because its product, the child, represents the parents' (natural) love and (natural) blood, as well as their (cultural) marital union.[4] Upon further reflection, however, the apparent unity or merger of the two realms in sexual intercourse becomes problematic. Apart from its role in reproduction, sexual intercourse involves symbolism that may actually preclude an ultimate union of either the two realms of nature and culture or the two gender categories.

Frequently, cultural approval of sexual relationships relies either upon separations of natural bonds or upon the maintenance of a distinction between nature and culture. One example of the conscious separation of nature and culture is found in the terminology of the American sex-kinship system. Relatives are defined according

26

to their (blood) natural or (law) cultural connections in terms that distinguish between biological parents or siblings and parents- and siblings-in-law. These terminological distinctions affect behavior and expectations; blood relationships cannot be severed, although in-law relationships, which might be as close or as satisfying, can be terminated for cause. Another example is the taboo against certain sexual liaisons. If two people are united by blood (in nature), for example, fathers and daughters, the culture disapproves their sexual alliance.[5] Homosexuals, unified in nature by the fact of their identical sex, are also considered illegitimate sexual partners. Legitimate sexual intercourse, on the other hand, relies upon a separation in nature (the lack of a blood connection and differences in biological sex, for example) for its acceptance in culture—legal marriage.

Female Is to Male as Nature Is to Culture[6]

The two sexes partake of the symbolic opposition between nature and culture, including both their separation and their distinction from each other. The two realms have specific associations with male and female gender identities. The female gender is associated with nature because of the female role in reproduction and the nurture of the young. Those apparently natural functions imbue all female-sphere activities (as well as the female psychic structure) with "natural" symbolism.[7] Consequently, the female herself appears to partake of nature's apparently irrational, intangible, involuntary qualities. Relationships formed by these creatures of nature also share in its repetitive, involuntary, and subjective characteristics.

The lack of an obvious male reproductive role, on the other hand, removes the male from the symbolic realm of nature and places the male gender identity into the cultural realm.[8] Male activities are characterized as conscious, rational, and public. Male labor is identified as legitimate work for which money is an appropriate reward. Male relationships, too, share in the cultural symbolism of rationality and conscious selection. Male-identified public work relationships are subject to behavioral standards and can be terminated for inadequate performance.

Heterosexual Intercourse, Sex Roles, and the Oppositions of Cultural Domains

The domains of home and work also share in these symbolic distinctions of the sexes, and of nature and culture, through various interdependent associations. Because it is the locus of childcare and family concerns, home qualifies as a natural domain. Woman's association with home (whether it is voluntary or involuntary) is, therefore, an association with the natural domain. Work, on the other hand, is the locus of achievement, rewards, and other public characteristics of culture. Man's association with work (and lack of association with home) therefore identifies him symbolically with the cultural realm. A key root metaphor of the female home/family domain is love—a personal, nonmaterial, unifying, and spiritual feeling among family members that produces "diffuse and enduring solidarity."[9] As part of the "natural" realm, relationships in the home are involuntary and exempt from objective, cultural criteria and tangible rewards. The male domain of work, on the other hand, is symbolized by money—an objective, impersonal, political, unsentimental, and nonmoral substance that empowers workers to develop the voluntary relationships in which criteria must be met, judgments made, and rewards bestowed.[10] Because love and money appear to represent separate domains, they are symbolized as opposites. When they are united, their combinations are viewed as illegitimate and are sometimes called prostitution—the selling of something that should be given for love. To avoid such illegitimacies, separation of their respective domains—including separations and divisions between male and female activities associated with those domains— often seems the best policy.

Gender associations with the domains of home and work are reinforced by the assignment of sex roles, which appear "natural, in the American view . . . the various tasks of protecting the home, of providing the necessities of life, of giving care and instruction to the young should be divided according to the natural talents, aptitudes, and endowments of those involved . . . certain of these tasks naturally fall to men, certain to women." Because nature rather than human culture is credited with prescribing sex roles, one's genitals, rather than one's wishes or personality, tend to determine one's cultural role.[11]

A logical result of these symbolic layers of difference and opposition between male and female gender identities is a cultural
prohibition against the ultimate reconciliation of gender symbolism.
As long as divisions between the realms of nature and culture must
be maintained, then the domains of home and work and the symbolic
gender identities of male and female remain differentiated. The association of the female with the home setting, for example, signifies
both her separation from the work domain and her apparent dis-
qualification for it, especially its most "cultural" aspects. Such associations can even determine her experience in the work domain
should she enter it; certain jobs might be considered beyond her
ken, and those with a domestic flavor may be hers alone. Likewise,
woman's association with love from the home domain sets her both
apart from and in opposition to the male's association with money.
Hence, although she performs a pseudo-domestic job, her pay scale
may not match that of her more cultural, male counterparts. Frequently, women workers receive intangible rewards in deference to
their alleged discomfort with money. Just as frequently, even wom-
en's technical jobs, such as the operation of office machinery, appear
domestic just because women are doing them. In such a context,
the two symbolic gender categories may appear not just different,
but also incompatible. Therefore, in order to function properly, the
sexes, like the domains they represent, may be segregated in order
to ensure that they will remain distinguishable from one another.

Sexual intercourse may mediate the oppositions and distinctions
implied in the symbolic system of opposed genders, but intercourse
might do cultural damage if a sexual union ultimately blurred gender
distinctions. Movies, for example, frequently portray sexual relations
as opportunities to assert gender difference (real man versus real
woman) rather than to reduce it. Conflicts between the sexes are
not resolved (that is, differences are not camouflaged) in celluloid
intercourse; they are, rather, exacerbated (that is, differences are
flaunted) through its repeated performance. The metaphor of the
"war between the sexes," which is occasionally invoked in both
media and in life, suggests that the appeal of heterosexual intercourse
is enhanced by the maintenance of symbolic gender distinctions,
even irreconcilable oppositions, rather than through a reconciliation
of those differences. Sexual difference, based in biology, must be

accompanied by symbolic, culturally induced gender differences in order to ensure the validity of sexual intercourse.

From Opposition to Hierarchy

As already discussed, hierarchy is a critical feature of this system of sexual and cultural oppositions and distinctions. Neither the social domains nor their symbolic elements, including gender, exist in separate-but-equal relation to one another. Rather, in the prestige systems of most human cultures, including American culture, activities considered cultural, such as industrial labor, are not just different from, they are more valued than, activities considered natural, such as childcare.[12] Based on the symbolic associations of gender with the two realms, maleness (culture), therefore, often appears superior to femaleness (nature).

According to recent feminist scholarship, the typical preference for culture over nature frequently creates prestige systems in which women and their traditional activities are actually eliminated from the rankings. In most systems, in fact, women are defined only in terms of their relationships to men—as daughters, wives, and mothers—and, therefore, by their relationship to male status. To say that a man is a warrior or a banker is to give him a rank. To say that a woman is a mother, without reference to her husband or his occupation, is to place her outside of the rankings on the merits of her occupation. Motherhood can actually reinforce a woman's marginality in the world of male prestige. Even in cultures in which women are clearly instrumental in male acquisitions of prestige—by being available as suitable brides, for example—women are less likely to be actors than prizes or pawns in the male game.[13]

The women's movement in twentieth-century America has done more to admit women to male occupational statuses once denied them than to elevate the status of female occupations. Even within those male occupations, however, references to a woman's role usually includes an adjective denoting her sex: she is a female banker or a lady lawyer. Such phrasing sends at least two messages. First, the woman is unusual; she is encroaching upon an occupation expected to be held by a male. Second, she is not the "real" banker or lawyer; thus she is less effective, powerful, or talented than a man in the role. In both ways, her prestige is mitigated by her sex and judged by a male norm.

One way out of this female invisibility, which is illustrated in the celibate systems, occurs in those cultures that privilege a woman's kinship roles (sister, daughter) over her marital roles (wife, mother). If the role of sister or daughter takes precedence over the role of wife, a woman often qualifies for greater prestige on her own merits.[14]

Gender Opposition, Separation, and Hierarchy in the Domain of Religion

The patterns of gender opposition, separation, and hierarchy surrounding the symbolism of sexual intercourse are also reflected in the symbolism of mainstream American religion. One key symbolic change imposed by Christianity on Western culture is its transformation of religious faith from the natural (nonprestigious, involuntary) realm of blood relationships to the cultural (spiritual, rational, prestigious) realm of human experience. In contrast to Judaism, in which the believer's birth to a Jewish mother (blood, nature) must accompany his or her voluntary adherence to a strict code of conduct (culture), Christianity represents a shift "away from the particularistic, bio-genetic criterion of substance [or blood] as the defining feature . . . [and toward] a re-alignment so that commitment to the code for conduct becomes paramount as the defining feature, and the substantive element is re-defined from a material to a spiritual form."[15]

Based on the gender associations entailed in this shift, it is clear that Christianity subordinates the female realm — natural, material, and involuntary — to the male realm — spiritual, nonmaterial, and voluntary. In symbolic terms, the Christian triumph of spirit over matter, particularly in the context of heterosexual symbolism, implies the triumph of maleness over femaleness in the religious domain (Table 1).

Summary: Symbolism of Sexual Intercourse

Ultimately, heterosexual intercourse fails to reconcile maleness and femaleness as gender categories. It cannot even balance the genders as equal complements; hierarchy is implicit in gender differences

TABLE 1. A SUMMARY OF GENDER-BASED SYMBOLIC SETS
IN HETEROSEXUAL CULTURE

nature	culture
female	male
home	work
private/domestic	public
nurture	competition
love	money
personal	impersonal
emotional	rational
involuntary relationships	objective relationship criteria
intangible rewards	tangible rewards
blood	spirit
intuitive, pious	spiritually transcendent
emotional bonds	legal bonds
use-value labor	exchange-value labor
duty	commitment

because of the assignment of the sexes to stratified domains. Evidence from the symbolic systems of home, work, and religion reveals that the bridge created by intercourse between the sexes is at best temporary and cannot, ultimately, alter symbolic patterns of opposition and hierarchy. In fact, women's exclusion from cultural prestige systems is the direct result of reproductive/sexual relationships to men. Having defined woman as heterosexual and reproductive, American culture has also relegated her to domestic status, to an un- or underpaid economic role, and to involuntary personal alliances. To use Simone de Beauvoir's famous terms, the heterosexual woman symbolizes immanence as opposed to transcendence. Although that immanence may produce positive emotional and psychological benefits for many women who participate in the heterosexual/reproductive system, as well as for society, it also symbolizes female confinement to the undervalued side of the cultural/symbolic ledger. The symbolism of celibacy found in Shaker, Koreshan, and Sanctificationist documents can best be understood in light of this gender system in heterosexual American culture.

SEXUAL SYMBOLISM IN THE HISTORICAL RECORD

The next question in the analysis of heterosexual symbolism is whether Shakers, Koreshans, and Sanctificationists living in the late

32

nineteenth century would have understood sexual intercourse in the symbolic terms just discussed. Based on cultural currents of the time, one can extrapolate the operation of heterosexual intercourse as a key symbol in the white, Protestant, nineteenth-century American culture that these white, Protestant communards would have known. It is possible to examine the workings of heterosexual symbolism in the cultural domains of family, work, and religion by surveying trends within those domains during the century.

Separation, Opposition, and Hierarchy in the American Family

> After expelling man from paradise . . . God arranged for the establishment of churches and states. In creating these institutions, God did not abolish the family. . . . Instead he developed churches and states out of the family, which continued to be, in the Puritans' opinion, "the very *First Society* that by the direction and Providence of God, is produced among the children of man."[16]

The late-nineteenth-century culture had its roots, of course, in the colonial culture that preceded it. And it seems clear that from the colonial period forward, the nuclear family form was regarded not only as the basic unit of reproduction in American culture, but also as a primary unit in American civic life. Thus, the family has historically combined natural and cultural symbolism. Colonial laws enforced the role of father as head of household and required that parents perform their duties and bestow their affection according to community standards. Early settlers also encouraged unmarried people (especially women) to join established families so that everyone in the community would be appropriately bonded in the socially sanctioned way.[17]

By the nineteenth century, specific community rules had been replaced by the force of custom and the requirements of industry; the separation of home and work mandated by industrialization provided a less jural but equally powerful imposition of social needs upon the family domain. Increasingly throughout the century, the familial (natural) values of love and morality contrasted with the (cultural) work values of money and achievement.

Within the family, the dominant natural symbol, blood, has both endured and evolved over time. The colonists probably placed more

33

value on familial ties of blood—kinship relations—than did their nineteenth-century descendants.[18] In fact, because the Calvinists took literally the biblical edict uniting a "man and wife [into] one flesh," they probably interpreted marriage itself as a blood relation. They prohibited marriage between a man or woman and the siblings of his or her dead spouse, suggesting that relatives later considered in-laws were once considered blood relations.[19]

Sexual intercourse has always been regarded as a legitimate, culturally approved feature of mainstream American family life, especially for the purpose of procreation, based on the mainstream Christian interpretation of nature. Acceptable levels of sexual and procreative activity within marriage have varied, however. Historians have suggested that the 50 percent decline in the fertility rate of white American women between 1800 and 1900 may have resulted from women's increasing willingness to assert their identities as separate persons, with rights to self-determined lives, throughout the century. Nineteenth-century women also increasingly interpreted ideals of feminine morality in terms of chastity and modesty. Such an interpretation, not coincidentally, helped to reduce women's experience of the hazards of childbirth and limited the number of children they had to rear. There is no evidence that birth control technology was any more advanced than it had been in the preceding century.[20] This voluntary control of reproduction is one important link of celibate Shaker, Koreshan, and Sanctificationist women to women in the mainstream who were seeking autonomy through a modification of the reproductive mandate.

The American family ideal has also been a source of, and an arena for, the concept of gender distinction and, in varying periods, of gender separation. The history of sex roles within the family can be seen as an indicator of the importance of sexual differentiation and separation in American culture. Eighteenth-century married couples performed different tasks according to sex, but because their homes and workplaces were generally combined (a pattern that reappeared among the communards under study), complete separation between males and females was neither possible nor desirable. Some scholars have interpreted this fact as evidence of slightly more egalitarian relations between Colonial husbands and wives than between their nineteenth-century counterparts, who were more likely than their forebears to differentiate between and to oppose domestic and non-domestic work, both in terms of location and of value.[21]

By the late nineteenth century, an ideology of separate, complementary spheres for men and women replaced the shared mixed-sex workplace of eighteenth-century Americans, except perhaps in rural areas. Industrialization did much to remove men's work stations from the home and to limit women's work to the home. The ideal of the home then became almost a defense against the increasingly corrupt and competitive male world of work. In spite of its reputation for conflict and corruption, however, the workplace was more prestigious than the domestic realm of women, a fact that prevented sexual equality and promoted female dependence on males. The ideal home was increasingly defined in contrast to the workplace, as a haven away from the stresses and excesses of commerce and industry. Home was offered to men as a reward for and retreat "from the corroding cares of business, from the hard toil and frequent disappointments of the day."[22]

The books of Catharine Beecher provide an insight into this ideology, which suggested that women's family roles were the very source of human morality. Hoping to institutionalize and expand the separate female sphere, Beecher even sketched blueprints for model family dwellings, which included home, church, and school in a single building under the control of a loving wife.[23] But Beecher's expansion of the domestic realm made few encroachments upon the domain of work, and thus upon the ideology of female weakness and dependence. Later, women's domestic feminism, with its roots in "educated motherhood," would take them outside of their homes and into the public sphere, but even then remuneration was scarce for the social reform activities that might have lent them prestige. Men professionalized the educational, social welfare, and medical work that women pioneered, while women's lesser cultural status dictated their roles as mere technicians and "handmaidens."[24]

The fate of women who violated the boundaries of their domain by pursuing paid employment reveals, among other things, the seriousness with which the symbolism of opposition between public work and private family roles was taken. Even single women whose livelihood depended upon their own labor suffered from the taint of women's lesser public status and from the pressures and limitations placed upon them by their families. As women, they were prohibited from the profitable and prestigious realms of science, art, and politics. For their support, they turned to the few occupations open to them, which tended to be low-paid and dead-end. The equation of woman with her reproductive capacity weighed heavily even upon those women who chose the celibacy of singlehood as a means of enhancing their freedom. As their childbearing years waned, some single women worried about the unnaturalness of their state. Others felt continued demands upon their time and loyalty by their natal families. Single women remained daughters and sisters and retained the responsibilities, as well as the support, inherent in those roles.[25]

Married women were more heavily penalized than other women for their forays into paid employment, even if the very survival of their families depended on their income. Because of childcare needs, such women often accepted nominal payment for piecework done at home. Women's low cultural status also kept the salaries of women who worked in factories lower than those of men, even for the performance of the same work. Women who wished to become involved in the political arena, particularly if their actions were intended to achieve equal rights for women, faced obstacles that illustrate the magnitude of their threat to mainstream notions of femininity and domestic life. Suffragists were routinely called not only aggressive, but also unfeminine, un-Christian, and emasculating.

Notions of the Christian family reinforced these examples of symbolic gender opposition, separation, and hierarchy. In the Puritan family, male dominance was mandated in the covenant model of Calvinism. Husbands were supposed to be loving rulers of their voluntarily submissive wives, just as God lovingly rules His voluntarily submissive children.[26] In the nineteenth century, the hierarchy of males and females in the family setting carried the Christian metaphor even further, attributing to capitalism a hierarchy of gender-related values with roots in Christianity. Therefore, the nineteenth-century urban family (woman's domain) was, ideally, voluntarily submissive to the values of the (male) workplace. Within the family, the man's contribution of economic support signified the more prestigious values of work. The economic security of a nonearning wife frequently depended upon her ability to provide a home environment that facilitated the work of her employed husband.

Thus, in the nineteenth century, the men and women who met

in the marriage bed probably saw themselves not only as distinct from one another, but also as symbolic opposites and unequals, at least in terms of social status. Given the network of symbols mandating gender separation, opposition, and hierarchy during the nineteenth century, it seems clear that heterosexual intercourse would have been hard-pressed, then as now, to symbolize a fusion of sexual symbolism, even if it were perceived as a moment of physical and spiritual union by the partners themselves. Again, the unifying aspects of intercourse can better be understood as mediation rather than as resolution of the many oppositions the act represents. In fact, the ultimate reconciliation of differences, muting of distinctions, or blurring of domains might have invalidated the sexual act in the context of the period's cultural requirements.

Separation, Opposition, and Hierarchy in the Domain of Work

As industrial capitalism overtook the system of direct manufacture in the 1820s, the American system of work enforced many forms of difference, opposition, and hierarchy that had implications for the sexes. In fact, even when the distinctions and separations of the capitalist system were ostensibly unrelated to sex—as in the class system—they were frequently couched in terms of gender. Analogies between gender and other culturally defined dualities are characteristic of systems, like those in the industrialized West, in which gender categories are defined as unreconcilable opposites.[27] In such systems, for example, men without power may be derided as feminine or chided as "wimps" or "weak sisters," terms that insult them by impugning their masculinity. Social classes without economic power may also be cast into supportive roles that appear feminine in the system of production. The Shakers and Koreshans were aware of such analogies in American culture and criticized them. Writers in both groups understood the connection between class hierarchy at work and gender hierarchy in the nuclear family, which was increasingly molded to support the system of work.

Private ownership of property also contributed to gender hierarchy by women's economic independence and by further confining her to the domestic realm. Communal land ownership had flourished in many seventeenth- and eighteenth-century towns, but by the nineteenth century, private family ownership of land and its concomitant, primogeniture, held sway. Primogeniture restricted property inheritance to eldest sons and only infrequently benefited eldest daughters. This method of inheritance reinforced the exclusion of women from the economy and established female dependence on male relatives, by either blood or marriage.[28] Perhaps more important was the fact that common law limited married women's right to acquire and control property. These limitations, coupled with restrictions on women's educational and work opportunities, cemented the inverse relationship between a woman's sexuality (as expressed in her marriageability) and her economic independence. Coerced into marriage and reproduction, a nineteenth-century woman was also forced into economic dependence.

At the same time, the increasingly isolated nineteenth-century family was more often required to support the values of the workplace, further diminishing the status of woman's supposedly complementary sphere. The homemaker was expected both to enforce and to facilitate in her employed husband a workmanlike sobriety, punctuality, and dedication to the profit of his employer.[29] Good families were supposed to produce and support good workers and good citizens.[30] The family's role in providing services for the benefit of the worker and his employer did much to confine women to unpaid labor in the home and to separate them from and subordinate them to their husbands. A single working woman who married was expected to leave the labor force. Her new role as wife obviated her role as a paid worker; she was to nurture a worker rather than be one.

In this system of separation and difference, the husband was perceived almost as the woman's employer, a position that gave him power and authority over her and thereby reinforced sexual hierarchy. At the same time, however, the wife was frequently thrust into the position of ensuring the husband's (and her own) economic survival by enforcing unpleasant routines upon him. Thus, although ostensibly uniting them in a single cause—family economic support—the demands of the workplace, like intercourse itself, contributed instead to the opposition of the sexes.

Separation, Opposition, and Hierarchy
in the Domain of Religion

Playing into the other symbolisms of the sexual system in eighteenth-
and nineteenth-century America was a mainstream Protestant ethos
that supported both the work and family domains through its own
system of separations, differences, and hierarchies. The ethos of
Protestantism has been a powerful reinforcing agent in American
culture. According to many historians, it has served as a "summarizing symbol" of the culture by crystallizing both the commitment
and the attitudes of the American people.[31] Although Protestants
were never the only religious group on the continent, nor were they
the first, the Protestant/Puritan origins of the American character
constitute a myth that might as well be true.[32] Even in today's multi-
ethnic nation, many non-Protestants function in terms of that ethos
which, all evidence suggests, must have had a greater impact in earlier
centuries.[33]

As in the world of work, the development of American Protestantism reveals a number of symbolic oppositions with gender implications. The sects that emigrated from Europe to the New World
contained dual symbolic strains. One was inherited from the En-
lightenment; it emphasized rationality, voluntary choice, equality
among all believers, and the virtues of progress. Another, conflicting
strain was embodied in the impulse toward evangelical conservatism,
individual revelation, and the elitism of the saved.[34] Female gender
identity had ties with intuition and revelation, but it was male gender
identity that meshed with voluntary choice and rationality. The
relationship between spirit and matter was also hotly debated, a
conflict with hidden but potent gender associations. Emphasis upon
the spirit suggested a preference for male-type transcendence; emphasis upon matter (body, blood) validated female symbolism and
supported female forms of piety and religious commitment.

American Protestantism also encouraged the maintenance of the
symbolic gender divisions and hierarchies of the traditional nuclear
family. A Christian woman was expected to know and keep her
place in the domestic realm, to remain silent in church, and to
submit to the will of her husband. To be a Christian woman was
to be the daughter of Eve and to fulfill, in all humility, the curse of
Eve by submitting to men and accepting painful childbearing duties.

Womanhood also implied to many theologians a disability in reason that, presumably, reinforced woman's need for religious faith and piety. A Christian man, on the other hand, was destined to rule his home in a God-like manner even if (or, perhaps, especially if) such rulership contrasted with his subordinate role in the workplace. Men's religious roles were based on their superior reason and conscious commitment to Christianity. Male religious power allowed men the privileges of stewardship, which occasionally required a compromise of a religious value for economic ones.

Fortunately for men, mainstream Protestantism willingly supported the economic goals of capitalism, while simultaneously promoting the familial roles of women. In eighteenth-century America, the Puritan Ethic equated economic success with religious virtue, despite the inevitable irony contained within the equation: prosperity sometimes produced the sins of luxury and avarice that marred godliness.[35] As industrialization progressed, the connection between religion and the competitive, capitalist economy only increased. Behavior that interfered with either prosperity or production was pronounced un-Christian from many pulpits. Employers were regarded as stewards of their flocks, and they often exercised their stewardship by requiring employees to attend church. Public piety became a demonstration of devotion to the job. Religious denominations even united in support of capitalist values in such organizations as the Society for Industry, Frugality, and Temperance.[36]

Religion's support for the separation of gender roles thus contributed to opposition and hierarchy between the sexes. Through its preference for the transcendent spirit, Christianity helped to stratify the symbolism of nature and culture and, therefore, of male and female. The merger of religion and work also created gender hierarchy. With men tied by God's plan to the more prestigious domain of work, and women relegated to the home by both industrial and religious value systems, wives experienced both secular and divinely ordained subordination to their husbands.

The Religious Loophole

It seems clear that the symbolic relationship between sexual intercourse and opposed and unequal gender identities with which this chapter began generally applied to white Americans in the nineteenth century. To be a reproductive female in that period was to inhabit a realm that was labelled natural and domestic and was, therefore, considered less prestigious than, and supportive of, the realm associated with males. Even nonreproductive women in a heterosexual culture were identified with reproduction and family duties. Because the female domain was perceived as natural, no wages accompanied woman's prescribed activities in her domain, a fact that enforced her economic dependence on men and denied her an economic base upon which to build public, political, and social power. The symbolism of nineteenth-century gender identities also implied the separation of male and female spheres of activity. The bridging of those spheres, in any permanent way, threatened to merge the symbolism of love and money, suggesting prostitution, and otherwise to create dangerous and socially disruptive combinations. Nineteenth-century morality virtually depended upon women's maintenance of a separate (domestic) sphere. Because of these requirements of opposition and distinction, heterosexual intercourse, although ostensibly designed to unify them, served to divide the sexes. Sexual intercourse obtained its legitimacy from the separate, opposed, and differentially valued spheres of males and females.

The component symbols of the religious domain, however, provided a kind of loophole in the system in which women found themselves. For a variety of reasons, female symbolism began to intrude upon the spiritual (male, cultural) world of American Protestantism, and some Protestant women were able to utilize their religious roles in order to extricate themselves from the domestic, reproductive cycle. In spite of Christianity's continued preference for a transcendent spirituality with symbolic male overtones, American religion became more and more associated with immanent virtues that were labelled "female" by the culture. Female piety, as well as domesticity, was increasingly defined as religiously approved antidotes to male-identified traits that, in excess, threatened Christian values. Avarice, lust, and intemperance were logical outcomes of male life in nineteenth-century industrial capitalism.[37] At the same time, although the feminization of the religious domain may have made it a less comfortable place for them, men could not completely abandon religion. Their wives and employers, and possibly their consciences, insisted upon their participation in it.

In fact, the use of religion by many white Protestant women to free themselves and to influence their society forms the context in which Shaker, Koreshan, and Sanctificationist views developed. Religion was the domain in which women could exercise female traits with the power of a cultural (rather than natural) institution behind them. In various revival groups, women had opportunities to testify, preach, and convert their families and neighbors. Because male converts were also attracted to these groups, female religious leaders acquired some prestige by exerting influence over men.[38] In less traditional sects such as Christian Science, Spiritualism, and Theosophy—which recognized the female qualities of God and opposed the hegemony of the male clergy—women fared even better. In fact, "mind cure gave jobs to women by the hundreds of thousands."[39]

In addition to providing employment for women, albeit frequently unpaid, religion also helped to modify both actual and symbolic female domestic confinement. Protestant support for the worth of all believers and for the sacrifice of self for others encouraged women's self-respect and inspired them to extend their domestic values into public realms. Women performed missionary work, became involved in the abolition and temperance crusades, formed kindergartens, and engaged in various social reform movements, all in the name of the Protestant value system. Through such work, they also learned how to organize, how to make public presentations, and how to bond with other women for a common cause.[40]

In short, some women interpreted mainstream Protestantism as a deconstruction of itself. While limiting them on the one hand, it opened doors for them on the other. Religion also valorized allegedly female traits such as intuition and spiritual and emotional sensitivity, which were routinely devalued in other public domains.[41] Thus, religion may have forged a sturdier bridge between women's private, domestic lives and the male-dominated public, cultural realm than heterosexual intercourse ever did.[42]

This form of female spiritual power never completely liberated women from their less prestigious place in American culture, however. Any freedom and power obtained through female religious activities depended upon woman's continued commitment both to cultural expectations of gender-appropriate values and to her prescribed, religious, reproductive, and domestic roles. Women did not enter the clergy in mainstream Protestant denominations, for example. Rather, religion offered one way for a woman to be powerful while still living within acceptably female parameters. Still, the religious escape valve did provide many women with opportunities to extend female symbolism into public domains and thereby to become "cultural" by remaining within their "natural" sphere.

The celibate women in this study took the religious opportunity one step further than most Protestant women did by interpreting their religious responsibilities as grounds for renouncing rather than embracing the sexual and reproductive aspects of a female identity. They examined the symbolic premises of female confinement to the natural familial domain, and they rejected them as incompatible with the spiritual order. The Shakers, Koreshans, and Sanctificationists of the late nineteenth century substituted spiritual for sexual, natural (blood) or legal personal bonds, and they rejected sexual/reproductive foundations for female subordination in a separate, "natural" domain. The rejection of subordination and confinement did not necessarily mean the rejection of all traditional female activities, or of female gender identity, however. Rather, the incorporation of spiritual, transcendent symbolism into female gender identity by these groups sometimes promoted a kind of female superiority, particularly in spiritual affairs, that privileged feminine qualities.

NOTES

1. Sherry B. Ortner and Harriet Whitehead, "Introduction: Accounting for Sexual Meanings," in *Sexual Meanings: The Cultural Construction of Gender and Sexuality,* ed. Sherry B. Ortner and Harriet Whitehead (Cambridge: Cambridge University Press, 1981), pp. 7-8. This source builds upon arguments made by Ortner in "Is Female to Male as Nature Is to Culture?" in *Woman, Culture and Society,* ed. Michelle Zimbalist Rosaldo and Louise Lamphere (Stanford, Calif.: Stanford University Press, 1974), pp. 67-87, esp. p. 70.

2. Classic statements of the cultural relativist point of view on these topics include Peggy Sanday's "Female Status in the Public Domain," in *Woman, Culture and Society,* ed. Rosaldo and Lamphere; and Judith K. Brown's "A Note on the Division of Labor by Sex," *American Anthropologist* 72, no. 5 (1970): 1073-78 and "Leisure, Busywork and Housekeeping," *Anthropos* 68, no. 5 (1973): 881-88.

3. For a complete articulation of this symbolic theory, see David M. Schneider, *American Kinship: A Cultural Account*, 2d ed. (Chicago: University of Chicago Press, 1980), pp. 32, 38; and Ortner, "Female to Male," p. 84.

4. Ortner, "Female to Male," p. 84.

5. Ibid., pp. 39-40.

6. This heading adapts the title of Ortner's "Female to Male." Although Ortner's is the definitive description of this analogy, Schneider had noted gender hierarchy in American culture in his 1973 work with Raymond T. Smith, *Class Differences and Sex Roles in American Kinship and Family Structure* (Englewood Cliffs, N.J.: Prentice-Hall, 1973), p. 104.

7. Ortner, "Female to Male," pp. 73-83. Criticism of Ortner's work is a dominant theme of Carol MacCormack and Marilyn Strathern's *Nature, Culture and Gender* (Cambridge: Cambridge University Press, 1980), particularly in an essay by Carol MacCormack, "Nature, Culture and Gender: A Critique" (pp. 1-24). MacCormack objects to Ortner's use of structuralism because it ignores data that disprove its models, including Ortner's own woman:nature::man:culture model. For example, women can be seen as mediating between nature and culture rather than as languishing in the natural realm. Women also play active roles in marriage and agree to their own "exchange." Structural analysis also fails to account for female power in a number of societies, MacCormack argues. I share Ortner's contention that such failures do not necessarily invalidate the endurance of a symbolic system (see "Female to Male," pp. 70-71).

8. Ortner, "Female to Male," p. 79.

9. Schneider, *American Kinship*, p. 61.

10. Ibid., pp. 48-49. Schneider does not discuss this aspect of the home-work symbolic system, but it seems clear that, based on his system, prostitution appears immoral in American culture partly because it mixes the respective home-related symbol of love with the work-related symbol of money.

11. Ibid., pp. 35, 36, 43. The belief that specific qualities are inherent in members of each sex is stronger in working-class families, according to Schneider's later work. See Schneider and Smith, *Class Differences*, p. 106.

12. See Ortner and Whitehead, "Introduction," in *Sexual Meanings*, pp. 14-21.

13. Ibid.

14. See Sherry B. Ortner, "Gender and Sexuality in Hierarchical

Societies: The Case of Polynesia and Some Comparative Implications," in *Sexual Meanings,* ed. Ortner and Whitehead, p. 400.

15. David M. Schneider, "Kinship, Nationality and Religion in American Culture: Toward a Definition of Kinship," in *Forms of Symbolic Action, Proceedings of the 1969 Annual Spring Meeting of the American Ethnological Society,* ed. Robert F. Spencer (Seattle: University of Washington Press, 1969), p. 122.

16. Internal quotation from Cotton Mather, 1709, in Edmund Morgan's *The Puritan Family,* new ed. (New York: Harper and Row, 1966), p. 133.

17. Morgan, *Puritan Family,* pp. 27, 143-56.

18. John Demos, *A Little Commonwealth: Family Life in Plymouth Colony* (New York: Oxford University Press, 1970), p. 121; Morgan, *Puritan Family,* p. 150.

19. Morgan, *Puritan Family,* pp. 150-52.

20. Carl N. Degler, *At Odds: Women and the Family in America from the Revolution to the Present* (New York: Oxford University Press, 1980), pp. 181-98. No comparable data exist for blacks of the nineteenth century. Because the women of the communities under consideration in this work were white, comparisons with mainstream women will be limited by race, as they are by religion, to the majority white, Protestant population.

21. See Jessie Bernard, "Stations and Spheres," in her *The Female World* (New York: Free Press, 1981), pp. 77-93.

22. William G. Elliott, Jr., *Lectures to Young Women,* 1853, in Jeffrey Kirk, "The Family as Utopian Retreat from the City: The Nineteenth-Century Contribution," in *The Family, Communes and Utopian Societies,* ed. Sallie TeSelle (New York: Harper and Row, 1971), p. 21.

23. Kathryn Kish Sklar, *Catharine Beecher: A Study in American Domesticity* (New Haven: Yale University Press, 1973), pp. 263-65.

24. Sheila M. Rothman, *Woman's Proper Place: A History of Changing Ideas and Practices, 1870 to the Present* (New York: Basic Books, 1978), pp. 147-57.

25. Lee Virginia Chambers-Schiller, *Liberty a Better Husband, Single Women in America: The Generations of 1780-1840* (New Haven: Yale University Press, 1984), pp. 116-22, 171-73, 197-202.

26. Morgan, *Puritan Family,* pp. 43, 91-97, 106.

27. Ortner and Whitehead, "Introduction," in *Sexual Meanings,* ed. Ortner and Whitehead, p. 58.

28. Paul Faler, "Cultural Aspects of the Industrial Revolution: Lynn, Massachusetts, Shoemakers and Industrial Morality, 1826-1860," *Labor History* 15 (1974): 372.

29. Paul E. Johnson, *A Shopkeeper's Millennium: Society and Revivals in Rochester, New York, 1815-1837* (New York: Hill and Wang, 1978), pp. 122-24; also, Edmund Morgan, "The Puritan Ethic and the American Revolution," *William and Mary Quarterly*, 3d ser., 24 (1967): 42.

30. Schneider, *American Kinship*, pp. 44-45.

31. Sherry B. Ortner, "On Key Symbols," *American Anthropologist* 75 (1973): 1342.

32. Sidney Ahlstrom, *A Religious History of the American People* (New Haven: Yale University Press, 1972), pp. 38-39. Ahlstrom observes that Catholicism came with the Spanish in the sixteenth century and dominated Hispanic America well before the Jamestown settlers even set sail in 1607. Catholics constituted the largest single denomination in the United States even as late as 1850.

33. Ahlstrom, *A Religious History*, p. 8.

34. For a detailed discussion of these strains of thought, see Anthony F. C. Wallace, *Rockdale* (New York: Alfred A. Knopf, 1978) and Philip Greven, *The Protestant Temperament: Patterns of Child-Rearing, Religious Experience, and the Self in Early America* (New York: Alfred A. Knopf, 1977).

35. Morgan, "Puritan Ethic," p. 3ff.

36. Faler, "Cultural Aspects," p. 369.

37. See Johnson, *Shopkeeper's Millennium*, p. 108, and Greven, *The Protestant Temperament*, p. 125ff.

38. Johnson, *Shopkeeper's Millennium*, pp. 96-102, 108.

39. Mary Farrell Bednarowski, "Outside the Mainstream: Women's Religion and Women Religious Leaders in Nineteenth-Century America," *Journal of the Academy of Religion* 48 (June 1980): 217. Bednarowski's evidence in this area is compelling. She reports that there were 127 female spiritualist mediums in practice by 1867, the same year that Mary Baker Eddy began the Christian Science movement that would give roles to scores of women lay readers. Bednarowski also describes the influence of Helena Blavatsky, cofounder of the Theosophy movement.

40. So many writers have illustrated these points that only a few can be named here. See especially Barbara Welter, *Dimity Convictions: The American Woman in the Nineteenth Century* (Athens: Ohio University Press, 1976); Carroll Smith-Rosenberg, "The Female World of Love and Ritual: Relations Between Women in Nineteenth-Century America," *Signs* 1 (Autumn 1976): 1-29; Sheila Rothman, *Women's Proper Place: A History of Changing Ideals and Practices, 1870 to the Present* (New York: Basic Books, 1978); and Nancy Cott, *The Bonds of Womanhood:*

"Woman's Sphere" in New England, 1780-1835 (New Haven: Yale University Press, 1977).

41. Ann Douglas, *The Feminization of American Culture* (New York: Avon Books, 1977), p. 86.

42. Amanda Porterfield, *Feminine Spirituality in America: From Sarah Edwards to Martha Graham* (Philadelphia: Temple University Press, 1980), pp. 13-15, 129-53. Porterfield explores various ways in which women in America transformed the hegemonic Christian message into a personal spirituality that validated them.

· 2 ·

SEX AND OPPOSITION:
THROUGH THE CELIBATE LENS

"Sweep from out the soul its selfish aiming!"

[Ann Lee] fell upon her knees, her eyes blinded by the super-
natural radiance. The conviction was borne in upon her
then . . . that the life of the celibate . . . and the taking up of
the cross against the world and the flesh was the only way of
regeneration.[1]

Although Shaker, Koreshan, and Sanctificationist believers were committed to celibacy primarily for religious reasons, the ideals of all
three groups reveal that they also understood celibacy as a symbol
of resistance to the divisiveness, hierarchy, and opposition they associated with heterosexual American culture. This chapter sum-
marizes the criticisms of sexual culture by members of the three
groups. This discussion will reveal that many of these communards
shared Ann Lee's observation and identified celibacy as their means
for taking up the "cross against the *world* [as well as] the flesh."

In explaining their religious motivations for celibacy, all three
groups in varying ways equated sin and sex on the one hand, and
salvation and celibacy on the other. Shaker legends describe Ann
Lee's nine years of "constant travail of spirit and body" over the
question of sin. Finally, she had a vision of "Adam and Eve in the
Garden of Eden committing the act that resulted in their expulsion
from the Garden and in saddling mankind with a heritage of sin."[2]
Lee understood both the role of sexuality in the curse of humankind
and the role of celibacy in reversing the curse, thereby hastening
the advent of the kingdom of God. Koreshanity was born in a similar
moment. Cyrus Teed (Koresh) experienced a beatific vision of the
Motherhood of God, in whose "gloriously regal" and "majes-

tic . . . sacred presence" Teed discovered his own preference for chastity and his own desire to "overcome all things in [himself] of the old sensual proprium."[3] Martha McWhirter, founder of the sanctified church, also had a parallel vision, shortly after the deaths of two of her children and a brother. She interpreted those events as a sign from God that she must purge her life of sin, including the sin of sex. McWhirter's understanding of sex as sin probably came from her understanding of Wesleyan doctrine, which defined sanctification, in part, as the casting out of "the old Adam, or carnal nature."[4] In McWhirter's view, celibate sanctification promotes genuinely spiritual rather than sexual unions between people, as well as spiritual unions between human believers and God.

Sex was more than sin to Shakers, Koreshans, and Sanctificationist believers, however. It was often characterized as a central evil of American culture. The records left from this period by all three groups reveal believers' disgust with the social consequences of sex in American family, work, and religious life. Their disgust resulted from their belief that each of those domains was tainted by heterosexual symbolism manifested as vicious competition, avarice, and other interpersonal and social evils. They saw celibacy, on the other hand, as the premise for alternative social values, including altruistic love, cooperation, and spiritual bonds among people on earth and between humanity and God.

THE SHAKER CRITIQUE

We may prate of individuality and freedom; but where is the independent man or woman? Surely they are not the heads of families; for who makes greater sacrifice than the true parent?[5]

When they put the Trinitarian God and Christ into the American Constitution on whose coin they have unlawfully put, "In God we trust," instead of "in Gold we trust"; which would, at least, be a truth and not a lie—liberty of conscience will be gone.[6]

Shaker writers of the late nineteenth century criticized American culture as an indulgent, privatized society, the foundations of which, in the isolated nuclear family, promoted selfishness, sexism, cupidity, and even war. Although Shakers generally understood separation on

49

the earthly plane—including the separation of the sexes—as a root metaphor of the divine order, they did not necessarily equate separation with irreconcilable opposition or hierarchy. Rather, they reserved the concepts of hierarchy and opposition for the divine rather than the human order, and they rejected all inequities and oppositions in human relations when they were unrelated to the system of divine order.

From Nature/Culture to Spirit/Flesh

In contrast to mainstream beliefs in an opposition between nature and culture, Shakers writing in the late nineteenth century considered both realms to be human creations that stood in opposition to true or divine nature. They classified reproductive humanity in the realm of human culture that is necessarily opposed to divine nature. As descendants of Adam and Eve, and therefore of the Fall, such persons cannot inhabit the divine natural realm. As followers of Ann Lee and Jesus, on the other hand, celibate communal Shakers can inhabit the realm of divine nature. (Shakers are post-millenial Christians; Ann Lee's conversion represents the Second Coming in Shaker doctrine.)[7] In 1887, Elder Daniel Fraser of New Lebanon explained that the two realms—divine and human—represent the orders of spirit and flesh that "lusteth" against one another and cannot be reconciled. Because conflict between them is inevitable, the orders must remain separate, and people must choose the order to which they will devote their lives. "Ye cannot live in two worlds at the same time," Fraser wrote.[8]

Earthly and Divine Love

Consistent with their concepts of separate spiritual and fleshly orders—representative respectively of divine or new nature and old nature—Shaker writers also distinguished between fleshly and divine love. Sexual or conjugal love, perverted by the curse of Adam, belongs to old nature. Its key symbol is, of course, heterosexual intercourse. All sex acts only replicate original sin and offer evidence, according to an 1889 text by Martha Anderson of New Lebanon, of "the sensual part of man," "his perishable self," the "grossness that clings to his nature," and "the remnant of his animal heredity."

Those who "still grovel in low loves and sensuous pleasures" are "incapable of comprehending the high destiny of the soul." Natural (generative) acts are merely "instinctive," according to Anderson, and they emanate from the "basilar region of the brain."[9] Elder Frederick Evans of New Lebanon, like several other Shakers, identified sexual love as "lust" and labeled it an "inferior" form of love. In a text of 1853 that contains the seeds of many of his later ideas, Evans explained that the "lust of generation is the one great evil that marred all the designs and works of God." Lust caused the flood, destroyed the laws of Moses, and ruined the early Christian church. A disdain for lust inspired the Shakers to follow the celibate example of Ann Lee and to abolish "generation itself" in their quest for spiritual lives.[10] True or divine nature requires a spiritual rather than a physical link among people as well as between people and God, according to Elder William Offord of New Lebanon in 1872.[11]

Even legitimate conjugal love was criticized by Shakers of this period and was rejected in favor of sibling love. "Those who admire husbands and wives, more than they do 'brethren and sisters in Christ' should not consider becoming Shakers," wrote Evans in 1878.[12] Because of its perverted attempt to unify the two orders of spirit and flesh, Shakers sometimes equated conjugal love with adultery and prostitution. Some saw the lust associated with conjugal love as the result of God's curse that prescribes male dominance in the marriage relationship. To them, the curse reveals God's own condemnation of sex in the context of dominance. Such believers understood Shakerism as a religion dedicated to the release—particularly of women—from the cursed combination. "Thousands of young women, ruined by the lust of men, are committing susiside [sic] to cover their disgrace," lamented Aurelia Mace of Sabbathday Lake in 1896. "The Testimony should be so powerful against that [old] nature that it would cause men and women to hate it with a perfect hatred—and to rise so far above it in Spirit as never to entertain one thought of indulgence."[13]

In short, as Daniel Fraser explained in 1887, "Marriage is not a Christian institution in Shaker belief."[14] That is, the sexuality that marriage is intended to legitimate is so sinful, self-serving, nonegalitarian, and destructive of spiritual values that the other goals of family life cannot redeem the institution. All familial roles and emotions are tainted by the "lustful life principle" of the nuclear family form, according to Evans's text of 1853. It is lust that converts a woman into a wife and mother, he explained. Therefore, the spiritual person should "hate with vehement indignation" not the woman, but the roles that reduce and limit persons to the "small and antagonistic . . . sphere" of the family.[15] Evans also observed that parental love interferes with the ideal "*universal* spiritual Gospel love." "A natural man first loves himself — then his wife, — his children, — his neighborhood, — his state, — his country, — his race. But, when he receives the love of God in Christ, his love extends to all the intelligent creation of God."[16] Daniel Fraser agreed: "The germ of the Adamic family is very limited in its unfoldings," he wrote in 1884.[17]

In addition to narrowness and sinfulness, the contribution to disorderliness of sexual love and its reproductive consequences also distressed some Shakers of the late nineteenth century. They believed erotic love and reproduction not only to represent base human nature, but also to encourage irresponsible and unpredictable acts. Sex was seen to produce consequences similar to those resulting from indulgence in other "appetites," including those for food and drink, and from the selfish waste of the earth's resources.[18] Further, Shakers also recognized that products of sexual intercourse — children — can create social disorder because heredity is not subject to rational control. "Either good or bad posterity" can result from sexual reproduction explained Evans in 1878. Further, he concluded, beings conceived in sin have little chance of becoming anything other than sinful themselves.[19]

From Selfish Family to Selfish Society

Shaker objections to sex extend beyond the family symbolic system to the closed and unfair society it produces. Martha Anderson summarized this view when she wrote that the nuclear, reproductive family is an "isolated fractional relationship which . . . makes [a] selfish society."[20] W. Watson Andrews, writing in the same undated Shaker publication, reinforced Anderson's view: "the family requires that a man be governed by the selfish sentiments, — exclusive care for himself and family. Directly or indirectly, whatever he plans or executes has for its object the support and comfort of his own household . . . his nature prompts him . . . to provide for his own in preference to another."[21]

Like Andrews and Anderson, Daniel Fraser, writing in 1884, interpreted the emotional climate of the family, valued by mainstream Americans for its "diffuse and enduring" qualities, as mere "family distinctiveness" resulting from the "power of the forces of animal emotional life."[22] Such distinctiveness was seen to promote private rather than communal emotional skills. Andrews further explained that the family is not a positive social model as Americans generally claim. Rather, the family is actually characterized by "its 'trouble in the flesh,' its cares, its anxieties, its fears and its sorrows; antagonistic in its nature and limited in duration."[23] Such a family form is more likely to produce "social miseries and prostitutions," according to Nicholas Briggs of Enfield and Canterbury, and to "fill our cities with crime, glut our prisons and insane asylums, people our pauper institutions and fill our cemeteries with premature deaths" than to exemplify ideal social behavior and organization.[24]

Evans went further than most writers of the period in identifying the selfish generative instinct that motivates the family as the cause for overpopulation, as well as for the perpetration of "bad and unphysiological food and drink, . . . vicious practices, . . . drugs . . . and lastly, eating *fellow creatures*." In the same text of 1866, he also accused physicians of being "a whole class of men [who] invent new diseases by the administration of . . . deadly substances" and, thereby, of contributing to unsavory forms of population control.[25] Without the selfish sexual and generative motivation, such practices would presumably no longer be necessary.

Several writers also identified private property, the logical concomitant of the family system in the generative order, as a social evil. Those enmeshed in the system of "flesh and blood cannot inherit the Kingdom of heaven," wrote Fraser in 1887; they must inherit something more tangible, like land.[26] According to Evans, it is "sin and self" that produce private property.[27] Families require the private ownership of property in order to ensure proper inheritances. War has become an acceptable means of protecting that property. Evans concluded in 1878 that "those . . . who believe it better to people the earth, with good or bad posterity, than to populate the heavens" are those "who love wars."[28]

A few writers also linked the concept of private property to the subordination of women. They saw the roots of male control over females as lying in the same Adamic curse responsible for lust and sin. When God told Eve that her "desire should be to her husband," he also required that "[the husband] should rule over her." Thus, according to Nicholas Briggs, God created male dominance, as well as lust, in the cursed family.[29]

Male perceptions of women as part of the private property within the family have also influenced other domains, according to several writers. Women's low wages and lack of the franchise, as well as the male "monopoly of business pursuits [and] injustice of the laws" can be traced to the family system that originated in the curse. Because Shakerism was designed to redeem humanity from that curse, one writer concluded that "whatever should subject the female, in any department of the animal kingdom, to male rule," as prescribed by the curse, should be abolished. A list of offending institutions must, of course, include the family.[30] "Man's supremacy has been tried for more than six thousand years, and it may be, six times six thousand years," wrote Briggs, "and it has failed."[31] Shakerism heralded the dawn of a new age characterized by new power relationships in familial settings.

Although most Shaker writers criticized the generative order throughout the nineteenth century, many were somewhat less critical after mid-century of those who continued to reproduce. "Whoever feels that the perpetuation of the species is a moral duty incumbent on him or her," wrote Alonzo Hollister of New Lebanon in 1892, "should seek a partner of like opinion, and discharge that obligation to the best of his ability, never infringing on the right of offspring to be well born and wisely educated." Shakers accepted the fact that generative people would continue to own property, because in Evans's words of 1853, "private or individual property forms the basis of, and is essential to, the marriage or generative order."[32] This recognition of a need by some for the nuclear family and its accompanying symbols did not imply an acceptance of the "forms and methods" of propagation, however. In fact, concluded Hollister, "physical passions and methods are [still] totally excluded from the higher mental and spiritual plane of life."[33]

Privacy and Avarice in the Work Domain

Shaker writers were especially aware of the influence of nuclear family values on the mainstream American domain of work. In fact, they understood the class system and private ownership of production in the American capitalistic economic system as extensions of the distinctions, hierarchies, and selfishness of the nuclear family. In 1878, Evans defined capitalism as a system that allows "the minority to accumulate and hold property so far beyond their normal wants, that vices, detrimental to all classes, are engendered by its possession."[34] Martha Anderson, writing in 1889, explained that such a system of private ownership of resources is unspiritual and leads to the holding of land by a few, "to the exclusion of their equals, by material force." Privacy of land ownership, in turn, sends "the landless into the labor market . . . subjecting them to the 'law of supply and demand,'" which she considered demeaning.[35]

Instead of understanding these marketplace exigencies as positive, as the mainstream did (and does), writers such as Daniel Fraser viewed them as "wage slavery." Writing in 1884, Fraser explained that the capitalist system, like the system of slavery, uses the worker to create property while he consumes "none, except what [is] necessary to create more."[36] Although, unlike slaves, workers receive wages, those wages only add insult to injury. Low pay prevents workers from buying their freedom from the system, as enterprising slaves sometimes could. Fraser also called the system of capitalism a satanic injustice and blamed it for "pauperism, social troubles, want and crime . . . standing armies . . . debts" and "other villainies," such as the monopolistic East India Company.[37]

As in the family, the antidote to such poison in the work domain is altruistic love which, according to Martha Anderson, can "counteract and hold in check the lower forces that bind and enslave the spirit in the gross realm of materiality."[38] If sex creates gross materiality, then celibacy can promote cooperation in the sharing of worldly goods and labor, as well as the fruits of labor.

The Shaker Critique of Mainstream Protestantism

Shakers of the late nineteenth century were painfully aware of the role played by mainstream Protestantism in the troubled symbolic systems of the work and family domains. Therefore, the practices of mainstream Protestantism became central to the Shaker critique of American culture. Like the Koreshans and the Sanctificationists, the Shakers were less critical of mainstream religion for its importance in American culture than for its distortions of true Christian values. Many Shakers considered the support of a divisive, selfish, competitive culture by mainstream religion an unholy alliance. They saw dissonance between the true values of Christianity and the false values of sexuality, family, and industrial capitalism. As Evans explained in 1853, "religion has been more wounded, *in the house of its professed friends,* by illogical doctrines, flowing from persons whose minds were beclouded and darkened by their sensual and wicked lives, than by all the infidel writers in the creation."[39] Fraser echoed those sentiments in 1887 when he wrote that any criticism of "what is called religion is a public service."[40]

Evans repeatedly articulated an important premise in the Shaker religious critique of the period. He explained that most Christians, in supporting competitive, privatized culture and in reaping the profits of that system, simply miss the point of Christ's message. At the core of their error is the false belief that salvation can occur while the sin of generation continues. Evans criticized as lazy and avaricious those Christians who worship Jesus in order to atone for their perpetual sin of Adam and yet continue to commit it. Such Christians exploit the "temporal advantage—*the loaves and fishes*" of religious life, he wrote in 1853.[41] In 1871, Evans explained that most Christians fail to recognize the "inevitable concomitants" of the sin of sex, including "marriage, selfish property, war, creating rich and poor, bond and free, on the basis of 'male and female'; [and live] to drink those things which afford the most present satisfaction." He defined the true purpose of religion: "to make a man's foes, his generative lusts, and their products, to be those of his own household."[42] In 1887, Fraser explained that non-Shaker Christians resemble the Pagan or Gentile Christians of the past by practicing "monopoly . . . slavery, usury, polygamy, war and sexual abominations."[43] Such a view was based on the earlier assertions of several writers that only Shakers were the true descendants of the Primitive Church of Jesus.[44]

Also implicit in the late-nineteenth-century Shaker critique of mainstream Protestantism is the denunciation of an all-male Trinity.

An earlier, rather charming example of such a view appears in a poem by Kentucky Shaker Richard McNemar from the 1830s, in which the poet ridicules the very idea of three males producing God's creation without female help. Such a concept not only excludes and deprecates femaleness, McNemar said, but it also violates all the rules of a clearly dual-sexed universe.[45] Texts from the later period are less explicit on this point, but the descriptions of both God and the Christ Spirit as bisexual that do appear indicate the continued unacceptability of the all-male Trinity.

Many Shaker writers were also offended by the mainstream Protestant interpretation of the Bible as the final word of God. Such a view implied to them a privileging of the past over the present. In 1872, James Prescott scoffed at the idea of an "infinite God [having] exhausted all his resources on the imperfect Jewish records, or on any age or nation."[46] Prescott refused to accept the Bible as a barrier between the ancients and modern believers, who have also witnessed new revelations of the true faith.

Many Shakers approved of one division in mainstream society, however, although they complained that they saw too little of it. Shakers supported the division between church and state mandated by the U.S. Constitution. They believed such a separation reinforces divine order by distinguishing between divine and earthly institutions. Evans argued that religious freedom is more likely to prevail when church and state are separated. "Let not the Clergy . . . seek to join together what God . . . has put asunder," he wrote in 1871.[47] Evans further advocated excluding "the priests of all religious denominations from civil power, [declaring] entire liberty of conscience, in matters of theology, from the Hindoo to the Atheist . . . and [banishing] theology from the Constitution of the United States."[48] He believed that the mixing of the two domains creates a kind of religious persecution by favoring hegemonic religion and denying nonstandard groups their rights "to be born; to live; and to [receive] an equal education; and [to participate in the] equal possession of the land."[49]

Shakers who expressed these criticisms of American culture were not content with the idea of mere reform of mainstream family, work, and religious domains. Rather, they sought a revolution in "reason and revelation . . . [in] Church and State systems and in all their institutions," as Evans wrote in 1889.[50] Mother Ann had ob-

57

served that "the foundations of the world 'were out of course,' " and she designed Shakerism to right them.[51] As a stabilizing influence, Ann Lee herself represented a center around which Christians could redesign the systems of family, work, and religion to create greater harmony with the divine order.

THE KORESHAN CRITIQUE

> We find the humanity eating, drinking, marrying and giving in marriage; atheistic in thought, blasphemous in speech, hypocritical and fallacious in religious tendency, and unmindful of impending catastrophes. . . . the world is slumbering in vice, pretence, infidelity, and frivolity.[52]

The Koreshan critique of mainstream American culture also focused on its divisiveness and selfishness, although without the overall analysis of divine and carnal nature provided by the Shakers. Like Shaker writers of the late nineteenth century, Koreshans identified the key symbol of sexual intercourse as the first human sin and defined all replications and results of that sin as "a violation of the sex law by the prostitution of sperm and germ for sensual reasons."[53] Also like the Shakers, Koreshans understood sex as the root of many familial and social evils.[54]

In the Koreshan view, sex for the sole purpose of reproduction was originally created by God as a force for good. In Eden, however, reproductive conjugal love was distorted into erotic lust which, in turn, perverted the "bond of true religious fellowship and unity" that should unite the sexes. After Adam and Eve added lust to sexuality, marriage became mere "legal adultery . . . a superficial and man-made ceremony . . . a legal license to monogamic prostitution" not of God's design. Such lust also wastes precious sexual substances, either in the service of passion or in the propagation of "offspring begotten under the influence of . . . a curse."[55] To Koreshans, celibacy could halt this waste and restore the pure bonding of male and female in spiritual rather than in physical reproduction. Through the practice of Koreshanity, Koresh explained, the biological processes of reproduction that normally lead to death and division are transformed into a spiritual process that leads to immortality and union.[56] Like the Shakers, Koresh also bemoaned the randomness of sexual generation: "the type improves in certain directions, while it degenerates in others," he wrote in 1896.[57]

Wasteful, lustful reproduction also inevitably creates an unspiritual family system, according to Koreshan writers. Koresh called the nuclear family unit a collection of hypocrites and sinners, bound together by "no mutual bond; no tie of reciprocity . . . but [rather by] passional emotion . . . [and] pride."[58] He was also skeptical about the quality of feeling existing among family members because he had seen it destroyed by outside influences and passions. "Let a member of a Protestant family join the Catholic church," he wrote in 1892, or support Belva Lockwood for president, "and [then] see how, as an electric shock, such a procedure makes the sacred family bond quiver."[59] Koresh also explained that the myth of family bonds bolsters blood relationships that would otherwise crumble from their own lustfulness and sinfulness.[60]

The Family and Sexual Hierarchy

Koresh considered marriage to be "sex slavery" for women.[61] Koreshan texts accused men of using male dominance in the cursed family system to "demand privileges, right emoluments, honors, opportunities and freedom, which they claim as good for and necessary to them and their welfare, while they insist that all these are not to be allowed to women."[62] Koreshans also identified all laws since the curse of Adam as man-made and male-aggrandizing. They felt that the extermination of sexual love, with woman as its "executioner," would end inequity between the sexes by snipping its root — sexual practice.[63]

In contrast to the Shaker belief that an earthly separation of spirit and flesh will restore divine order, Koresh envisioned divinity in their union. His scenario for the unification of the two realms is "theocrasis," a kind of spiritual alchemy. He wrote in 1900 that Mother God, whom he had seen witnessed years before, inspired him to believe that he, like Elijah and Jesus, had "the knowledge of transmutation . . . which, if manipulated, would unlock and disclose . . . [a] vital law" for the transformation of "matter of one kind to its equivalent energy, and in reducing this energy, through polaric influence, to matter of another kind."[64] Koresh believed himself to be a theocratic messiah, capable of transforming the evils of sexual society into spiritual perfection through the celibate science of Koreshanity.[65]

Likewise, Koresh envisioned the ultimate unity of the actual physical natures of the sexes in a "biune" being or hermaphrodite who would embody both maleness and femaleness but be a sexually neutral creature. Such "biunity" reflects God's unified, androgynous identity; "dualism [of the sexes] is not the extreme expression of the deific personality."[66] What mainstream culture regards as a God-given condition of distinction and unreconcilable opposition between the sexes is, to Koreshans, the result of God's curse. Distinctions between the gender identities and even the functions of the sexes are maintained only because they suit an industrial system that relies upon the division of labor by sex and the separation of home and work domains. Helen Gardener, a non-Koreshan whose work was frequently printed in Koreshan publications, explained in 1892 that "there is no distinction of right, or opportunity or privilege as to the occupation, life, liberty or the pursuit of happiness anywhere in nature between the sexes until we reach the one species of animal where one sex has been subordinated to the other by industrial conditions—by financial dependence."[67]

Koresh employed the metaphor of commerce in characterizing a new link between the sexes, wrongly divided by the curse. He advocated "true commerce" in both family and work domains as a means for achieving an equitable "collection and distribution of all the products of nature and industry."[68] In contrast, he saw the mainstream sexual, nuclear family as a system of false commerce or prostitution in which money and love are wrongly blended because of woman's need to barter her sexuality in marriage in order to achieve economic security.[69] He also blamed female financial dependence in the family for materialism and competitiveness among men. Such dependence, he felt, creates pressure on men to meet the financial obligations incurred by women.[70]

Cupidity and Capitalism

Like several Shaker writers of the period, Koreshans were highly critical of capitalism—especially competitiveness and private ownership—as an economic system. They blamed the values of the nuclear family system for the cupidity, waste, excess, sin, monopolistic practices, and hierarchical class structure in the productive sphere.

Like Shaker Daniel Fraser, Koreshan O. F. L'Amoreaux, writing in 1892, characterized the American commercial system as "a merciless system of exploiting labor for the benefit" of "classes who perform no labor."[71] Employing the metaphor of true commerce, Koresh explained in 1898 that the domain of work should represent "the collection and distribution of all the products of nature and industry . . . [and should] equitably provide for every man, woman and child in the world."[72] Instead, according to L'Amoreaux, the work domain has been dominated by notions of competition and private ownership. Therefore, rather than true commerce, usury, monopoly, and "a merciless contraction of the currency" reign supreme.[73]

Unlike Shakers who identified private land ownership as the key scenario of economic injustice, Koreshans blamed the purchase of labor in the capitalist system for the economic woes of American culture. In addition, they identified wage slavery in the privately owned mode of production as a logical extension of the principle of private ownership in the nuclear family system.[74] Koreshan writers also blamed war on the furthering of selfish commercial interests, rather than on the defense of land or property. Koreshans were not pacifists, however, for they envisioned "a great and final battle" before "universal peace" could be restored and false commerce could be obliterated.[75]

Perverse Protestantism

Like many Shakers, Koreshan writers blamed mainstream religions for contributing to the fragmentation and injustice of mainstream society. Unlike Shakers, however, Koreshans did not prescribe either religious tolerance or religious diversity as an antidote to such religious malpractice. Rather, they condemned the errors of sects other than Koreshanity and imagined that a universal conversion to their own beliefs would solve all problems.

Koresh did not restrict his criticism of religion to mainstream Protestantism, however. In 1892, he attacked the "paganization of Judaism and Christianity . . . the direct result of the falsification of doctrine . . . [as well as the] hundreds of Christian sects in which the doctrines of the church are made multifarious and nefarious — atheism, infidelity, materialism, spiritualism, theosophy, Christian Science, so called, and agnosticism, with the thousand other isms founded upon a misunderstanding of the laws of interpretation." Koresh considered the unnecessary separation of science and religion socially divisive. He blamed "the false so called sciences, — astronomy, geology, chemistry, sociology, and government" — for this separation.[76] Several writers accused Catholics, agnostics, and Jews of missing the point of religion entirely; one called agnostics "the consummate ass" of creation.[77]

Like many Shaker writers of the period, Koreshans criticized mainstream Protestantism for enforcing the curse of Adam rather than contributing to humankind's redemption from it. Several writers, including Amanda Potter in 1898, emphasized the special hardship for women inherent in Protestantism's coziness with establishment familial and economic practices.[78] Others ridiculed the all-male Trinity as a slippery, "three-headed personality" with conveniently interchangeable parts, or as an antiquated image, like "three old bachelors" who take credit for creation without acknowledging a female role in the process.[79] Koreshans also resisted the mainstream view of the Bible as literal truth; the group preferred to interpret its eternal but symbolic wisdom for themselves.[80]

Religion as Unity

While Shakers supported the separation of church and state, Koreshans defined religion as the key agent of unification for all areas of earthly and spiritual life. Koresh advocated theocracy as the ideal form of government. "Koreshanity is the union of church and state," wrote Koresh in 1900, "the reestablishment of the divine supremacy in the earth, the restoration of the kingdom of righteousness." Koreshans believed that true religion should be consistent with, not contrary to, science. Blended, the two disciplines can "comprise the constitutional bond of unity in a true consociation of men and women."[81]

As an agent of transformation from separation to unity, Koresh played a different role than Ann Lee. In contrast to Lee's characterization as a stable nucleus around which change could occur,

Koresh modeled the dynamic process of change itself. This difference certainly affected the structure of the two groups. Shaker theory emphasizes order and progress from one state to another. Koreshan theory emphasizes the constant interchange of one state or substance with another. Yet the critiques of mainstream American culture by the two groups share many characteristics. Both groups found narrowness, selfishness, and sin in the core institutions of American life, including the culturally sacred nuclear family, and believers in both groups prescribed celibacy as the principal means of preventing the spread of the family's poisonous influences throughout society.

THE SANCTIFICATIONIST CRITIQUE

> It must be admitted that among the marks of this society's growth are households divided and families broken up. It has excited the deepest of human passions to culmination in violence; and one would think it fortunate, if he considered their intensity, that they were appeased without the sacrifice of human life.[82]

> The Bible was studied and discussed by the little band of earnest women in the dreariness of their lives on the Western frontier, under the leadership of Mrs. McWhirter.[83]

Although the Sanctificationists experienced violent resistance to their celibate communism, they were less overtly critical of the mainstream culture that rejected them than were the other two groups. They did not set out to destroy the nuclear family system, for example. In fact, Martha McWhirter maintained her relationship with her husband, George, long after she discontinued having sexual relations with him. She was apparently willing to continue living with him as long as he wished.[84] Perhaps she believed that the sexual love they shared for twenty-five years of marriage could be transformed into the affectionate, nonsexual relationship of siblings or friends. Although he eventually moved from their home, George McWhirter initially supported that belief. He continued to profess his love for Martha, and he remained in their home for a few years after her commitment to celibacy. Eventually, however, "A stone wall grew up between us, he on one side and I on the other, and both of us loving each other," Martha McWhirter said.[85] Although they had been estranged for many years by the time he died, George McWhirter named his wife executor of his estate.[86]

The Unsanctified Family

Even though she was willing to continue in familial cohabitation, McWhirter had little interest in maintaining the family system at the expense of celibate sanctification. "If a husband should go to a wife and ask her for his sake, for the sake of her children and the peace of society to surrender her belief in sanctification as we teach it," she said in 1880, "I should say for her to do no such thing."[87]

Implicit in group beliefs is a critique of the sexual basis of the traditional American family system. As the Sanctificationists sought to replace physical with spiritual bonds between men and women, the importance of those physical bonds to mainstream marriage and family life became clear. In short, their attempt to exchange spiritual for sexual relations in marriage effectively eliminated family life in the women's lives. Husbands generally either initiated divorces from their celibate wives or withdrew support, and grounds for the divorces sometimes included charges of sexual deprivation by the husbands. Such grounds suggest the symbolic purpose of marriage in mainstream culture against which the women rebelled.[88]

Married Women and Economics

In addition to a possible hidden agenda of protest against the sexually based American family system, Sanctificationist records contain evidence of the sisters' very deliberate rebellion against the economic implications of the traditional marriage relationship. The women were openly critical of the mainstream prescription for female economic dependence in marriage. Several group members complained that the stinginess of husbands with household and pocket money kept wives servile and destitute. Some merely asked to share equally in the family income.[89] Others, like McWhirter, wanted to share in family businesses.[90] The men's apparent reflex response was to tighten the purse strings further, thereby demonstrating the economic tyranny of marriage for women.

In protest against the traditional male control of female economic security, the women formed their cooperative business and living arrangements. They exchanged the traditional, although fragile, financial security of marriage for the even riskier security of economic independence. In order to achieve that independence, the sisters first sold the products of their previously unpaid domestic labor, such as butter, eggs, rag carpets, and wood. Then they marketed their domestic skills starting with laundry services in 1882. From 1883 to 1887, they put themselves out to domestic service. They abandoned that practice in order to devote all of their time to their first hotel, which opened in 1886.[91]

Having replaced the economic traditions of marriage with their own economic system, the women had no interest in returning to married life, even when such a return might have been financially advantageous. Some of the men attempted to attract their wives back into nuclear family life with the lure of money, but they had little success.[92] McWhirter's daughter, Ada Haymond, who joined the group after her husband abandoned her, testified in her 1887 divorce proceedings that her husband's offer of money, should she return to the marriage, "would be no inducement to her to live with him."[93] Such offers only reinforced the degradation inherent in a system of marriage that provided no economic independence for women.

From Privacy to Community

The economic alternative chosen by the women also reveals an implicit critique of the mainstream work domain. The Sanctificationists' preference for communism contrasted with the values of competition and individuality in the society around them, as well as with the emphasis on the private ownership of property. The women had discovered the injustices of private ownership in their own lives when they tried to gain control over property they had owned before marriage or had owned jointly with their husbands. McWhirter discovered this injustice when she expressed a wish to build a small home for one of the abandoned women of her group on land she had brought into the marriage. She learned that the law granted her husband (like other husbands of the day) control of that property, even though it had been hers before marriage.[94] The group's communal style of ownership represents a revolt against a system in which true partnership was difficult for women within the context of marriage. By the time the group's constitution was written in 1902, the sisters embraced communism as the best route to a "thoroughly dignified, upright and commendable life."[95]

Eventually, McWhirter rejected as evil all control of a woman by her husband. She regarded such control as grounds for terminating the marital bond. "It was no longer women's duty to remain with a husband who bossed and controlled her," she said. "God made man and woman equal, and to woman in these last few days he has revealed his will concerning his own elect few."[96]

In short, the Sanctificationist cultural scheme signifies the women's disgust with the divisiveness and hierarchy they saw in mainstream life. Their testimonies reveal their horror at the connection in ordinary married life between sexual love and women's economic security, as well as at man's control over woman.[97] Commonwealth organization also reveals the women's opposition to female domestic servitude in marriage. They established a system of communal housework and child-rearing that counteracted the isolation and domestic drudgery of mainstream wife- and motherhood.[98] There is also evidence that some of the sisters sought refuge from the dominance of abusive or drunken husbands who, in mainstream society, were still deemed women's superiors, even when inebriated or violent.[99]

The Protestant Critique

The Sanctificationist critique of the family and work domains discussed earlier must be inferred from group records, because the group left no explicit social analyses. In fact, contemporary observers denied that the women paid overt attention to the culture around them. "The women have no politics and do not pretend to be reformers," wrote a somewhat naive journalist in 1901. "Nor do they interfere in any manner with the outside world."[100] In the religious domain, however, the group's criticisms of the mainstream are more direct. In fact, their initial act of rebellion occurred in the religious domain, through their rejection of sectarianism in the Methodist church.

The trouble erupted in 1870, when the Methodist church in Belton attempted to convert the Union Sunday School, run by George and Martha McWhirter, into an exclusively Methodist institution. The McWhirters refused to join. Other women involved in the Union school also withheld their support. Most members of the group were Methodists, but McWhirter's followers also included a few Baptists, a Presbyterian, and a Christian or "Campbellite." The church's decision distressed McWhirter partly because it violated her understanding of Methodism. She and her followers believed that celibacy and ecumenism were consistent with the tenets of that denomination. They understood sanctification as a purification of body and soul and as a sign of membership in the entire Christian community. The church, for its part, probably resented the religious leadership McWhirter's group exercised on their own authority. In the end, McWhirter's group solidified in their protest, remaining firm in their commitment to nondenominational principles. The Union school was finally abandoned by everyone except McWhirter's followers. By 1874, it became a meeting place for them alone.[101]

In the end, McWhirter was forced to break with the Methodist church after twenty-five years in order to demonstrate her devotion to what she believed were its deepest values. She refused to become sectarian in God's name.

The women's other objections to mainstream Protestantism reveal their abhorrence for literalism and opportunism in religious practice. Like Shakers and Koreshans, Sanctificationists believed in the Bible as a symbolic rather than a literal history. They objected to baptism by water and to the use of bread and wine in the sacrament on the same grounds; they regarded such things as symbolic, not literal or substantive. They also objected to what McWhirter called "Sunday Christians," indicating that they, like Shakers and Koreshans, believed in religion as a central metaphor rather than a convenient support for human institutions.[102]

THE SEXUAL CRITIQUE

Shaker, Koreshan, and Sanctificationist believers of the late nineteenth century embraced celibacy both as a symbol of the cross to be borne by true Christians and as a key symbol of new principles that would correct what believers saw as the errors of the sexual culture around them. Although the groups held varying views about the place of religion in secular affairs, they agreed that their religiously motivated choice of celibacy had social ramifications beyond religious practice. As they observed the American mainstream, they saw fragmented and divisive family, work, and religious domains. They believed that sex produces selfishness rather than mere privacy, ownership rather than equal partnerships, and competition rather than cooperation among God's children. They saw sex as symbolic of the subordination—particularly in economics—of women to men. Some even attributed war and other social evils to the emotions and values surrounding the symbolic system of heterosexual intercourse in American culture.

In direct contrast, believers in all groups connected celibacy with the spiritual unity and social equality of the sexes despite the physical separation of celibate men and women. They also understood celibacy as a symbol of unity in other cultural domains. In short, believers in these groups agreed that divisions in sexual culture could be bridged by celibacy. They did not always agree on the details of that unity, however. The variations of the groups' beliefs, with an emphasis on their differing ideas about male and female unity, will be the subject of the next chapter.

NOTES

1. Account of Ann Lee's 1770 conversion in Benjamin Youngs et al., *The Testimony of Christ's Second Appearing,* quoted in *Gleanings from Old Shaker Journals,* comp. Clara Endicott Sears (Boston: Houghton Mifflin; Riverside Press, 1916), pp. 13-14.

2. Marguerite Fellows Melcher, *The Shaker Adventure* (Princeton: Princeton University Press, 1941), pp. 10-11. The Shakers used the generic "he," "man," and "mankind," even when referring to the bisexual God.

3. Koresh [Cyrus R. Teed], *The Illumination of Koresh: Marvelous Experience of the Great Alchemist Thirty Years Ago, at Utica, N.Y.* (n.p., [1900]), pp. 12-21 (hereafter cited as Koresh, *Illumination of Koresh*).

4. George Pierce Garrison, "A Woman's Community in Texas," *The Charities Review* 3 (November 1893): 30; Eleanor James, "The Sanctificationists of Belton," *The American West* 2 (Summer 1965): 67; J. T. Smith, *Entire Sanctification (Heart Purity) and Regeneration as Defined by Mr. Wesley, One and the Same* (Marshall, Texas: Howard Hamments, Printer, 1895), pp. 9-10.

5. Martha J. Anderson, "Unselfish Interest," from *The Manifesto* 18 (February 1888), in W. Watson Andrews, *Communism* (n.p., n.d.), p. 5.

6. Frederick W. Evans, "Shaking the Old Creation," *The Manifesto* 19 (May 1889): 102.

7. Henri Desroche, *The American Shakers: From Neo-Christianity*

to *Presocialism,* trans. and ed. John K. Savacool (Amherst: University of Massachusetts Press, 1971), p. 77.

8. [Daniel Fraser], *The Music of the Spheres* . . . . *Dedicated to the Consideration of Robert G. Ingersoll, and to Others Like-Minded* (Albany, N.Y.: Weed, Parsons, Printers, 1887), p. 24.

9. Martha J. Anderson, "Altruism," *The Manifesto* 19 (April 1889): 77.

10. Frederick W. Evans, *Tests of Divine Inspiration; or, the Rudimental Principles by Which True and False Revelation, in All Eras of the World, Can Be Unerringly Discriminated* . . . . (New Lebanon, N.Y.: United Society Called Shakers, 1853), pp. 85, 87, 60.

11. William Offord, *Nature. God. Law.* (Canaan, N.Y., n.p., 1872). Library of Congress Manuscript Collection, Washington, D.C.

12. Frederick W. Evans, "Should All Be Shakers?," *The Shaker Manifesto* 8 (April 1878): 92.

13. Aurelia Mace, *Sister Aurelia's Journal,* Sabbathday Lake, 1896-1908, August 29, 1896. Sabbathday Lake Shaker Community Manuscript Collection, Sabbathday Lake, Maine.

14. [Fraser], *Music of the Spheres,* p. 25.

15. Evans, *Tests of Divine Inspiration,* pp. 87, 89.

16. Ibid., pp. 89, 88.

17. Daniel Fraser, "An Analysis of Human Society, No. 2," *The Manifesto* 14 (December 1884): 267.

18. Evans, *Tests of Divine Inspiration,* passim; see also Elijah Myrick, "The Celibate Shaker Life" [no pamphlet title] [Mt. Lebanon, N.Y.?, 1889?], p. 2.

19. Evans, "Should All Be Shakers?" p. 92.

20. Anderson, "Unselfish Interest," p. 6.

21. Watson Andrews, "Communism," in W. Watson Andrews, *Communism* (n.p., n.d.), p. 2.

22. Fraser, "Human Society, No. 2," p. 267.

23. Andrews, "Communism," p. 3.

24. N[icholas A.] Briggs, *God, — Dual* [East Canterbury, N.H., n.d.], p. 3.

25. Frederick W. Evans, *Celibacy, from the Shaker Standpoint* (New York: Davies and Kent, Printers, 1866), pp. 9-10. Evans instituted vegetarianism among the Shakers, partly on the basis of his identification with his "fellow-creatures." The "poisons" he referred to are food additives such as yeast, alkalies, and potash, which he regarded as detrimental to health.

26. [Fraser], *Music of the Spheres,* p. 25.

27. Evans, *Tests of Divine Inspiration,* p. 84.

CHASTE LIBERATION

28. Evans, "Should All Be Shakers?," p. 92.
29. Briggs, God, — Dual, p. 3.
30. "Woman's Rights," The Shaker 2 (July 1872): 53.
31. Briggs, God, — Dual, p. 3.
32. Evans, Tests of Divine Inspiration, p. 84.
33. Alonzo G. Hollister, "Shakerism," The Manifesto 22 (October 1892): 218-29.
34. Frederick W. Evans, "The Future," The Shaker Manifesto 8 (May 1878): 106.
35. Anderson, "Altruism," p. 77.
36. Daniel Fraser, "An Analysis of Human Society, No. 1," The Manifesto 14 (November 1884): 247.
37. [Fraser], Music of the Spheres, p. 10; Fraser, "Human Society, No. 1," p. 247.
38. Anderson, "Altruism," p. 78.
39. Evans, Tests of Divine Inspiration, p. 91.
40. [Fraser], Music of the Spheres, p. 11.
41. Evans, Tests of Divine Inspiration, p. 84.
42. Frederick W. Evans, "Running the World Out: Shakers — Salt," The Shaker 1 (June 1871): 41-42.
43. [Fraser], Music of the Spheres, p. 26.
44. See Youngs et al., Testimony of Christ's Second Appearing, quoted in Gleanings From Old Shaker Journals, comp. Sears, p. 14.
45. [Richard McNemar], ed., The Orthodox Trinity, with a Few Remarks on Certain Doctrines Therewith Connected, four-line quotation. [Watervliet, N.Y., n.d.], n.p.n.
46. J[ames] S. Prescott, "The Two Orders," The Shaker 2 (November 1872): 83.
47. Frederick W. Evans, "Religion and Spiritualism: A State without a Church," The Shaker 1 (March 1871): 20.
48. Evans, "Religion and Spiritualism," p. 18.
49. Evans, "Shaking the Old Creation," p. 103.
50. Ibid.
51. Mother Ann, quoted in Evans, "Religion and Spiritualism," p. 17.
52. Koresh? [Cyrus R. Teed], "How Can the Utopian Dream Be Realized?," The Flaming Sword 3 (May 7, 1892): 5.
53. Koresh? [Cyrus R. Teed], "The Human Race Is Degraded Through the Prostitution of the Sexual Function," The Flaming Sword 3 (May 7, 1892): 1; see also Koresh? [Cyrus R. Teed], "Geographical and Ethnological Confirmation of the Correctness of the Location of the Me-

tropolis of the Coming Pan-American Empire," *The Flaming Sword* 12 (August 5, 1898): 5.

54. "If Celibacy Obtains, How Will the Race Be Perpetuated?," *The Flaming Sword* 3 (March 26, 1892): 2.

55. Koresh [Cyrus R. Teed], *Judgment* (Chicago: Guiding Star Publishing House, 1900), pp. 6-8.

56. Koresh? [Cyrus R. Teed], "Revelation of the Mystery of Life," *The Flaming Sword* 3 (January 30, 1892): 1ff.

57. Koresh [Cyrus R. Teed], *Reincarnation, or the Resurrection of the Dead*, 2d ed. (Chicago: Guiding Star Publishing House, 1896), p. 5.

58. Koresh, *Judgment*, p. 6.

59. Koresh? [Cyrus R. Teed], "The Family Tie," *The Flaming Sword* 3 (April 9, 1892): 3.

60. Koresh?, "Mystery of Life," pp. 1ff.

61. Koresh [Cyrus R. Teed], "The Money Evil," *The Flaming Sword* 3 (May 7, 1892): 8.

62. Helen H. Gardener, "Sex Maniacs (Part 2)," *The Flaming Sword* 3 (June 11, 1892): 11. Reprinted from *The Woman's Tribune* (n.d.).

63. *The Flaming Sword* 3 (June 18, 1892): 9.

64. Koresh, *Illumination of Koresh*, pp. 1-5.

65. Koresh? [Cyrus R. Teed], "Cosmogony. [Part 1]," *The Flaming Sword* 3 (February 27, 1892): 6.

66. "God the Lord Alternately Male and Female; the Sons of God, Neuter," *The Flaming Sword* 3 (January 23, 1892): 1.

67. Gardener, "Sex Maniacs (Part 2)," p. 11. As will be discussed in chapter 3, Koresh was uncertain on the question of sex roles. His tacit approval of Gardener's sentiments did not prevent him from assigning women and children to domestic tasks in the community at Estero or from commenting, in one of his publications, that such an assignment simply and logically extended their traditional roles. See Koresh [Cyrus R. Teed], *The Koreshan Unity Cooperative* (Estero, Fl.: Guiding Star Publishing House, n.d.), p. 85.

68. Koresh?, "The Family Tie," p. 3.

69. *The Guiding Star* 1 (February 1888): 48-49.

70. [Koresh] [Cyrus R. Teed], *Response to Inquiries* (n.p., [1896]), p. 2.

71. O. F. L'Amoreaux, *The Flaming Sword* (February 13, 1892): 2.

72. Koresh? [Cyrus R. Teed], "Analysis of the Great Beast and His Image, Part III," *The Flaming Sword* 12 (August 26, 1898): 5.

73. L'Amoreaux, *The Flaming Sword*, p. 2.

74. See the unauthored excerpt from the Des Moines *Tribune* in *The Flaming Sword* 2 (April 30, 1892).

75. See *The Flaming Sword* 12 (October 21, 1898), p. 6, for the cryptic article that suggests this scenario.

76. Koresh?, "Great Beast, Part III," p. 4.

77. Lucie Page Borden, "The Anti-Semitic Movement," *The Flaming Sword* 12 (February 4, 1898): 7; Koresh [Cyrus R. Teed], "Analysis of the Great Beast and His Image, Part IV: The Beast and the False Prophet," *The Flaming Sword* 12 (September 9, 1898): 3; "Antichristian Religious Ceremonies," *The Flaming Sword* 3 (May 7, 1892): 2; "Sword Thrusts," *The Flaming Sword* 12 (March 4, 1898): 6.

78. Amanda T. Potter, "Observations and Reflections; Catching the Audience," *The Flaming Sword* 12 (September 30, 1898): 6; M. Sears Brooks, "Pagan Origin of Woman's Subjection," *The Flaming Sword* 3 (May 28, 1892): 9. Reprinted from the *Eastern Star* (n.d.).

79. "What Is Required that One May Become a Son of God?," *The Flaming Sword* 3 (January 30, 1892): 9; Koresh? [Cyrus R. Teed], "How Can Social Order Be Established? [Part II]," *The Flaming Sword* 3 (March 5, 1892): 4.

80. Koresh? [Cyrus R. Teed], "The Wife of God," *The Flaming Sword* 3 (March 26, 1892): 7; "A Few Points of the Koreshan System," *The Flaming Sword* 3 (March 19, 1892): 10.

81. Koresh, *Judgment,* pp. 17, 20.

82. Garrison, "Woman's Community in Texas," p. 29.

83. A. H. Mattox, "The Woman's Commonwealth," *Social Service* 4 (November 1901): 169.

84. A. L. Bennett, "The Sanctified Sisters," *The Sunny Slopes of Long Ago,* Publications of the Texas Folklore Society, no. 33 (1966): 143.

85. Margarita Gerry, "The Woman's Commonwealth of Washington," *Ainslee's Magazine* (September 1902): 138. Jayme Sokolow and Mary Ann Lamenna have argued that the McWhirter's had an unhappy marriage, but evidence on this point is contradictory. See their "Women and Utopia: The Women's Commonwealth of Belton, Texas," *Southwestern Historical Quarterly* 87 (April 1984): 379. It is probable, however, that several other women in the group did suffer abuse from their husbands.

86. Garrison, "Woman's Community in Texas," p. 32; James, "Sanctificationists of Belton," p. 73. Ernest Fischer finds no instruction about Martha McWhirter's role as executor in her husband's will. See Fischer, "The Sanctified Sisters," in *Marxists and Utopias in Texas* (Burnet, Texas: Eakin Press, 1980), p. 173. Documents found among the Commonwealth's papers support Garrison's view. Both George McWhirter's will, dated 1887, and a Fee Bill of the same year name Martha McWhirter "executrix" of her husband's estate.

87. Martha McWhirter, quoted in James, "Sanctificationists of Belton," p. 68.

88. For an example of such a divorce, see *Haymond v. Haymond, Southwestern Reporter* (June 13, 1889): 90-93.

89. James, "Sanctificationists of Belton," p. 67.

90. Sokolow and Lamanna, "Women and Utopia," p. 379.

91. Garrison, "Woman's Community in Texas," pp. 35-38.

92. Mattox, "Woman's Commonwealth," p. 169.

93. Testimony of Ada Haymond, *Haymond v. Haymond, Southwestern Reporter,* p. 91.

94. Garrison, "Woman's Community in Texas," p. 36.

95. *Constitution and By-Laws of the Woman's Commonwealth of Washington, D.C.* (Washington, D.C: Crane, 1902), pp. 3-4.

96. Martha McWhirter, quoted in Gwendolyn Wright, "The Woman's Commonwealth: Separatism, Self, Sharing," *Architectural Association Quarterly* 6 (Fall-Winter 1974): 37.

97. James, "Sanctificationists of Belton," pp. 68-69.

98. *Constitution of Woman's Commonwealth,* p. 10.

99. James, "Sanctificationists of Belton," pp. 68-69.

100. "Mrs. M'Whirter and Her Community of Celibate Women in Washington: They Migrated There from Belton, Texas: How They Work and Prosper in Their New Home," *The Waco Weekly Tribune,* July 20, 1901. George Pierce Garrison Papers, Barker Texas History Center, the General Libraries, the University of Texas at Austin. Private papers reveal that the women were aware of politics both in the United States and abroad. They followed the progress of the Spanish-American War, for example. Correspondence from 1898 even shows disagreement about the presidential candidates among group members.

101. Garrison, "Woman's Community in Texas," pp. 29-30, 31.

102. Ibid., p. 34.

· 3 ·

UNITY THROUGH CELIBACY:
COMMUNAL VISIONS

"Makes of all one common ground"

If sexual intercourse symbolizes a divisive and hierarchical society, then, logically, celibacy can be seen as the opposite, symbolic of unity, harmony, and equality. Where sexual culture stratifies social and economic classes, home and work, as well as male and female, celibacy promotes economic equity, public and private harmony, and sexual equality.

This conversion through celibacy is an implicit premise in the records of each of the celibate communities in this work. Believers in all three groups envisioned alternative cultural domains of home, work, and religion and theorized alternative relationships — predicated upon the possibility of unity — among them. Late nineteenth-century Shakers, Koreshans, and Sanctificationists designed communal families devoid of the sexual needs that create the opposed gender identities required in the nuclear family form. All three groups, in varying degrees, also rejected the idea that the domains of home and work must be separate and opposed. As a result, the hierarchy implicit in the respective association of those domains with nature and culture disappears. Believers understood celibacy as a premise for cooperative, communal economic theories, and egalitarian property ownership and distribution based on a spiritual rather than a physical bond.

In conceptualizing celibate unity, as in other ideas, the three groups differed. Many Shaker believers of the period envisioned a form of spiritual and symbolic gender unity based on the differentiation and separation of the sexes in most activities. The concept of gender differences in the Shaker system is not, however, predicated on ideas of female weakness and male strength, female economic dependence and male economic control. Rather, through the elimination of sex and marriage, the sexes are seen as differentiated but equal, as brothers and sisters, not husbands and wives. Some believers theorized that human gender distinctions would become perfectly balanced complements (not opposites) in Heaven, just as they are in the Godhead and Christ spirit.[1]

In contrast to this Shaker view, Koreshan writers promoted the achievement of sexual unity through celibacy by envisioning the elimination of both physical and symbolic gender differences. Theirs is a form of unity-through-identity. The Koreshan ideal is a biune, sexually neuter being who somehow blends the characteristics of both male and female, but who is neither male nor female. This sexually neuter being reproduces as Koreshans felt God originally intended, through internal, spiritual rather than lustful, interpersonal means. Although the process was never fully explained, Koreshans believed that celibacy contributes to spiritual reproduction by eliminating the very basis of lust and reproductive waste—sexual intercourse—thereby encouraging the conservation of sexual substances (sperm and ovum) for spiritual use. Such conservation, they believed, would make new methods of reproduction possible. As in the Shaker system, the gender unity achieved through celibacy becomes in Koreshanity a model for social unities of various kinds, including the unification of social classes and the resolution of competitive economic practices. Upon close analysis, however, the Koreshan biune being actually symbolizes traditionally male, rather than androgynous, characteristics. Thus the Koreshan system raises important questions about the benefits of androgyny for women.

The Sanctificationist system also promotes symbolic androgyny but their ideal of celibate unity merges male and female gender symbolism into an economically productive and independent human prototype. As will be discussed in chapter 4, that prototype assumes a female rather than a neuter or male identity. To Commonwealth believers, femaleness became the One and maleness the Other, a reversal of the more usual vision of the androgyne (evident in the Koreshan system) as a male- rather than a female-identified being. Another feature of the Sanctificationist system, as of the Shaker, is the promotion of unity only in the context of physical separation. For the Sanctificationists, the symbol of separation incorporates the root metaphors of individuality and autonomy, both within the essentially all-female group and between believers and the outside world. Unlike the Shaker version, however, Sanctificationist celibacy resulted in both the separation of believers from unsanctified men and in a prescribed limitation on expressions of intimacy among the women. As an all-female community, however, the Commonwealth also represents a form of sisterhood as a function of the celibate bond.

These summaries of the groups' approaches to unity condense scores of written documents by and about believers and represent hundreds of details. Celibacy as a symbol of sexual unity can be explored by means of those details.

SHAKER UNITY

> Their exclusion of marriage is proof . . . that . . . there is some
> rational connection between their control of the sexual relation
> and their prosperity.[2]

In Shaker texts, symbols of separation and difference intertwine with symbols of unification. This symbolic interplay is evident in Shaker views of a bisexual God and Christ Spirit. In both of these divine entities, Shakers believed that male and female gender characteristics coexist.

At first glance, Shaker views of sexual separation resemble the nineteenth-century doctrine of separate but complementary spheres for males and females, a doctrine that created opposition between the sexes and contributed to gender hierarchy. Shaker views of separation and of gender roles were not replicas of mainstream doctrine, however. Rather, in contrast to mainstream views of gender difference as the basis of hierarchy, Shakers flaunted difference to promote equality and unity of the sexes on the spiritual plane. Such spiritual unity is possible only in the context of the physical separation that celibacy requires.

The Metaphor of Progress in Shaker Thought:
From Jesus to Ann Lee

In order to establish the religious basis for their beliefs in gender unity, many Shaker writers of the late nineteenth century embraced the value of religious progress. Shakers recognized that their goals of equality and unity, among others, deviated from those of other Protestant sects. They rationalized that deviance as a sign of their advanced religious understanding; theirs was, simply, the most modern form of Christ's message to date. In establishing Shakerism as progressive Christianity, believers defined theirs as the fourth (regenerative) dispensation, following the first (initiative) dispensation of Adam, the second (covenant) dispensation of Abraham, and the third (redemptive) dispensation of Jesus.[3] An 1853 text by Frederick Evans described Shaker communities as representative of the Kingdom in which "all the righteous laws of the Four Dispensations culminate."[4]

The Shakers did not consider theirs to be the final dispensation of God, however. Therefore, they resisted attempts even by their own believers to establish a rigid Shaker theology. "This is not a creed," insisted Giles Avery of New Lebanon in 1883, "a boundary to faith beyond which *no further revelation may peer* .... Shakers do not perceive that a *formulated opinion of mere human conception,* anchored at the dock of finished creed, has cabled the *heavenly argosy of divine truth,* with all her cargo of revelations, within the finite harbor of present human attainments."[5] "Theology, ritualist forms, and credal systems, have not brought forth goodness," Daniel Fraser argued in 1887. "Hence, they are not religion."[6]

These views also help to explain the Shaker reluctance to accept the Bible as the last word of God. "The Bible of the Past can never supersede the necessity of the Bible of the present and of the future . . . if man progresses at all, he will ultimately reach a spiritual order," wrote James Prescott of North Union, Kentucky, in 1873.[7] The idea of a fixed text contradicted important concepts of Christianity as the Shakers understood it: continuous revelation and spiritual progression. "Avenues are open to the spirit world, through that to God," explained Anna White and Lelia Taylor of New Lebanon in their 1904 history of Shakerism. "New revelations are always possible, are expected, and are, in their economy, necessary, as man advances, individually and collectively, in light and knowledge of things human and divine."[8]

Even the belief in a female Christ Spirit was seen as consistent with religious progress. W. Watson Andrews explained in 1893 that Ann Lee represents "the quickening into spiritual life [of] the female nature, in humanity, as the male had been in the first advent."[9] "Though the whole world may sneer," wrote Harvey Eads of South Union, Kentucky, in 1879, the Shakers knew Ann Lee to be the proper person "to come in [Jesus's] spirit, power and gift."[10]

Believers who articulated ideas of religious progress did not condemn previous dispensations for their ignorance of the Shaker revelation. "Moses and Joshua were incapable of perceiving higher truths than an 'eye for an eye,'" explained Eads. "God could not give them the Christ light nor life . . . . According to this, you will say that Moses, who *slew* his enemies and Christ who *loved His,* were equally justified before God."[11] Each dispensation was, however, seen as an improvement over the previous ones. "The law of Moses is a system of commandments and penalties adapted to the order of generation," wrote Sarah Lucas in 1868. It therefore must focus upon "thou shalt nots." But "the Gospel is a system of grace and gracious invitation to a holy life. 'Whosoever will, let him,' is the language of the Spirit."[12]

Shaker ideas of progress beyond previous eras also included respect for their religious forebears. Many writers were eager to demonstrate this religious continuity. To that end, Ann Lee was symbolically linked with Jesus in many texts. Like Jesus, she was the child of working-class parents, and she performed manual labor throughout her life. Many writers saw her advocacy of celibacy, communism, pacifism, and spiritual, altruistic love as parallel to Jesus's advocacy of the same principles. Both had suffered, preached, and sacrificed for their beliefs, for which they were both physically and mentally abused.[13] Some writers also connected the two on the grounds of their adult baptisms. Neither Jesus nor Lee had been holy at birth, they explained; rather, both were reborn and anointed by the Christ Spirit in maturity. "Jesus is not Christ, *per se,*" wrote Evans in 1890; "Christ is a spirit from the Christ or resurrection heavens."[14] It was the hope of other Shakers that such anointment would also be their lucky fate.

Even Lee's illiteracy was sometimes seen as a possible link to Jesus; like her, Jesus left no written expressions of his message. To some believers, Lee's illiteracy only enhanced the legitimacy of her role: an illiterate who cannot study religion must receive her faith directly from God. Lee also continued Jesus's practice of the oral tradition. Believers repeated that tradition in various ways; the receipt of messages from departed believers, God, and other spirits in various periods of Shaker history may have been part of that tradition.

The Unity of Spiritual Progression Through Separation and Control

It is possible, therefore, to consider progress—both from and beyond previous religious periods—to be a root metaphor in these Shaker texts, a metaphor that also underlies the scenario of progression in Shaker belief. "The souls of all . . . have endless existence. Every soul is a subject for the spiritual resurrection to eternal life," explained White and Taylor.[15]

Spiritual progression in turn depends upon self-control on the earthly plane, and celibacy was seen as the principal evidence of such control. Celibacy requires separation, and that separation leads to spiritual unification of the believer and God. "Unless you are able to take up a full cross, and part with every gratification of the flesh, for the Kingdom of God," said Mother Ann, you should not try to be a Shaker.[16] "The object of Shaker life is self-conquest," wrote Alonzo Hollister in 1892; "salvation from all wrong doing, from selfishness, to be utterly rid of the carnal life and will, through a perfect moral, intellectual and spiritual obedience to the commandments of God, as taught by Christ Jesus." Self-control leads to eternal life, and, conversely, delivers eternal death "to the corrupt, fluctuating, passionate, conflicting, mutating and transient, pleasure seeking animal life of the world."[17] "The true cross is not of wood," explained White and Taylor, "but a life of self-denial."[18]

Self-control, symbolized by appropriate forms of separation, also enhances a believer's receptivity to the Christ Spirit according to several writers of the period. That receptivity, in turn, facilitates the entry into the spiritual domain. "The Shaker Order proves that . . . self-denial of spirit, works the soul gradually into the heavenly state," wrote William Leonard of Harvard, Massachusetts, in 1871.[19] By enacting the scenario of self-control, believers expected to be reborn "in the pure perfect, heavenly and eternal life of the angelic societies, whose greatest delight is in serving, and ministering to the happiness of others," according to Hollister.[20] In the angelic societies, many forms of spiritual unity are possible.

In addition to promoting spirituality, the scenario of spiritual progression emphasizes action against sin rather than the mere profession of the wish to stop sinning. Frederick Evans, for example, saw "no truth in the atonement theory" he witnessed in mainstream Evangelical Christianity. " 'Cease to do evil, and learn to do well'; 'work out your own salvation' — is the atonement needed," he wrote in 1890.[21] White and Taylor explained atonement as "at-one-ment. . . . Man works out his salvation and comes to be at one with God."[22] Celibacy signifies such action against sin.

Control of the appetites, including sexual ones, is not the equivalent of ascetism, however. Believers were well although simply fed and clothed, and they enjoyed the society of co-believers. Shakers of the period extolled the importance of physical and emotional comfort to a spiritual quest. Therefore, as Evans explained in 1853, the Society provided "a full supply of physical and spiritual necessaries, for the body and soul of every one of its members."[23]

Celibacy and Reason

By emphasizing reason as a root metaphor of their key symbol of celibacy, Shakers challenged what they saw as the unreasoned, passionate basis of reproductive family life and, by implication, of any religious sect that encourages immediate, emotional conversion of believers. They also suggested that celibate, rational human beings were closer to God — another sign of celibacy's unifying power.

Celibacy uses reason as a defense against the temptations of the flesh, which are the enemies of reason. Daniel Fraser explained in 1880 that the Apostle Paul himself recognized the "animal passions — 'warring against the law of [his] mind,' " as he struggled to overcome his own carnality.[24] In order to choose celibacy, believers must surpass mere human reason and follow the small spark of divine reason that lies dormant in everyone. According to Evans, recognizing that spark allows the believer to see the plan of the universe as designed by "divine intelligence" from "the mind of the creator, — God."[25] Sexual humanity cannot recognize divine rationality because their perceptions are clouded. They see the world through generative nature, which, as William Offord explained in 1872, has "no intelligence . . . no rationality . . . no responsibility . . . [no] motives, intentions, plans or *will*."[26]

To live in accordance with "all-wise and *intelligent God*," continued

Offord, Shakers must replace desire with will.[27] Even Eve might have escaped her cursed fate as a submissive subordinate to man by rationally transforming her sexual desire for her husband through that divine spark of rational will. The Christ Spirit provides believers with a second chance to dedicate themselves to divine reason, for it, too, models the transformation of sexual desire into voluntary compliance with the "law of vital force."[28]

A believer's voluntary acceptance of divine reason through celibacy and other forms of restraint and self-control also symbolized for some writers the transformation of mere flesh into a higher and more durable life form that expresses the merger of human and divine realms. Offord explained that "living according to the laws of hygiene, dietetics, and cleanliness; and entirely abstaining from all exciting, intoxicating, and benumbing narcotics, spices and compounds: such as alcohol, tobacco, [and] opium," in addition to abstaining from sex, promotes health and long life.[29] In the late 1880s, Giles Avery assessed the effect of celibacy on longevity in several Shaker communities. Compared with the average lifespan in mainstream America of less than sixty years, Avery reported that, in New Lebanon, "the number of deaths from 1848 to 1850 was 29 persons, and their average age was 70½ years—this included both sexes." He also found that, among 200 persons in Alfred, Maine, 100 were more than seventy years of age, thirty-seven were aged eighty to ninety, and thirteen were aged ninety to ninety-seven. "The average age of the 200 is 62 years, 9 months, 6 days, 2 hours," he wrote. Furthermore, he found that these Shaker elderly "[had] good use of their limbs, [were] able to go out of doors, and [capable of] a good day's work of choice."[30]

Frederick Evans also linked celibacy with the increased longevity of the human family as a whole. Because celibacy signifies the death of selfish family relations and their evil accomplice, private property, it also eliminates key premises for war. The end of war through celibacy would reduce the mass destruction of human life, according to Evans, thus proving that celibacy actually increases rather than decimates the population.[31]

Reason was also linked by Shaker writers to believers' exercise of voluntary and conscious choice in joining Shaker communities and adhering to Shaker ways. A Green and Wells' text of 1879 explained that only voluntary sacrifice, not that made "by any undue constraint or persuasion," can be seen as a "sacred privilege." In turn, they suggested, voluntary sacrifice instills reason in the entire society, encouraging the values of justice, goodness, and truth.[32]

As support for the symbolic link between celibacy and divine reason, several writers cited historical precedents for the celibate commitment. "That there is a law in our nature responding to a virgin life is evident," wrote Daniel Fraser in 1880; "it has cropped out in all ages from the earliest historic times; it was manifested in the theraputae [sic] of Egypt, among the Jews in the Nazarites, and was developed as a permanent institution in the communities of the Essenes." These and several other examples demonstrated to Fraser "the innate veneration of the human spirit for a life of absolute purity."[33] In 1866, Evans described the long history of celibacy in the Christian tradition. Begun by Jesus, his 8,000 converts, and other "proselytes," the celibate ideal lasted 1,600 years before Martin Luther found it "an impossibility," Evans explained.[34]

Celibacy, Order, and the Separation of the Sexes

The achievement of unity with divine reason and the spiritual domain depends on various forms of separation, including the separation of the sexes. Separation promotes celibacy, and celibacy, in turn, promotes spiritual unity. The models for human gender difference in Shaker texts are creation itself and the divine order on which creation is based. According to Evans, writing in 1890, the importance of the duality of sex can "clearly [be] seen by revelation, and by the things that are made . . . animals, vegetables and minerals are all dual—male and female."[35] In Creation, sexual dimorphism symbolizes bisexual qualities of the Godhead and of the Christ Spirit. Shaker policies, recorded in various versions of the Society's *Millennial Laws*, enforced the differentiation and distinction of the sexes in reflection of divine order in its earthly form. Rules limited the interaction of the sexes, separated men and women at table and in other parts of the house, and assigned them to different tasks.

The Shaker version of sex separation and differentiation does not require symbolic gender opposition, however, because celibacy requires no mutually exclusive distinctions between males and females, as sex does. In fact, in the Shaker view, gender opposition promotes sexuality and thus works against celibacy. Gender differentiation in

Shaker texts, therefore, generally links believers with divine bisexuality, understood as a balanced and unified duality. Evans observed in 1871 that "the difference of sexes is brighter and more exquisite in proportion as the person is high and the sphere pure."[36] But, he and others suggested, the greatest distinction leads to the highest plane and, therefore, to the greatest unity.

Shaker concepts of gender difference did lead to prescriptions for separate and distinct gender roles. Women were expected to perform indoor, domestic work while men performed outside chores. Women often served the men, made their beds, mended their clothes, and prepared their food.[37] Although these traditional-looking roles do resemble mainstream gender roles, they were not interpreted by Shakers as evidence of the weakness or dependency of one sex upon the other or the greater value of the tasks performed by men. Texts from the late nineteenth century suggest that Shaker believers were increasingly reluctant to interpret sexual difference and separation—mandated by the divine order—as hierarchy. As Anna White wrote in 1891, "the occupations of men and women may differ very materially; but does this go to prove that those of women are of the least importance? Not by any means." Men's duties may be "sterner," she continued, but women's are "all important responsibilities." Furthermore, duties were divided to promote mutual economic and spiritual interdependence: "the man is as equally dependent upon the woman as is the woman upon the man," according to White.[38] Shaker views of the symbolic merger of family and work domains facilitated this egalitarian view.

Further, in the context of the Shaker ideal of spiritual union between celibate male and female believers, the differentiations between, and separations of, males and females defined in Shaker texts of the period do not result in the association of the sexes with stratified realms such as nature and culture, as they do in mainstream society. Male and female celibate believers are united in their beliefs as denizens of a post-millennial world in which all realms are spiritually unified. By reframing the world in which they lived, Shakers reframed the meaning of gender distinction and separation. Difference is divine; opposition and hierarchy are cursed. Celibacy ensures the maintenance of the first and reduces the risk of stumbling into the latter two.

Celibacy Promotes Other Separations

The most important separation required by celibacy, and one that does entail the stratification of human spheres, is the separation of the reproductive order of humanity from the celibate order. Evans wrote in 1866 that each order of humanity represents, respectively, the "natural and the spiritual [orders], each having its own laws," which would be violated if the human orders were to be blended.[39] If the orders were mixed, spirit and flesh would come into unholy alliance. Sarah Lucas prescribed the maintenance of boundaries between the order of "the old man Adam, which is of the earth, earthy," and the regenerative order of celibates or "the New Man, Christ, the Lord from Heaven."[40]

Evans's desire to maintain the separation of church and state included his wish to separate these two orders. He wanted no connection between (divine) church and (earthly) civil government. Like Jesus, he wished to be dissociated from the "worldly corruption and bitter, political, enduring antagonisms" that inevitably accompany the state.[41] The need to keep spiritual life separate from earthly life also formed a basis for argument against Shakers' voting and participating in political wars. As Evans explained in 1880, a person can serve only a single cause in an ordered universe. The choice to serve God precludes the choice to serve government.[42]

Several writers realized that the separation of the celibate, spiritual population from reproductive, earth-bound humanity implies an irony: the celibates need the reproductive in order to populate their communities. Giles Avery explained in 1883 that, although Shakers are spiritually advanced over reproductive persons, they remain dependent upon them for their members.[43] Such a prospect troubled some writers more than others. Sarah Lucas, for example, believed that God approves of "the married relation, when the laws of God and nature are strictly observed, and no carnal intercourse indulged except for issue."[44] With similar optimism, Evans predicted in 1890 that the two orders would continue in an interdependent relationship, with "the generative order, perfected [presumably by devoting itself only to reproductive sex]; and the resurrection order, as a spiritual granary into which the great human harvest will be gathered."[45] He was more expansive than most, however, when he imagined in 1866 that "millions might then live celibate lives in Shaker communities, dotting the land with paradises, as oases in the desert of selfishness."[46]

In spite of occasional tolerance of those in the reproductive order, however, Shaker writers were adamant that an individual cannot belong simultaneously to both the generative and the spiritually regenerative orders. Once the commitment is made to the spiritual life, the life of the flesh becomes unthinkable. As Daniel Fraser wrote in 1880, "That which is flesh is flesh, and that which is spirit is spirit."[47] Sarah Lucas observed that "we cannot belong to both; for 'all in Adam die; but all in Christ are made alive.' "[48] In 1880, Harvey Eads expanded on the reasons for separation: "All philosophers agree that spirit and body are distinct and contradictory substances. The body loves the excesses that disgust the spirit—the body has the pleasures, the spirit the pain . . . . The work of the former is below, and is performed in the dark—the work of the latter is above, and is performed in the light."[49]

Because of the need for separation between spirit and flesh, several writers opposed allegedly spiritual marriages in such groups as the Mormons and Oneidans. Such marriages would only confuse the categories of the spiritual and fleshly orders, and, according to an 1872 text by James Prescott, lower the standards set by Jesus and bring "down the divine below the human."[50] In 1853, Evans called spiritual marriage a "vile prostitution of the principle of virgin purity," thus employing the term used in mainstream culture to designate the mixing of love and money to refer, instead, to the inappropriate mixing of spirit and flesh.[51]

Spiritual Unity and the Shaker Celibate Family

Because the spiritual unity of the sexes is the goal of gender differences and gender roles, it is not surprising to find Frederick Evans envisioning in 1866 a New Heaven in which "the man is not without the woman, nor the woman without the man, any more than in the old [original] creation."[52] On the same grounds, it is also not surprising to learn that the Shakers insisted that the sexes live under the same roof in every house in every Shaker community. If separation and opposition had been the ultimate goal, they would have divided men and women permanently and completely. Instead, they demanded togetherness without intercourse (social or sexual): unity in difference.

Several writers described the Shaker form of celibate cohabitation as an improvement even upon the celibacy of Jesus's time because it challenged believers' control over the flesh and maintained a healthy tension among the difficult concepts implicit in God's plan: earth and heaven, separation and unity, group and individual, pain and ecstasy. Evans explained in 1866 that, in Shaker communities, "the males and females, instead of coming under vows of perpetual chastity, and then being kept so separate that they could not infringe them, are all together as are brothers and sisters in a natural family."[53] In a text of 1883, Giles Avery contrasted Shaker communities to cloisters and nunneries that tended to "abnormalize the sexes."[54] In Shakerism, the sexes learn to live according to the nonsexual, spiritual qualities of their gender characteristics.

Reflecting the ideal of spiritual unity, believers described themselves as members of families that were bound by nonphysical, cognatic rather than sexual, conjugal love. In "spiritual regenerative society," wrote W. Watson Andrews in 1891, the "harmonial bond is love—love to God, supreme, and neighbor as self in the communistic relation, with its freedom from . . . the cares, the anxieties, the fears and the sorrows of the family relation. Harmonial in nature and continuous in duration, its pleasures are necessarily unlimited and abundantly satisfying . . . ."[55]

The form of love most advocated by Shaker writers is nonsexual, affectionate, sibling love, the closest approximation on earth to the divine and unifying love of God and of the Christ Spirit. Anna White defined it as a love "every pure heart believes in and enjoys, before passion has sullied the soul with its poisoned breath, [and] which the first Christians felt for each other."[56] She also identified sibling love as the "bond and seal to unite the whole."[57] Sarah Lucas defined the love felt by gospel siblings (Shaker brothers and sisters) as an impartial "expansion of love, not requiring us to love our natural relations less, but to love others more, and all on a different and higher principle."[58]

Shaker sibling love broadens the definition of family that many Shakers found so limited in its nuclear form. "Only the relation of husband and wife, — the married relation, — is to be forsaken," Lucas explained, "and not the person or persons." Spouses can, therefore, become siblings in Christ and be loved with Christian rather than erotic love.[59] In fact, as Evans wrote in 1871, "genuine Christianity began its career by dissolving the marriage tie, and making the man and woman nearer and dearer relatives — brother and sister."[60] Where sex limits love by requiring ownership and a confining affectional fidelity, celibacy widens the field and opens the heart.

In contrast to what Shakers witnessed in the conduct of blood and in-law relations in mainstream family life, several writers encouraged "the perfect harmony of good will, a spirit of passionate concern for and joy in, each other's being; which shall rule in every member of the society of ideal beings. It is love . . . fully present . . . equal shining along every line of the space it inhabits," as Hollister explained in 1892.[61] If this kind of love "destroys the family, root and branch," then so be it; that destruction is simply the "fulfilling of the Law" of divine nature, according to Green and Wells.[62]

Reason and the Celibate Family: Work/Family and Male/Female

If celibacy signifies the presence of divine reason in the individual, then the celibate Shaker family system can be seen as a sign of collective rationality. Celibacy creates voluntary families, formed rationally through selection and choice. The celibate family contrasts with the passion and involuntarism of blood relationships in the mainstream nuclear family form. Even the "parents" of Shaker households — elders and elderesses — earned rather than inherited or assumed their rights to leadership.[63] For blood ties, the Shaker system substitutes the deliberate act of adoption. The accident of biological birth is superseded by the conscious act of conversion, reflecting the adult baptisms of Jesus and Ann Lee.

By infusing family life with the concepts of voluntarism and reason, the Shakers effectively infused their family domain with relational qualities — including the imposition of objective criteria — associated by mainstream Americans with the work domain. Several texts support this blending of family and work relationship concepts. In a memorial volume of 1912, Lelia Taylor expressed typical feelings for two recently deceased gospel relations, connected by common belief rather than blood. Of Sister Eunice Canterell, Taylor wrote, "We loved her,—ready and willing to perform any little act of kindness to a brother or sister that lay in her power." Of Eldress Mary Ann Gillespie from the Maine Ministry, she explained, "her heart was full of love for all humanity," a quality that earned her the love of others. Taylor concluded that she herself loved best "those who have through suffering and tribulation kept the gospel for me."[64]

More like co-workers than typical relatives, Shaker converts formed commitments to Shakerism only after careful consideration and evaluation. In their 1879 *Testimonies,* Green and Wells explained that "no flattery nor any undue influence is used, but the most plain and explicit statement of [the Society's] faith and principles are laid before the inquirer: so that the whole ground may be comprehended, as far as possible, by every candidate for admission."[65] As early as 1830, when practices were codified and stabilized, the Shaker admissions process required three steps. New members joined the novitiate, junior, and senior orders, each step representing an ascending degree of commitment of self and property to the community. Similarly deliberate methods of membership continued throughout the century.[66]

The theory of leadership in Shaker families also blends symbolism from the family and work domains. Supervisors in the Shaker family system treated their workers as loved children of God. William Offord explained in 1873 that "the perfect spiritual order is parental. . . . What is meant [is] an interior spiritual, or heavenly order of society, which, equally with the natural order, requires father and mother, and children, to constitute it a *family* or order."[67]

The Shaker family leadership model can also be seen as an infusion of public principles of social democracy and representative government into the family domain. Each Shaker family was led by elders and eldresses, usually two of each sex, who governed each communal house, which was composed of twenty-five to 150 brethren and sisters.[68] Both sexes in those roles were expected to "focalize rays of divine love, connect the soul to God, [and] impart the germ of heavenly life," as well as to "direct, control, inspire" those under their care.[69] Domestic affairs of the community as a whole were handled by deacons and deaconesses, and trustees of both sexes handled commerce and other dealings of the community with the outside world. A major requirement for exercising family leadership was freedom from "any involvements with those without." People who were considered advanced in their family leadership qualities might qualify for higher community posts, as in the Central Ministry.[70] Shaker family leadership was seen as a training ground for more public responsibilities rather than, as in the mainstream, an exercise of merely private skills.

The Shaker custom of adopting orphans who were unwanted by mainstream society also demonstrates a view of the family as both a public and a private domain. Believers prided themselves on performing this service, pointing out to critics of their nonprocreative celibacy that they were caring for children who had been abandoned by their blood relations.[71] Although they required work from these children, as from all community members, the Shakers did not view the adoption of an immature, pre-rational child as a lifetime agreement. The children became Shakers only if they voluntarily and consciously committed themselves to Shakerism at the age of twenty-one. Nonrational allegiance, even among the young, was not a Shaker value.

Late-nineteenth-century Shaker texts reveal Shakers' visions of a new family system, founded on celibacy, that counteracts the evils of mainstream family life by enlarging its symbolic sphere. The Shaker family blends rationality with love, love with work, and leadership with the maintenance of family ties. While nuclear families depend upon passion and "natural" compulsion for their bonds, Shakerism relies upon choice, voluntary association, and earned love. These principles not only promote enduring family relationships, but they also unify symbols that are opposed in mainstream views of work and family, and therefore of the males and females who inhabit those stratified domains. Thus, to the Shakers, the physical separation of the sexes through celibacy actually promotes their symbolic unity.

From Familial to Social System

If the closed, selfish, sexually based nuclear family produces privatized, competitive social and economic systems, then, Shakers reasoned, the celibate communal family system can produce a cooperative, communal, unified society. Rather than interpreting the family as a haven from society, the Shakers extended their familial values into the social system in order to promote unities where divisions and oppositions traditionally occur.

Frederick Evans was perhaps the most ardent advocate of unity as a goal of social design. In 1888, he envisioned a single-class society, as opposed to the multiple, stratified social classes of mainstream American life. He wanted "no rich, no poor," and he imagined that "all would be capitalists and laborers."[72] In 1890, Evans further explained that the unification of social classes he advocated would produce a society with "no hereditary power or privileges; each receiving as his or her 'works shall be'; the chief and greatest being those who make themselves the most useful and necessary to the community of government; so living that the public cannot live without them." Just as private ownership of land symbolized, to Evans, an unjust, fragmented society, universal rights to land symbolized social harmony and justice. "If a man has a right to live," continued Evans, "he has a right to land; the rights of life and of land being inseparable."[73] William Leonard extended those rights to include all property. "Where there is unity of spirit there must be a unity of interest to show to all that we are the disciples of Christ, children of one family, all making one sacrifice, and gaining one eternal spiritual inheritance."[74]

Although few were as adamant as Evans and Leonard, many believers characterized the existing Shaker social system as a unified social plan because it insisted on equal representation by both sexes and because it united symbols of the divine and earthly planes. Most Shaker industries depended on the work of both sexes. In the herb industry of Sabbathday Lake, for example, men raised and harvested the herbs, while the women dried and packaged them for sale. The famous Shaker furniture was not designed merely to be beautiful, but to unite form and function and, therefore, to unify work and spiritual values.

Looking back from their vantage point of 1904, White and Taylor identified the cooperative aspects of Shaker economics as one of the Shakers' greatest contributions to humanity. "The time will doubtless come," they wrote, "when separate business interests will be united [in a] wider cooperation."[75] "In the religious, as in the scientific and business world," wrote Anna White in 1900, "the day of individual interests, of small holdings, has passed, the day of concentration and conservation of energy has dawned, the beginning of a world-wide realization of God's great law of cooperation."[76]

Through the blending of the home and work domains in Shaker

communities, the Shaker system also symbolizes the unification of domestic (use-value) and productive (exchange-value) labor. Using an artisanal mode of production, the Shakers manufactured and marketed many products inspired by their own domestic needs. They are credited with the invention of the clothespin and the flat broom, for example, and they were granted patents for a large, industrial-type washing machine, a tilting button for chair legs, and a counterbalanced window sash.[77] Other Shaker goods also have strong home-use connotations: herbs, wool, furniture, and preserved foods. Furthermore, women's domestic work was scheduled, regulated, and overseen just like all other work.[78] Such evidence suggests the equal worth of use-value and exchange-value labor and accompanying elevation of female status from the natural domain to the cultural domain of human endeavor.[79]

Indeed, most unities of symbolism from family and work domains in the Shaker cultural system signify an elevation of female symbolic status because they counteract a fundamental premise of low female cultural prestige — confinement to the natural domain and exclusion from the economic domain in which capital is produced. All Shakers were considered workers, and all workers contributed equally valuable labor to the community/family. The historian Edward Andrews has explained that in Shaker communities, "there was no gulf between producer and consumer: the craftsmen themselves were members of the 'family' unit."[80] The family unit is the work unit; family activity (love) and work activity (money) are merged.[81] No premise for low female status remains, even when that status is connected with domestic labor.

Other Celibate Unities

According to writers of the late nineteenth century, Shaker celibacy also symbolizes the unity of the economic and religious domains. In contrast to mainstream American Protestantism, however, which promoted competition and reinforced the ethos of individual achievement, Shaker religion encouraged cooperative effort and shared wealth. The theory of communal work, made possible by the celibate family structure, signified to William Leonard the unity of believers in "all things spiritual and temporal," thus opening "wide the door to contentment, health and happiness" in the community.[82] In fact,

Leonard characterized work as the equivalent of spirituality. "Work is Christian worship," he wrote in 1871.[83] Another writer explained in 1892 that it was as workers that Shakers could best emulate God, the master worker.[84] Leonard also explained that work unites believers with Jesus, who was born to laboring parents; the Apostles, who labored with their hands; and with Ann Lee, who admonished believers to put their "hands to work and hearts to God."[85]

The spiritual values of celibacy were seen by some as agents for dramatically transforming and unifying American society. Frederick Evans speculated that spiritual unity might ultimately occur among celibate and reproductive people if celibate values were allowed to prevail. In a text of 1878, Evans envisioned "a class of intellectual celibates, male and female, [who will] be the leaders, rulers and instructors of the people . . . the legislators."[86] Such celibate rulers will "limit the population to the quantity of land and the resources of food in the national kitchen."[87] In addition, they will bridge the historically separate orders of church and state and of generation and regeneration by effectively "marrying" the then spiritual state and taking full responsibility for governance. Those in the married order will thereby be freed to devote full time to the rearing of children. (He did not, incidentally, restrict such child-rearing only to women.)[88] Evans dubbed the celibate leaders the "White Cross," and insisted that both sexes be represented in their governance structure—"the Senates, female; the Houses of Representatives, male; the President and Governors, dual."[89]

Evans also envisioned other social reforms—all of them devoted to unifying that which is divided in a world dominated by sexual values. He described "a Supreme Court of arbitration" for settling international disputes, and national schools, communal child-rearing centers, land limitation (no more than a hundred acres per citizen, "or such other amount as the wisdom of Congress may fix upon"), and citizenship for all adults, including Indians and women.[90]

Celibacy: The Key to Unity

All unities imagined by Shaker writers, including social and personal relations, depend upon the symbolism of celibacy. In their view, celibacy signifies an end to the possessiveness and jealousies of sexual culture and ushers in a spiritual era, a New Earth in which genuine unity is possible. "It was this principle of *virgin purity* that enabled Jesus Christ and his Apostles to have all things in common," wrote Evans in 1853. "Virgin purity is the root of all religious communion because sexual relations confine the love principle in man to a small circle, of which *self* is the centre."[91] For many writers, the affection possible in celibacy parallels the altruistic love of Jesus for his disciples: " 'I call you not servants; but I have called you friends' (John 15:15)," quoted William Leonard.[92]

Celibacy also symbolized to nineteenth-century Shakers the separations and the self-control necessary to a spiritual union—of male and female gender symbolism, of believers and God, of the symbolism of home and work and nature and culture. Ironically, these unities depend upon the separation of elements whose mixing on earth violates divine order and, thus, divine unity. The Shakers felt that by merging spirit and flesh, sexual intercourse constitutes such a violation, and its practice poisons the entire culture. Thus, they believed the elimination of sex frees humanity from human-formed restrictions to the spiritual union God intends, even as it requires sexual distinctiveness and separation on earth.

Koreshan Unity

> We know that what we teach is diametrically opposed to everything taught in astronomy, in religion, in theology, in sociology, and in political economy, by the world's teachers . . . . If what we teach be true, then we are the true teacher. . . . We know it all, or we know nothing aright.[93]

> Celibacy, or the forsaking of sensualism, being the fundamental doctrine and practice of these churches [i.e., the Shakers, the Economites, the "Brotherhood of the New Life," and the Koreshans] they must, of necessity, be the primal builders of the new societal structure.[94]

The unity resulting from celibacy in Koreshan belief is both more concrete and more abstract than the Shakers envisioned. In Koreshan theory, celibacy signifies unity between the sexes because of its role in the ultimate obliteration of gender differences and in the blending of gender characteristics in an androgynous, hermaphroditic being allegedly capable of reproduction via spiritual rather than sexual means. In Koreshan thought, that process requires celibacy so that the necessary unification of spirit and flesh (so taboo in Shakerism) can occur internally in each person. The Koreshan mandate for celibacy is a precursor to and catalyst for biunity; the separation of the sexes in celibacy paves the way for their ultimate unification by giving time for the development of the spiritual powers that lead to biunity. The Koreshans also identified celibacy as the agent of transformation from sin to sinlessness.

Unlike the Shaker process of celibate unification, Koreshan celibate transformation includes the merger of matter, the sperm and ova of sexual reproduction, with spirit, the energy of religious faith. They believed that spirit and matter, properly merged, would create the human hermaphrodites capable of physiological reproduction without interpersonal sex.

Because the unifying processes of Koreshanity occur within a single person rather than between persons, the Koreshans spent little time redefining familial or other relationships. Therefore, their picture of an alternative family domain is sketchy. Believers did discuss the communistic ideals of a celibate community and of a society converted to Koreshanity, however, and like many Shakers they felt the redirection of sexual energies would be productive of a unified, cooperative, rather than a selfish, competitive society.

Celibacy and Theocrasis

The unifying qualities of celibacy are evident in Teed's 1869 divine revelation, an experience he had been anticipating for some time. While he worked in his medical laboratory, Teed felt that he witnessed God one evening in that year. The vision revealed God in female form and demonstrated to Teed the dual gender of the Godhead. Unlike most Shaker discussions of the bisexuality of God, however, Teed conceptualized God as an androgyne who appears alternately as male or female depending on the need of the human situation in which the appearance occurs. Therefore, Teed explained, the manifest sex of God at any one time is insignificant.[95] From this divine biunity, Teed developed his model for the mix-gendered, but sexually neuter, biune human being.

Teed's vision of God associated celibacy with alchemy, a "scientific" process of transformation and unification he had been seeking for years in laboratory experiments. Writing of his experience thirty years later, Teed recalled his pledge of celibacy to the Divine Mother God who appeared before him: "My Mother, behold my obedience! In thy hand I experience the chasteness of thine own virginity, communicated to me in the respiration of thy Holiness . . . . I am repelled from my former evils and falses [*sic*] with such agnostic recedence [*sic*] that I turn my face to thee. . . . in thee I find my rest forever."[96]

He then explained that his commitment to celibacy was analogous to his work as an alchemist; he saw celibacy and alchemy both as processes of unification. In his experiments, Teed applied principles of alchemy in order "to define the correspondential analogy between the domain of what scientists denominated physics and that denominated biology, for the purpose of applying to the sphere of life, the principle that a short time before [he] had discovered to obtain in electro-alchemy."[97] These scientific correspondences convinced him of the potential for a law of transmutation between organic life and the physical laws of the universe, as well as between matter and spirit. As a man of religion, Teed moved easily to the conclusion that substances of biological reproduction could be transformed into essences under spiritual control. He saw celibacy's conservation of sexual substances as the necessary catalyst for such a process. By extension, celibacy's transformative powers could be applied to social organization and gender relations, promoting unity, harmony, and equality.

Celibacy's transformative and unifying symbolic role was frequently related in Koreshan texts with a general theory of transformation that Teed called "theocrasis," which he defined in 1900 as a "subtle combustion, that resolves the material and organic form to its most refined spiritual essence." He believed that the prophets, including Enoch, Elijah, Jesus, and himself, had obtained "knowledge of the mystic law which, in electro-alchemy he had tested and exemplified."[98] In renaming himself Koresh (a translation into ancient language of the name Cyrus), Teed also identified himself as a messiah who would redeem the race both through his own powers of transformation and through the conversion of his followers to the transformative powers of celibacy.[99]

Unlike the Shakers' belief in a democratic form of divine anointment, Koresh saw himself as the primary theocratic force among celibates. "Life cannot exist without a supreme head," an

"ARCH-POLARIZER, a man who possesses the central thought of the divinely communicated wisdom of the age, and can harmonize and control the activities of . . . [society] as the heart . . . controls the energies of the body," he wrote in 1892. "Herein lies the messianic principle."[100] He conceded that the power could be shared by female celibates, however. As Lucie Page Borden explained in 1898, female celibates would be the first to develop a "spermo-germinal channel," or conduit for both sperm and ova, for the direction of sexual commerce into spiritual reproduction.[101] But even such females were never granted powers as sweeping as those Koresh attributed to himself.

As might be expected, the exact processes of spiritual reproduction were never fully explained. Koreshans understood spiritual repro-duction as an example of the "universal law of correlation," which one writer defined as the "transmutation of the energies of the sun to the matter of the earth, and the metamorphosis of these material elements again to solar energy." Spiritual reproduction entails the "perpetual interchange of the impregnative function to the capacity in turn of being the receptacle of a subsequent vitalizing influx."[102] Lucie Page Borden wrote in 1898 that this interchange can be en-hanced by the transformational potential of various "mental de-grees." She explained that "the three environing membranes of the brain, the pia mater, arachnoid, and dura mater, are foundations of . . . the celestial, spiritual and natural" realms of the body. She called the innermost celestial or solar realm "the abode of the Gods, the Lord's sphere of divine love," and considered it both the center of divinity and the center of spiritual reproduction in the person.[103]

The Biune Genus

The Koreshans felt that the being who results from spiritual repro-duction, induced by celibacy, is biune, both androgynous and her-maphroditic, a being in whom the falsely divided male and female powers and characteristics—the result of lust in Eden—are reunited through celibacy. In the 1890s, Koresh explained in several texts that the biune androgyne will restore humanity to its original con-dition before the Fall, as a "genus having the principles and forms of sex so blended as to constitute them neuter beings, biune man-ifestations, not dual."[104] They are the "first fruits of the resurrection" and, therefore, advanced beyond the descendants of Adam and Eve.[105] Koresh saw the biune genus as a reflection of divine biunity, both in God—in whom the "masculine and feminine . . . are equal"— and Jesus—"the highest type of manhood, the united sex, . . . the immortal being, the very Life of lives."[106] Therefore, in addition to achieving unity between human male and female qualities, the biune genus also brings humanity closer to Koreshan models of the divine spirits.[107] At the same time, biunity brings humanity closer to the ultimate divine quality, immortality. Celibacy in the biune being forestalls death, according to the Koreshans, whereas sexuality invites death. In this symbolic association, Koreshans go beyond Shaker Frederick Evans who merely claimed that celibacy produces longevity, not immortality. Koresh explained in 1892 that the spiritual, unlike the carnal, need not die in order to reproduce. "Mortality depends upon the transmission of the germs of being to the structuring of a new organism. Immortality depends upon the conservation of the life potency, and through it, the preservation of the already formulated entity and consciousness."[108] Another writer explained in the same year that "dying, rotting human life . . . must become . . . wholly transmuted to the quality of the higher life, by becoming the stock upon which some other higher form of life is grafted." Therefore, humanity, like the seedling apple, can save "its own life . . . by being grafted upon some other stock."[109]

Another function of celibacy, according to Koreshan writers, is its role in obliterating the sexual desire that perpetuates the opposition of the sexes and prevents their union. Celibacy replaces desire with "new and overwhelming" spiritual desires in the biune being.[110] This role also associates Koreshan celibacy with the exercise of reason and with the transformation of irrational, "natural" passions into rational, voluntary, "cultural" and spiritual motivations.

The Biune Jesus

The Koreshans saw the model biune celibate as Jesus himself. Several texts defined Jesus as the symbol of unified gender identities. First, Koresh explained, Jesus was conceived through a hermaphroditic process, in which Mary's "virginally generative" and "parthenogenetic" ovum joined the male Word within her. The process was completed only after Jesus's baptism by John, another act of celibate reproduction that contributed force, the pneuma, to Jesus's final birth. Thus, in Jesus the male pneuma and the female psyche—the two forces "by which the sons of God are manifest"—converge.[111] Second, because he had retained his virginity, Jesus embodied the purest forms of both maleness and femaleness, untainted by sexual merger. This interpretation of sexual "essences" contrasts with mainstream cultural expectations that real men and women will express their gender identities through sexual prowess and reproductive experience. Koreshans found the purest form of gender identity in persons who were the least overtly sexual in behavior.

In an interplay between symbols of tradition and progress that is reminiscent of some Shaker texts, Koresh explained that his messianic mission was both consistent with religious history and progressive toward a spiritual future. In his view, Jesus's original apostles had failed in their mission as spiritual descendants of Jesus's "seminal essence." They had allowed the seed of the Holy Spirit to die.[112] Koreshans were the apostle's true descendants, and they would succeed where the originals had failed. They would redirect the sexual essences—Jesus's seed—that ordinarily flow down into the body up to the spirit, thereby forming the "truths of life created from love."[113] Koresh also eagerly identified himself symbolically with Jesus as "the point of terminal conversion" and as the messiah.[114] Most importantly, as a biune prophet, Koresh felt his spiritual powers to be the equivalent of Jesus's. Koresh also considered himself to be one of the few who, like Jesus, "while he tried to govern others, was capable of governing himself."[115]

Celibacy and the Unities of the Koreshan Social Order

Like Shakers of the period, Koreshans saw the symbolic unities of celibacy as keys to various other unities possible in an ideal economic and political order. Koreshan texts discussed these social unities in terms of theocrasis, that transformational and unifying process, by employing the metaphors of centrality and commerce.

According to Koreshan theory, economic and political theocrasis, like reproductive theocrasis, must occur through a center. In reproductive theocrasis, that center exists in the body. In economic and political theocrasis, the center is a prophet, such as Jesus or Koresh, or a geographic point or channel in the physical world. One center of political and economic theocrasis is located in the structure of the universe, which Koreshans believed to be a hollow sphere. Koresh wrote in 1898 that "the World is a cell, its vitellus like the egg, with an environ or shell." He believed that earthlings live on the inside of that cosmic ovum, however, and walk on its inner shell rather than on the outside.[116] He further asserted that God had selected the vitellus of the cosmogonic egg and had built the universe around it.[117] This universe operates on a system of energy transmission from that center or vitellus to the periphery and back to the center. Also located at the vitellus are the spirits of Jesus, God, and Koresh. The latter believed that proper communication through the center, along paths of universal energy, would promote social exchange and unification.

Koresh identified the location of the Koreshan community in Estero, Florida, as another center for economic and political theocrasis. Koresh explained in 1898 that Estero was chosen as the home of Koreshan Unity because of its location in "the wake of the world's commercial intercourse." Further, Estero is located in America, whose capital, Washington, D.C., lies in a direct line from the West Indies — the original gateway to the New World. Thus, to Koreshans, Estero qualified as the Divine Imperial seat. Florida also represented the intersection of agriculture — "the function of the liver" — and commerce — "the function of the heart."[118]

When all centers are operating properly, Koreshans viewed the result as "true commerce" in which goods and services could be distributed according to the principle of equilibrium. They saw Jesus's communism as an example of such true commerce; like his Koreshan followers, Jesus ensured that " 'distribution was made unto every man according as he had need.' "[119] In a text of 1892, the concept of equilibrium was applied to ideal labor practices in a theory of "equitable uses . . . in which there may be established an equitable adjustment of labor and capital [to] . . . insure an equilibrium which can but become the potentializing energy of the human race."[120] Unless such an equilibrium could be accomplished, warned another writer, a revolution of labor would restructure the social system. In fact, he continued, "The battery of organic disintegration is [already] being formulated through the application of the science of Koreshanity; its magneto-electric currents are beginning to vibrate the atoms of dissolution, and the solvent potencies of alchemicovital tension will enter upon the general reagency of materio-spiritual metamorphosis in the proximate future."[121]

Based on this view of true commerce through equilibrium, Koresh preached the virtues of communistic economic practices and the redistribution of wealth as applications of Jesus's altruistic form of love and of the unifying potential of celibacy. He explained in 1896 his wish that communistic/altruistic practices replace "the love of self [implicit in the family system] dominantly portrayed in the eagerness of human greed for mammon."[122] Overlooking his own monopolistic values, Koresh also hoped to destroy mammon and promote equitable uses through both the "destruction of *fictitious* money" and the Koreshan "government's ownership of every system of industry and every department of economy."[123] He ultimately wished to eliminate competition and avarice and to promote altruism over individual ambitions.

Consistency in Korshan views of unity would require that the principle of communism and the root metaphors of true commerce and equilibrium be applied to the critical duality of sex. Based on such metaphors, sex roles could disappear, blended in a biune economic system, or they could be defined as equitably balanced in terms of social value and prestige. As it happens, neither form of unity appears in Koreshan texts, and this oversight weakens the value of Koreshanity for a feminist vision. Koresh wanted all work roles in the community to be voluntary. He also wanted the cooperation of all persons "upon the basis of united life."[124] But he did not discuss the equitable distribution of sex-specific work roles. A pamphlet describing life in Estero reveals that women did nontraditional work as store managers, draftspersons, engineers, dentists, artists, and doctors. But they were also responsible for the domestic work of the community. The rationale presented for the assignment of women to domestic work sounds familiar; women should do such work because they have more experience in it.[125]

Koresh probably ignored the implications of true commerce for sex roles for reasons of expedience. In doing so, however, he failed to associate symbolism from the work domain with domestic roles, as the Shakers did. Therefore, Koreshanity fails to elevate the symbolic status of domestic workers from the natural to the cultural realm. Unlike Shaker women, who could see their domestic toil in a new, cultural light, Koreshan female domestic workers had a weak theoretical basis for considering their domestic work as anything other than private and traditional. If applied correctly, however, the Koreshan system could provide such a theoretical base.

In the end, Koreshan doctrine suggests an expansion of female roles and gender identities into male territory without an equivalent expansion of maleness into the female world. In addition to its obvious benefits to men, this imbalance may reflect a greater flexibility in female gender identities. Women risk losing less of their culturally defined femininity by moving into the domain of productive work than men risk of their culturally defined masculinity by moving into the domain of domestic work. The Shakers handled this problem by allowing the sexes to remain associated with their traditional work while infusing that work with new meaning. Without such a strategy the Koreshans implied that traditionally female work remained beneath the dignity of, and somewhat threatening to, male believers.

Church and State

Another form of social unity advocated in the Koreshan celibate system is the unification of church and state. "Religion is our bond of moral obligation," wrote Koresh in 1896, "and we enthuse our secular life with religious fervor."[126] Koreshans considered the separation of church and state to be a "foolish idea," because "under a true governmental system, [the two] are as inseparable as the body and soul in the individual."[127] Such a sentiment contrasts markedly with the Shaker analysis of the need for the separation of those institutions—if not their ideals—as representatives, respectively, of spirit and flesh. In addition to promoting the unity of church and state, Koresh also wished, as has been discussed, to blend science and religion. He believed religion to be, simply, the science of God. And "the science (knowledge) of God," he wrote in 1896, "is the science of man."[128]

Many Koreshans saw little hope of uniting the celibate, androgynous Koreshans with the rest of the world, however. "Of course many thousands will not come into a celibate or communistic mode of life," explained one believer in 1892, "so that the masses need not have any solicitude regarding the perpetuation of the race."[129] Another writer, who resembled Shaker Frederick Evans in this view, predicted the continuation of two classes, the married and the un-married.[130]

Unlike Evans, however, Koreshans outlined no plan for interdependence or even for coexistence of the two orders. Overall, their theories, which predicate a variety of transformations upon a radical unification of existing dualities, seem to argue for universal conversion—the ultimate unity of all persons in Koreshan celibate culture.

SANCTIFICATIONIST UNITY

> Now, if the carnal mind—the old Adam—remains, then all things have not become new—there is one thing still old. But all things have become new; therefore, the carnal mind (Old Adam) does not remain.[131]

The key symbol of celibacy, as developed in the Woman's Commonwealth, suggests two forms of unity. One is the unity of androgyny. In embracing celibacy, the sisters discarded old models of humanity, including those that distinguish between the worth and rights of males and females. Their standard of celibate sanctification was designed to eradicate all other distinctions among persons except those of religious conversion. In their experience, however, only women were willing or able to accept the rigors of celibate sanctification. Therefore over time, a second unity—female solidarity or sisterhood—emerges in the Sanctificationist cultural system.

In contrast with the other two groups, the sanctified sisters did not base their concepts of celibate androgyny on a divine model. There is no evidence that they envisioned a bisexual God or Christ. They apparently gave little thought to the sex of either God or Jesus.[132] In the context of their religious views, however, it appears that the sisters merged their secular feminist goals of female independence and autonomy with female-identified religious values, thus creating a bond between their model of an androgynous being and God. The Commonwealth economic system also reveals the unification of home and work symbolism and, therefore, of many aspects of male and female gender identities that are traditionally segregated in separate domains.

Celibacy as Sanctification

Sanctification is a basic root metaphor for the group's approach to symbolic gender unity through celibacy; it is the inspiration for the commitment to celibacy. The Commonwealth view of sanctification resembles the Wesleyan Entire Sanctification that is traditional in Methodism, but it represents an unorthodox view of the concept. Wesley's definition of sanctification implies a gradual, progressive process rather than the sudden conversion McWhirter and her followers reportedly experienced. Wesleyan sanctification derives from the state of justification in which God forgives the sins of repentant believers. Once completed, the process of justification becomes sanctification, a state of regeneration or spiritual rebirth.[133] For McWhirter and her followers, however, such spiritual rebirth occurred suddenly and dramatically. Stories about McWhirter's primary revelation, following the deaths of two children and a brother, suggest it was a case of spontaneous regeneration. According to one version, she felt faith infuse her body and soul while she kneaded biscuit dough one morning. She had been suffering torments about her lack of faith the night before. She believed herself to be in a continuing state of sanctification because of her ongoing intention not to sin, as evidenced by her commitment to celibacy. As she testified in 1887, "where there is no intent there is no sin."[134]

The inclusion of celibacy in the Commonwealth version of sanctification also contrasts with the usual Methodist interpretation. Wesley did speak of the purifying effects of sanctification that allow regenerate man to be "purified from pride" and to have his love of the world "changed into the love of God."[135] Wesley explained that, in the sanctified person, passion becomes meekness; hatred, envy; and malice, love.[136] He also discussed the importance of casting out the "old Adam" and "carnal nature," but he made no explicit reference to the living of a celibate life. In fact, nineteenth-century commentators on Wesley's text, whom McWhirter might well have read, warned against interpreting such terms in a sexual way, because they refer to the disciples, who were already celibate.[137]

In spite of her unorthodox views, however, McWhirter's concept of the sanctified person is consistent with Wesley's definition of the recipient of the "second blessing." Like that new man, she and her followers had "a new life, new senses, new faculties, new affections, new appetites, new ideas and conceptions. [The] whole tenor of action and conversation is new, and he lives, as it were, in a new world. God, men, the whole creation, heaven, earth, and all therein, appear in a new light, and stand related to him in a new manner, since he was created anew in Christ Jesus."[138]

As time went on, however, McWhirter increasingly turned to her own rather than to Methodist interpretations of the sanctified life. Echoing a statement by Koresh on a similar topic, she said, "I know that what we teach is right. We are perfect. There is no adding anything new to what we have."[139] She finally decided that sanctification required her to separate herself from, and rebel against, any church sacraments or practices, including marriage, that did not respect the sanctified person's authority over her own spiritual life. "God never reveals to his people that they should turn back to their old modes of life, and therefore there is no possibility of my being directed to go back into the Methodist church and live as I did when I was a member of that body," she said.[140]

As the sisters increasingly followed their own consciences, inspired by God, they increasingly asserted their right to serve as their own authorities on all religious matters. From the start, therefore, their commitment to sanctified celibacy, with its emphasis on separation, symbolized their commitment to religious autonomy without the backing of institutionalized forms of Christianity. As will be discussed in the following chapters, this autonomy contributed to a female form of religion in the community.

The Celibate Marriage

Although it does not endorse celibacy, Wesleyan doctrine does imply that sanctified believers should be separated, at least spiritually, from unsanctified persons. This separation is meant to be "for their sakes to the work before [them];" that is, to facilitate God's work.[141] McWhirter and her followers did intend to separate themselves in spiritual ways from their old relations, but they did not originally consider legal separation or divorce from unsanctified spouses necessary to their religious mission. Even their commitment to celibacy, based in part on the same biblical text (1 Corinthians 7:12-15) used by Mother Ann to justify Shaker celibacy, did not require them to dissolve their marriages. "Our belief and our actions have been that if we are married to an unbeliever, when we are called into this state of Christianity, we let them remain with us as husbands," testified McWhirter in 1887. Furthermore, she explained that believers were happy to perform their wifely and motherly duties as long as they could practice celibacy. But, she continued, "If the husband chooses to leave us on account of our religion, we let them go."[142]

Most, if not all, of the husbands did choose to leave. Perhaps predictably, the husbands were less satisfied with the nonsexual unity in a celibate marriage—even though it included the performance of domestic duties—than were the wives. This attitude may reflect differences in male and female perceptions of marriage in the nineteenth century, when sexual interest of any kind was more likely to be a male than a female concern. If so, the Sanctificationists took the typical female position to an extreme by advocating marital union based only on friendship and sibling love. Their husbands also took the male stereotype to an extreme, however. Among others, B. W. Haymond, McWhirter's son-in-law, took his marital rights to court. The alienation of his wife's affections by the Commonwealth was one of his complaints. Partly on the grounds that she refused to accept sex as a necessary component of marriage, Haymond sought divorce and custody of their children. Male observers, commenting upon the situation in later years, sympathized with that perspective. One commented that the women's choice of celibacy constituted "an assault upon that most radical principle existing between men and women—love."[143] Clearly, the love he meant is the sexual kind. Another, looking back forty years later, sympathized with Haymond's suit against his wife, Ada, predicated as it was on the loss of his "sexual rights."[144]

Several estranged husbands also carried another facet of the sexual stereotype of their era to an extreme by reacting violently to the cohabitation of their former wives with a few male group members. In 1879, Matthew and David Dow, immigrants from Scotland, moved to Belton and joined the Sanctificationists. At that time, the women were living in the McWhirter house without George McWhirter, who had already left. Within a few weeks, although there was and is no evidence of any sexual activity between the women and the Dow brothers, the house was attacked by several of the former husbands, and the brothers were brutally flogged.[145] No indictments resulted from the assault, although the Dows were confined to an asylum in Austin for their own protection.[146]

The acceptance of the Dow brothers by the women demonstrates that although celibacy failed to unify the women and their husbands, the possibility of celibate unity between sanctified men and women was a goal of the community. Other attempts at such unity dot the group's history. In addition to the Dows, who temporarily left both the group and Belton shortly after their violent encounter, several men joined the sisters.[147] One man, probably a caretaker, stayed ten years.[148] There were four male members in 1892.[149] One Joseph Barlow, whose wife was also once a member, lived in the community intermittently between 1884 and 1903. McWhirter's son, Robert, was a resident as a boy and again after the move to Washington. He also worked with and for his mother, running a boardinghouse and other business interests in New York for many years.[150] Eventually, two Shaker men from New Lebanon stayed in the community as well. Always, however, male membership depended upon acceptance of the women's conditions. "They are welcome if they are willing to live the life we do," said McWhirter in 1902.[151] As it happened, few men could or would qualify. Too many men, according to McWhirter, suffer from "bossism."[152]

The Sanctificationist Alternative Family

In the absence of sex and marriage, the women initially suffered economic hardship, and they were forced to develop alternative familial and economic arrangements in order to survive. As in the other two groups, the family they preferred was based on economic communism. In contrast to the Koreshan and Shaker experience, however, the Commonwealth practice of communism followed long after the commitment to celibacy. The sisters did not gather into community until 1879, thirteen years after McWhirter's sanctification.[153] That gap in time may represent the women's initial efforts to achieve independence and autonomy within celibate marriages. The women were also driven to communism as a defense against their ostracism by the citizens of Belton, especially between 1878 and 1887.[154] It was apparent to the women that their economic chances in a hostile environment would be enhanced by collective rather than separate business endeavors.[155]

The initial experiment with economic communism entailed the partially protected investment of individual assests in the common fund. If a member left the community, she could claim a portion of the group's assets. The experiment proved very successful as both an economic and a familial arrangement. In fact, the sanctified sisters were so financially successful that they soon decided neither to seek nor to accept economic assistance from former husbands. That stance created controversy, too. For example, Sister Johnson was committed to the asylum in Austin for refusing her husband's insurance money, and McWhirter angered her husband by insisting on being the breadwinner for herself and her children while the couple was still living together.

Several sisters, including McWhirter, did claim rights to control property that they either had brought to their marriages or had owned jointly with their husbands, however. Such claims, they believed, had moral if not legal bases. The women, therefore, claimed rights specifically granted to men but denied to married women under a social system that associated married women with immature children.[156] The women's goal in making those claims to property was never personal gain. Property and income were shared equally among them. After the move to Washington, in fact, matters were arranged so that an individual investment could not be recovered, even if a member left the community. The group's 1902 constitution reveals the spiritual and altruistic qualities of Commonwealth economics: "The communistic life produces in the fullest measure, honesty, sobriety, spirituality, happiness and a keen sense of justice, and leads all who are thoroughly in sympathy with this life to strictly adhere to the Golden Rule."[157]

As in the other two dual-sex groups, Sanctificationist communal values depend on a form of physical separation. In their case, community entails separation, both within the group and between believers and outsiders, as a means of spiritual unification. Within the single-sex group, the sisters established a form of separation from one another by an insistence on individual autonomy instead of basing separation on sex. Nonmembers were excluded because of their unsanctified state. As it happened, unsanctified men were the primary group of outsiders from which the women separated themselves.

Although the Commonwealth was a sisterhood, the relationships among the women, although warm, were, like the relationships between men and women in the other two groups, apparently subject to regulation. Such regulation, although not specifically focused on sexual activity, echoes the other forms of separation already discussed that facilitate the commitment to celibacy. Having abandoned the conjugal relationship in which "interest" means sexuality and its concomitants, dependence and subordination, the women ultimately preferred "disinterest" as a sign of equality and personal autonomy. Group by-laws stipulate that "members shall not show any interest in one another, other than that of a purely friendly nature, nor shall they permit any person not a member . . . to show them, or either of them, any special attention or interest other than that of a purely friendly nature." In this deliberately dispassionate context, family members could expect to be provided with food, clothing, and lodging, as well as with "care and attention in sickness and misfortune, and in infancy and old age." Children brought into the group were treated as wards of the organization until their majority.[158] The constitution's silence about the mother-child relationship, coupled with the group's communal approach to child-rearing, suggest that the women may also have wished to avoid excessive intensity in that relationship.

These regulations have special significance in light of the fact that so many communal sisters were also blood relatives — sisters, or mothers and daughters. In fact, throughout the group's history, the great majority of the women were closely related to at least one other member of the group. In 1880, for example, there were seven mother-daughter pairs and five pairs of blood sisters. Out of twenty-nine members, twenty-one were blood relations.[159] According to the membership list of 1896, there were eight mother-daughter groupings (some mothers had three or more daughters with them) and four groups of blood sisters (one pair had no mother in the group). Only four members in that year had no blood relative in the community. Out of a total of twenty-five, twenty-one group members were blood relations. The 1902 prohibition against "special attention or interest" was issued, therefore, in the face of a strong potential, particularly for women from a small town, for intimacy among the members.

Further evidence of attempts to create separation among Commonwealth members can be found in their living arrangements. Unlike the Shakers, who slept in large single-sex dormitories, the women of the Commonwealth preferred individual bedrooms, or rooms shared by two sisters, that opened onto common work and eating rooms.[160] Such an arrangement permitted greater solitude and autonomy within the overall atmosphere of interaction and cooperation in work and leisure.

Like the other groups, the Sanctificationists modeled their interpersonal bonds on the relationships of Jesus and his disciples.[161] They apparently interpreted discipleship as a form of friendship and sibling love that requires no intimacy to seal the religious commitment.

The prescription for disinterest reflects the sisters' wish to incorporate objective performance standards and other values from the domains of work and religion into their celibate family setting. Though they stood fast by family members who followed their precepts, they willingly severed familial bonds with those who did not meet their standards. Eventually they codified those standards and prescribed a six-month probationary period during which mutual evaluation of old and new members could occur.[162] Men were, apparently, particularly subject to group standards and particularly ill-suited to meet them.

Like the Shaker system, then, the Commonwealth family discards the passionate, involuntary, irrational, and physical bonds of marriage and family and transforms existing relationships into sibling relationships of dispassionate friendliness by utilizing certain values from the cultural domain. The obvious need of the women to care for existing children reduces the voluntary nature of some Commonwealth relationships. Yet the women did what they could to transform such obligations into rational, consistent, and communal bonds. In so doing, they transposed those bonds from the purely natural to the cultural domain.

Celibacy and Work

In addition to the women's insistence on the right to property ownership and use of membership standards and criteria, the Sanctificationist system includes a direct association of domestic arrangements with business interests. Therefore, as in the cultural systems of the other two groups, the Commonwealth domestic domain par-

109

takes of workplace symbolism that unifies male and female gender identities.

Like their business interests, which were first incorporated in the Belton Investment Company and the Central Hotel Company of Belton and then in the Woman's Commonwealth, their family unit resembled a corporation, complete with a board of trustees. McWhirter was its president until just before her death. Conversely, their businesses grew primarily from their professionalization of female-identified domestic skills. Like the Shakers, the Sanctificationists marketed products with domestic origins, including butter, eggs, rugs, firewood, and bread. Even more than the Shakers, they commercialized cooking and housekeeping skills in their boardinghouses, hotels, and laundries. Their domestic abilities and business acumen ultimately earned them financial security. Their cooking and housekeeping eventually won the hearts of the rejecting citizens of Belton, who began patronizing their dining room and recommending their clean and comfortable beds to travelers.[163]

While they were marketing domesticity, however, the women also developed some nondomestic skills including dentistry, millinery, teaching, and shoemaking. The development of such skills in the context of a domestic industry recalls Catharine Beecher's vision of the ideal home. The Commonwealth experience goes beyond Beecher, however, by providing economic independence for the productive female laborer. By incorporating such varied skills in a unified home/work domain, the Commonwealth symbolizes the same give-and-take between home and work that exists in the Shaker system: work symbols extend into the home just as home symbolism reaches into the domain of work. This exchange of symbolic functions also represents the transformation of use-value work into exchange-value labor, with accompanying implications of unity between female and male gender systems.[164]

The Sanctificationist domestic domain also incorporates economics into family membership. The constitution requires all members to perform some manual labor in the community, without compensation, and to contribute all income from outside occupations to the group. Thus, on the one hand, domestic labor is identified as an economic contribution, although unpaid. On the other hand, the women assumed the economic identities of men by being required to contribute money to the support of the group as a whole.

The Commonwealth system allowed women to earn economic security through their labor rather than their performance of sexual and reproductive duties. Prostitution is thereby removed from the sanctified family because sex rather than money is banished from the home.

Celibate Sisterhood: An Overview

The celibate sisterhood of the Sanctificationists signifies the unity of women in struggle against some important symbols of nineteenth-century nuclear family life. As in the other two groups, the Sanctificationists discovered true familial unity in a spiritual bond among physically separated beings rather than in the false and fragile union promised by sexual intercourse. Sanctified sisterhood also signifies economic cooperation among women rather than female dependence on men. It represents a group effort to dissociate female economic security from female reproductive physiology. The women learned the hard way the difficulty of altering the gender and economic hierarchies implicit in mainstream marriage and nuclear family life. In fact, traditional family life was first threatened and then destroyed by the women's decision to control their own sexuality and their own economic destinies. As a group, the sisters enforced female control in those areas. They upset the power differential in the traditional nuclear family by rejecting the economic imbalance of marriage.

With celibacy as the foundation of their improved cultural status, however, the sisters could ill afford the physical intimacy that modern feminists associate with sisterhood, especially in female separatist groups. The sisters' purpose was not alternative sex but, rather, the transformation of all sexual desire into religious, economic, and personal power.

The Commonwealth differs from the other two groups in this study in its members' apparent disinterest in spreading their opinions to the outside world. Commonwealth sisters did no proselytizing; in fact, they rarely discussed their beliefs with nonmembers, whom they expected to misunderstand. They published no magazines or tracts. Apparently, they were content with their small membership, which peaked at fifty in 1880 and averaged less than thirty.[165] As the years went by, the sisters concentrated more on the well-being and fate of their limited membership than on expanding their system. Their modesty may suggest that the women understood both the threat of their system to mainstream culture and the benefits possible from a quiet cultural revolution. It may also reflect their seriousness about the major tenet of sanctification — solidarity against the unsanctified.

CELIBACY: THE GREAT UNIFIER

The study of these three communities elucidates the significance of celibacy as a symbol of unity despite its association with physical separation. The traditions of American culture associate the heterosexual act with the unification of the sexes, but Shaker, Koreshan, and Sanctificationist documents all identify such unification as illusory. Believers saw heterosexual intercourse ensnared in a web of oppositions that polarize and stratify the sexes and other socially defined groups. These celibates recognized that the legitimacy of heterosexual intercourse in mainstream culture both requires such symbolic oppositions and supports those oppositions through traditional sex roles within the family and, most important, through the erection of barriers between the family (nature) and work (culture) domains. By extension, such symbolic oppositions contribute to divisions among other groups of people, including social classes.

Celibacy, on the other hand, undermines the need for symbolic opposition between male and female, even though it requires the physical separation of men and women. Celibacy also eliminates the need for symbolic differences between home and work, nature and culture, and other symbolic pairs. It actually provides the basis for the symbolic merger of the sexes and of the symbolic sets associated with each gender identity.

The celibates of the three groups did not completely abandon concepts of difference and separation between men and women in their attempt to promote unity, however. The Shakers advocated ideas of gender difference within a spiritual framework in which male and female believers could ultimately be united. But because they did not identify celibate females as more carnal (or natural) than males or celibate males as more spiritual (or cultural) than females, their mandates for separation did not include the prescription for hierarchy implicit in gender differentiation in mainstream America.

The Koreshans, on the other hand, believed that celibacy actually unites the sexes in physical ways by promoting the production of a neuter, biune androgyne. The Koreshan form of gender unity, however, like that of the others, does depend upon the separation of the sexes (as currently constituted) necessary to the celibate commitment.

Finally, the Sanctificationists created gender unity within themselves as sanctified sisters by incorporating into their distinctly female ideal the rights, occupations, and privileges men have so long enjoyed. Their celibate ideal also entails separation, however, both from nonbelievers and among themselves. The creation of interpersonal distance protected the women from an excess of unity that might produce dependence, just as it so often did in marriage. Thus, they emphasized individual autonomy and personal independence even though they sought unity in sisterhood.

Important to the merging of gender symbolism in celibate systems is the accompanying unification of symbolism from the home and work domains and, therefore, from the realms of nature and culture. It is in these symbolic mergings that the first clues of celibacy's symbolic effect on female cultural status become apparent. Celibacy allows female gender identity to incorporate freedom of choice, productive work, property ownership, and other rights of full cultural membership usually associated (particularly in the nineteenth century) with males. In an age devoid of birth control technology, celibacy's emphasis on the conscious control of biological processes through the exercise of the will also signifies the possibility of women's control over the reproduction that so often controlled them. In an age that defined woman as a creature designed around her uterus, celibacy's inclusion of reason into the familial/reproductive domain emphasizes the mind, rather than the body, as a root metaphor of female gender identity. It is here that the Koreshan system is weakest, because its obliteration of specific gender characteristics limits the transposition of female symbolism from the natural to the cultural domain.

The emphasis on reason within the symbol of celibacy provides yet another basis for the unification of male and female gender identities. As rational, disciplined celibates, women could less easily be stereotyped as mindless or weak, and thereby denied full membership in the cultural realm.

NOTES

1. The theory of separate-but-equal is a tricky one. There is evidence that it was imperfectly applied in Shaker practice. It was also probably taken more seriously at the end of the nineteenth century in Shaker theory than earlier in the group's history. Marjorie Procter-Smith surveyed the violations and controversies surrounding the Shaker theory of sexual equality, and she concluded that Shaker men probably had more economic control than women in spite of theories to the contrary. Nevertheless, she also concluded that Shaker women experienced greater equality than did mainstream women of the period. See Marjorie Procter-Smith, *Women in Shaker Community and Worship: A Feminist Analysis of the Uses of Religious Symbolism*, vol. 16, Studies in Women and Religion (Lewiston, New York: The Edwin Mellen Press, 1985), pp. 47, 66-67.

2. John Humphrey Noyes, *History of American Socialisms* (Philadelphia, 1870), pp. 139f., quoted in Edward Andrews and Faith Andrews, *Work and Worship: The Economic Order of the Shakers* (Greenwich, Conn.: New York Graphic Society, 1974), p. 204.

3. Some writers identified the second stage as the dispensation of Moses; see Richard McNemar's *The Kentucky Revival; or, A Short History of the Late Extraordinary Out-Pouring of the Spirit of God in the Western States of America* (1808), excerpted in Robeley E. Whitson, *Shaker Theological Sources* (Bethlehem, Conn.: United Institute, 1969), p. 4.

4. Frederick W. Evans, *Tests of Divine Inspiration; or, The Rudimental Principles by Which True and False Revelation, in All Eras of the World, Can Be Unerringly Discriminated. . . .* (New Lebanon, N.Y.: United Society Called Shakers, 1853), pp. 59-60.

5. Giles Bushnell Avery, *Sketches of "Shakers and Shakerism": Synopsis of the Theology of the United Society of Believers in Christ's Second Appearing* (Albany, N.Y.: Weed, Parsons, Printers, 1883), p. 13.

6. [Daniel Fraser], *The Music of the Spheres . . . . Dedicated to the Consideration of Robert G. Ingersoll and to Others Like-Minded* (Albany, N.Y.: Weed, Parsons, Printers, 1887), p. 29. Apparently Evans believed in at least a modicum of theology. When Anna White confessed to him that she had no interest in theology, Evans admonished her to develop such an interest so that she might better understand her Shaker ex-

perience. See Lelia S. Taylor, ed., *A Memorial to Eldress Anna White and Elder Daniel Offord* (Mt. Lebanon, N.Y.: North Family of Shakers, 1912), p. 56.

7. J[ames] S. Prescott, "The Two Orders," *The Shaker* 2 (November 1872): 83.

8. Anna White and Lelia S. Taylor, *Shakerism: Its Meaning and Message* (Columbus, Ohio: Press of Fred G. Herr, 1904), pp. 306-7.

9. W. Watson Andrews, "Second Appearing of Christ," *The Manifesto* 23 (August 1893): 185.

10. Harvey L. Eads, *Shaker Sermons: Scripto-Rational. Containing the Substance of Shaker Theology. Together with Replies and Criticisms Logically and Clearly Set Forth . . . .* (Shakers [Watervliet], N.Y.: *The Shaker Manifesto* [Albany, N.Y.: Weed, Parsons, Printers]), p. 83.

11. Eads, *Shaker Sermons*, p. 175.

12. [Mary Frances Carr], *Shakers, Correspondence Between Mary F. C[arr] of Mt. Holly City and a Shaker Sister, Sarah L[ucas] of Union Village*, ed. R. W. Pelham ([Union Village, Ohio?], 1868), p. 21.

13. Very early Shaker journals emphasized tales of such beatings and related the joy with which they were accepted as signs of true religious sacrifice. See especially the journal excerpts in Clara Endicott Sears, *Gleanings from Old Shaker Journals* (Boston: Houghton Mifflin, 1916), passim. The historian Edward Andrews has speculated that Lee's death was probably hastened by the numerous, severe beatings she suffered. Edward D. Andrews, *The People Called Shakers* (New York: Dover Publications, 1963), p. 49.

14. Frederick W. Evans, *Two Orders: Shakerism and Republicanism. The American Church and American Civil Government, Coequal and Separate. The New Heavens and Earth* (Pittsfield, [Mass.]: Press of Sun Printing, 1890), pp. 8-9.

15. White and Taylor, *Shakerism*, pp. 259-60.

16. *Testimonies Concerning the Life, Character, Revelations and Doctrines of Our Ever Blessed Mother Ann Lee and the Elders with Her* (Hancock, Mass: J. Talcott and J. Deming, Jrs., 1816), p. 296.

17. Alonzo G. Hollister, "Shakerism," *The Manifesto* 22 (October 1892): 218.

18. White and Taylor, *Shakerism*, p. 258.

19. William Leonard, "Labor Is Worship, Part Second," *The Shaker* 1 (September 1871): 66.

20. Hollister, "Shakerism," p. 218.

21. Evans, *Two Orders*, pp. 8-9.

22. White and Taylor, *Shakerism*, pp. 258-59.

23. Evans, *Tests of Divine Inspiration,* p. 60.
24. Daniel Fraser, "Is Virgin Life Contrary to Law? No. 1," *The Shaker Manifesto* 8 (April 1878): 81.
25. Evans, *Tests of Divine Inspiration,* p. 58.
26. William Offord, *Nature. God. Law* (Canaan, N.Y., n.p. 1872), pp. 2-3, Library of Congress Manuscript Collection, Washington, D.C.
27. Offord, *Nature. God. Law.,* p. 24.
28. *The Higher Law of Spiritual Progression* (Albany, N.Y.: Van Benthuysen, 1868), p. 30.
29. Offord, *Nature. God. Law.,* pp. 6-7.
30. Giles B[ushnell] Avery, "Longevity of Virgin Celibates" in Elijah Myrick, *The Celibate Shaker Life* ([Mt. Lebanon?, 1889]), p. 8. According to the historian Carl Degler, male life expectancy in the nineteenth century was about fifty-six years; female life expectancy was a few years longer. Carl Degler, *At Odds: Women and the Family in America from the Revolution to the Present* (New York: Oxford University Press, 1980), p. 453. Therefore, Avery's statistics do seem fairly impressive, although he proved no cause-and-effect relationships. Avery also attributed Shaker longevity to their abandonment of distilled and fermented liquors, tobacco, and port.
31. Frederick W. Evans, "The Future," *The Shaker Manifesto* 8 (May 1878): 109.
32. Calvin Green and Seth Y. Wells, *A Brief Exposition of the Established Principles and Regulations of the United Society of Believers Called Shakers* (New York: E. S. Dodge Printing, 1879), pp. 6-7.
33. Fraser, "Virgin Life," p. 81.
34. Frederick W. Evans, *Celibacy, from the Shaker Standpoint* (New York: Davies and Kent, Printers, 1866), p. 8.
35. Evans, *Two Orders,* pp. 8-9.
36. Frederick W. Evans, "Religion and Spiritualism: A State without a Church," *The Shaker* 1 (March 1871): 19.
37. For a discussion of sex roles in earlier periods, see Procter-Smith, *Women in Shaker Community,* pp. 56-57.
38. Anna White, "Woman's Mission," *The Manifesto* 21 (January 1891): 3-4.
39. Evans, *Celibacy,* p. 7.
40. [Carr], *Shakers,* p. 20.
41. Frederick W. Evans, "Why Do Not Shakers Vote?," *The Manifesto* 10 (October 1880): 218-19.
42. Evans, "Why Do Not Shakers Vote?" See Also Green and Wells, *Brief Exposition,* p. 6. The Shakers were among the earliest American conscientious objectors. In the Revolutionary War, they refused to swear

allegiance to the Colonial cause because they felt they owed their allegiance to God alone. Edward R. Horgan, *The Shaker Holy Land: A Community Portrait* (Harvard, Mass.: Harvard Common Press, 1982), p. 27. They were also conscientious objectors in the War of 1812, the Civil War, and all subsequent armed conflicts in American history. Henri Desroche, *The American Shakers: From Neo-Christianity to Presocialism*, trans. John K. Savacool (Amherst: University of Massachusetts Press, 1971), p. 95. The states of Massachusetts, Maine, Connecticut, and Ohio granted the Shakers official status as conscientious objectors by 1821. Andrews and Andrews, *Work and Worship*, p. 165.

43. Avery, *Sketches of "Shakers and Shakerism,"* p. 13.

44. [Carr], *Shakers*, p. 19.

45. Evans, *Two Orders*, p. 3.

46. Evans, *Celibacy*, p. 11.

47. Fraser, "Virgin Life," p. 80.

48. [Carr], *Shakers*, p. 20.

49. Harvey Eads, *A Shaker Letter* ([Shaker Village, Canterbury, N.H.: Canterbury Shakers, 1880]), p. 4.

50. Prescott, "Two Orders," p. 83.

51. Evans, *Tests of Divine Inspiration*, p. 87.

52. Evans also wrote that "reproduction in the one [earth] is physical— in the other [heaven] spiritual," but neither he nor other Shaker writers surveyed carried this idea of spiritual procreation as far as Koresh did, to suggest actual spiritual progeny. Evans, *Celibacy*, p. 6.

53. Ibid., p. 8.

54. Avery, *Sketches of "Shakers and Shakerism,"* p. 12.

55. W. Watson Andrews, "Communism," *The Manifesto* 21 (December 1891): 271.

56. Anna White, quoted in White and Taylor, *Shakerism*, p. 372.

57. Ibid.

58. [Carr], *Shakers*, p. 8.

59. Ibid., pp. 10, 18.

60. Frederick W. Evans, n.t., *The Shaker* 1 (March 1871): 20.

61. Alonzo G. Hollister, *Mission of Alethian Believers, Called Shakers* (Mt. Lebanon, N.Y., 1892), excerpted in Whitson, *Shaker Theological Sources*, p. 42.

62. Green and Wells, *Brief Exposition*, pp. 6-7.

63. This is another area in which Shaker doctrine and practice struggled. Because of the hierarchical leadership pattern within the sect, leaders of communities and even of families were chosen by the Central Ministry and sometimes imposed upon less than enthusiastic followers (see Andrews, *People Called Shakers*, pp. 193, 237). Even this form of

oligarchy, however, contrasts with the leadership of a nuclear family, which requires no achievement standards or outside judgments in the assignment of leadership roles.

64. Taylor, *Memorial to White and Offord*, pp. 49, 31.

65. Green and Wells, *Brief Exposition*, p. 8.

66. Andrews and Andrews, *Work and Worship*, pp. 32-33.

67. William Offord, *Harmonial Philosophy* (Union Village, Ohio, 1873), pp. 14-15. Library of Congress Manuscript Collection, Washington, D.C.

68. Andrews and Andrews, *Work and Worship*, p. 26. In practice, some of the world's standards intruded, and men took on more of the economic and public duties. But that was not the plan. See Proctor-Smith, *Women in Shaker Community and Worship*, pp. 66-67, 208, 223.

69. Desroche, *American Shakers*, p. 176.

70. 1845 *Millennial Laws*, in Andrews, *People Called Shakers*, pp. 253-54. Again, failures of exact equality in the Shaker leadership practice does not negate the theory of equality. Even those failures represent an improvement upon the sanctioned male dominance of the mainstream family.

71. June Sprigg, *By Shaker Hands* (New York: Alfred A. Knopf, 1975), p. 177. Some children left with the Shakers were actually indentured to the communities — clothed and housed, given Bibles, and trained for occupations that they could pursue in the outside world if, at age twenty-one or before, they decided to leave the community. Viola Woodruff Opdahl, "William Pillow: His Life Among the Shakers," *The Yorker* 15 (November-December 1956): 25. Eighty percent of children raised in Shaker communities left to join the world at age twenty-one or before, however, a statistic that implies that the commitment to Shaker life may have been easier to make once sex and reproduction in the generative order had been tried and found wanting. Flo Morse, *The Shakers and the World's People* (New York: Dodd, Mead, 1980), p. 245.

72. Frederick W. Evans, *Shaker Reconstruction of the American Government* (Hudson, N.Y.: Office of the *Register* and *Gazette*, 1888), p. 6.

73. Evans, *Two Orders*, pp. 6, 5.

74. William Leonard, *A Disclosure on the Order and Propriety of Divine Inspiration and Revelation, Showing the Necessity Thereof, in All Ages, to Know the Will of God. Also, a Discourse on the Second Appearing of Christ, in and Through the Order of the Female. And a Discourse on the Propriety and Necessity of a United Inheritance in All Things, in Order to Support a True Christian Community*.... (Harvard,

[Mass.]: United Society, 1853), pp. 66-67. Leonard's *Disclosure* seems to be an earlier version of a work that was attributed to Frederick Evans in 1878. See Frederick W. Evans, "Christ in the Order of Male and Female," *The Shaker Manifesto* 8 (June 1878): 137-38.

75. White and Taylor, *Shakerism*, p. 393.

76. [Anna White?], *Present Day Shakerism* (Mt. Lebanon, N.Y.: [ca. 1900]), p. 35.

77. Horgan, *Shaker Holy Land*, pp. 98-99.

78. See especially Frederick Engels's interpretation of the importance of exchange value to the development of male dominance—quoted in Charnie Guettel, *Marxism and Feminism* (Toronto: Canadian Women's Educational Press, 1974), pp. 11-13.

79. See, for example, 1845 *Millennial Laws* in Andrews, *People Called Shakers*, pp. 270-74. If control of products is a mark of economic power, there is some doubt that Shaker women achieved economic equality with Shaker men. There is evidence that Shaker women did control the income from the sale of their own production, however, at least during some periods. That fact places them well ahead of many mainstream American women. See Procter-Smith, *Women in Shaker Community*, p. 67.

80. Edward Andrews, "Designed for Use," *New York History* 31 (July 1950): 339.

81. The Andrewses have also noted that the Shaker work domain combined economic values with individual artistic expression through the Shaker metaphor of usefulness. This term in Shaker texts implied economy of time, material, and methods as well as the individual craftperson's values of neatness and cleanliness, simplicity and proportion. All of these qualities were combined into the simple, elegant beauty of Shaker products. Andrews and Andrews, *Work and Worship*, p. 141.

82. Leonard, *Disclosure*, pp. 67-68; William Leonard, "Labor Is Worship. Part First," *The Shaker* 8 (August 1871): 58.

83. Leonard, "Labor Is Worship. Part First," p. 58.

84. Bostwick [no f.n.], n.t., *The Shaker Manifesto* 9 (February 1881): 30.

85. Leonard, "Labor Is Worship. Part First," p. 58.

86. Frederick W. Evans, "Shaker System," *The Shaker Manifesto* 8 (April 1878): 76.

87. Evans, "Future," p. 109.

88. Evans, "Shaker System," p. 76.

89. Evans, *Shaker Reconstruction*, pp. 5, 7. The term *White Cross celibacy* apparently derived from a group of the period called the White Cross and compared by Catherine Allen to the Salvation Army. Both

groups, Allen claimed, directed their energies towards "the preservation of the life principle of all reforms—social purity." The White Cross was better than the Salvation Army, however, because it was "separately organized for males and females." See Catherine Allen, *Fragrance from the Altar of Incense: Shaker Contributions to the "Flaming Sword"* ([Mt. Lebanon, N.Y., 1892]), p. 13.

90. Evans articulated these ideas in a number of articles and tracts. He discussed the concept of the supreme court of arbitration and their potential contribution to disarmament in "Shaker System" (p. 70.) His most complete discussion of land limitation, a concept that was also applied to Shaker communities, can be found in "The Shaker Land Limitation Act," *The Manifesto* 17 (March 1887): 68. The proposal for national schooling for all children up to age twenty-one can be found in *Shaker Reconstruction* (p. 6), in *Two Orders* (p. 5), and in "Shaker System" (pp. 79-80). Evans also discussed the elimination of lawyers— "any differences between individuals or nations being settled by arbitration"—and the ordination of all adults as priests. The latter had formed a class of social parasites and freeloaders, he contended. See *Shaker Reconstruction* p. 6.

91. Evans, *Tests of Divine Inspiration*, pp. 86, 88.

92. Leonard, *Disclosure*, pp. 66-67.

93. "Sword Thrusts," *The Flaming Sword* 12 (March 4, 1898): 6.

94. Koresh [Cyrus R. Teed], "Cosmogony [Part I]," *The Flaming Sword* 3 (February 27, 1892): 6.

95. Koresh? [Cyrus R. Teed], "The Wife of God," *The Flaming Sword* 3 (March 26, 1892): 2; Koresh [Cyrus R. Teed], "The Biune Genus," *The Flaming Sword* 3 (May 7, 1892): 2.

96. Koresh [Cyrus R. Teed], *The Illumination of Koresh: Marvelous Experience of the Great Alchemist Thirty Years Ago, at Utica, N.Y.* (n.p., [1900]), p. 13.

97. Koresh, *Illumination of Koresh*, p. 3.

98. Ibid., pp. 19-20.

99. Ibid. Koresh considered himself a messiah not only because of his revelation, but also because of a passage in the Book of Isaiah (44:28): "Cyrus, He is my Shepherd who shall fulfill all my purpose," Koresh, *Judgment*, p. 5. Based on that passage, containing his given name, Cyrus Teed changed his name to Koresh, the Hebrew transliteration of the original Persian translation of the name. Howard D. Fine, "The Koreshan Unity: The Chicago Years of a Utopian Community," *Illinois State Historical Society Journal* 48 (June 1975): 215.

100. Koresh, "Cosmogony [Part I]," p. 6.

101. Lucie Page Borden, "The Civil War of the Dual Nature," *The Flaming Sword* 12 (June 17, 1898): 6.

102. "God the Lord Alternately Male and Female; the Sons of God, Neuter," *The Flaming Sword* 3 (January 23, 1892): 1.

103. Borden, "Civil War of Dual Nature," p. 6.

104. Koresh, "Biune Genus," p. 2.

105. Koresh, *Judgment,* p. 11.

106. "God Alternately Male and Female," p. 1; Koresh [Cyrus R. Teed], *Reincarnation, or the Resurrection of the Dead,* 2d ed. (Chicago: Guiding Star Publishing House, 1896), p. 2.

107. Koresh, *Reincarnation,* p. 33.

108. Koresh, "Biune Genus," p. 2.

109. "Fatherhood and Sonship," *The Flaming Sword* 3 (January 30, 1892): 7.

110. "Fatherhood and Sonship," pp. 38, 41-42.

111. Koresh, *Judgment,* p. 14. Koresh used the word "sons" generically, but he explained in various texts that these sons would be neuter beings, embodying both masculine and feminine essences, rather than males. Koresh, "Biune Genus," p. 1.

112. Koresh, *Judgment,* p. 11.

113. Koresh, *Reincarnation,* p. 25.

114. Ibid., p. 19.

115. Koresh?, "How Can Social Order Be Established? [Part I]," *The Flaming Sword* 3 (February 13, 1892): 3.

116. Koresh?, "Quiet Talks with the Editors of Our Exchanges," *The Flaming Sword* 12 (February 11, 1898): 11. Koresh presented elaborate proofs of his theory that the earth is a hollow sphere (see, for example, Koresh, "Cosmogony [Part I]," p. 6). He designed a device, consisting of a series of poles linked together with rope, to demonstrate the concave curvature of the earth's surface. Although the proofs seem incomprehensible to the average reader, he accepted them as ironclad.

117. Koresh? [Cyrus R. Teed]. "Geographical and Ethnological Confirmation of the Correctness of the Location of the Metropolis of the Coming Pan-American Empire." *The Flaming Sword* 12 (August 5, 1898): 3.

118. Koresh [Cyrus R. Teed], *The Koreshan Unity. General Information Concerning Membership and Its Obligations* (n.p., [1902]), p. 6.

119. Mizpah [pseud.?], "Koreshan Communism," *The Flaming Sword* 3 (April 16, 1892): 8.

120. Koresh?, "Social Order [Part I]," p. 3.

121. "Devachan and Nirvana. (Ye Do Therefore Greatly Err: Neither Knowing the Scriptures nor the Power of God in that Aion, Age, They

Neither Marry nor Are Given in Marriage, but as the Angels in Heaven)," *The Flaming Sword* 4 (August 13, 1892): 3.

122. [Koresh] [Cyrus R. Teed], *Response to Inquiries* (n.p., [1896]), p. 5.

123. Koresh? [Cyrus R. Teed], "A Brief Summary of the Koreshan System," *The Flaming Sword* 3 (April 16, 1892): 15.

124. Koresh [Cyrus R. Teed], *The Koreshan Unity*, p. 7.

125. Koresh [Cyrus R. Teed], *The Koreshan Unity Cooperative* (Estero, Fla.: Guiding Star Publishing House, n.d.), p. 86.

126. [Koresh], *Response to Inquiries*, p. 6.

127. Koresh?, "Social Order [Part I]," p. 2.

128. Koresh, *Reincarnation*, p. 33.

129. Koresh? [Cyrus R. Teed], "How Can the Utopian Dream Be Realized?," *The Flaming Sword* 3 (May 7, 1892): 5.

130. "Devachan and Nirvana," p. 3.

131. Explanation of the doctrine of John Wesley in J. T. Smith, *Entire Sanctification (Heart Purity) and Regeneration as Defined by Mr. Wesley, One and the Same* (Marshall, Texas: Howard Hamments, Printer, 1895), p. 18.

132. Eleanor James interviewed friends and descendants of Commonwealth members in the course of her research. Eleanor James, "The Sanctificationists of Belton," *The American West* 2 (Summer 1965): 73. She recalls no mention of a female God or Christ (author's telephone interview with Eleanor James, November 1983). Available texts and testimonies likewise do not mention gender as an attribute of the Deity.

133. Smith, *Entire Sanctification*, p. 22.

134. For one story of McWhirter's conversion see "The Life and Spiritual Experience of Martha McWhirter Leader and Founder of the Women's Commonwealth . . .," n.p., n.d., p. 2 (typewritten). See also Martha McWhirter, "McWhirter's Answers to Interrogatories in B. W. Haymond v. Ada Haymond, #3037, in the District Court of Bell County, Texas, 17 October 1887," interrogatory no. 35.

135. Because Wesley wrote using the masculine pronoun, I have paraphrased him that way here.

136. Smith, *Entire Sanctification*, p. 15.

137. Ibid., pp. 8-9.

138. Smith, *Entire Sanctification*, p. 19. Perhaps Wesley's male bias was one reason that McWhirter felt the need to adopt a female version of Methodism.

139. Martha McWhirter, quoted in James, "Sanctificationists of Belton," p. 68.

140. Smith, *Entire Sanctification*, pp. 35-56.

141. Ibid., p. 10.
142. McWhirter, Haymond v. Haymond, interrogatories 8, 10.
143. A. L. Bennett, "The Sanctified Sisters," *The Sunny Slopes of Long Ago*, Publications of the Texas Folklore Society, no. 33 (1966): 136.
144. George W. Tyler, *The History of Bell County*, ed. Charles V. Ramsdell (San Antonio: Naylor, 1936), p. 394.
145. Bennett, "Sanctified Sisters," p. 141.
146. Tyler, *History of Bell County*, p. 394. A. L. Bennett reported that one husband was indicted but subsequently acquitted for the assault. Bennett, "Sanctified Sisters," p. 141.
147. Garrison reported that one of the Dow brothers returned to Belton in 1885 to run the group's laundry business. He remained only until 1886. At that point, the sisters repossessed the business and ran it more profitably themselves. George Pierce Garrison, "A Woman's Community in Texas," *The Charities Review* 3 (November 1893): 40. Mathew and another brother, Allan Dow, lived in Belton in subsequent years and stayed involved in projects for the community throughout the century.
148. Margarita Gerry, "The Woman's Commonwealth of Washington," *Ainslee's Magazine* (September 1902): 139; Bennett, "Sanctified Sisters," p. 141; A. H. Mattox, "The Woman's Commonwealth," *Social Service* 4 (November 1901): 167.
149. James, "Sanctificationists of Belton," p. 72.
150. W. Chmielewski, "The Sanctified Sisters," n.d., p. 41 (typewritten).
151. Martha McWhirter, quoted in Gerry, "Woman's Commonwealth of Washington," p. 139.
152. "Life and Spiritual Experience," p. 14.
153. Garrison, "Woman's Community in Texas," p. 35.
154. Bennett, "Sanctified Sisters," p. 139; Gerry, "Woman's Commonwealth of Washington," p. 135; Garrison, "Woman's Community in Texas," pp. 34-40.
155. I make this assertion based on national figures for women of the period. Although slightly less than 20 percent of nineteenth-century women, aged fourteen or over, participated in the paid labor force, only 2 percent of married women were so employed. Mary F. Cox and Sharlene Hesse-Biber, *Women at Work* (Palo Alto, Calif.: Mayfield Publishing, 1984), pp. 14-28. These statistics indicate that the concept of going to work was a departure from the norm for married women.
156. "Life and Spiritual Experience," pp. 18, 10; Gerry, "Woman's Commonwealth of Washington," pp. 135-36.

157. *Constitution and By-Laws of the Woman's Commonwealth of Washington, D.C.* (Washington, D.C.: Crane, 1902), p. 3.

158. Chmielewski, "The Sanctified Sisters," pp. 45, 17.

159. *Constitution of Woman's Commonwealth,* pp. 22, 9, 10.

160. Gwendolyn Wright, "The Woman's Commonwealth: Separatism, Self, Sharing," *Architectural Association Quarterly* 6 (Fall-Winter, 1974): 41. Wright, an architectural historian, discusses the use of space in Commonwealth boardinghouses and hotels.

161. Mattox, "The Woman's Commonwealth," p. 170.

162. Ibid., p. 11. There is little evidence that this procedure was ever invoked. Very few new members joined the community after 1902.

163. Garrison, "Woman's Community in Texas," pp. 39-40.

164. "Happy Home without Husbands"; Garrison, "Woman's Community in Texas," pp. 44-45. Wright has also observed an atypical merging of public and private areas within the women's buildings; for example, they used their front parlor as a community meeting room, the town's first library, and a Sunday socializing spot. Wright, "The Woman's Commonwealth," pp. 40-41.

165. Garrison, "Woman's Community in Texas," pp. 38, 41-42.

· 4 ·

FEMALE CELIBACY:
SEXUAL EQUALITY AND FEMALE
REDEMPTIVE POWER

"Crowning conscience with her trusty broom. . . ."

Celibacy defies mainstream expectations of unity of the sexes through heterosexual intercourse by promoting the symbolic and spiritual unity of males and females through sexual abstinence. This chapter explores another effect of celibacy that was particularly defiant of mainstream symbolism in the nineteenth century. That is, the symbolic mechanisms used to create gender unity through celibacy in the Shaker, Koreshan, and Sanctificationist systems also promoted the equal status of the sexes in contrast to mainstream gender hierarchy. Furthermore, in a reversal of the mainstream's preference for maleness, the celibate systems tend to favor femaleness whenever gender hierarchy is indicated. A celibate female is credited with redemptive powers in these systems, and her powers are identified as necessary correctives for centuries of male dominance.

The Shakers and Koreshans were explicit about the connection of female subordination and male dominance to original sin. In their view, woman became subject to man primarily because she was directed to focus her desire upon him. Therefore, in those two systems celibacy was characterized as a technique for short-circuiting the curse of gender hierarchy by attacking its cause, female sexual desire. The Sanctificationists addressed the same effect of inequality, especially in economic matters, but existing records make no explicit association of gender hierarchy with original sin. McWhirter was clear about the fact that God created men and women as equals, however, and about the association of sex with women's economic and political inferiority to men. Thus, each in their own way, all

125

three groups favored the dissociation of female gender identity from sexuality as a corrective to the social and spiritual inequality of men and women. If sex and reproduction cause hierarchy in the gender identities and roles of male and female, then celibacy, particularly among females whose desires were named in the curse, can promote equality between them.

All three groups also carried this logic of sexual equality through celibacy one step further. In varying ways, the Shakers, Koreshans, and Sanctificationists all suggested that female celibacy not only combats gender hierarchy, but it also empowers woman to redeem a world oppressed by generations of male dominance and its secret companion, male lust. Female celibates are superior to celibate males because the latter cannot easily escape their gender history of lust and the abusive exercise of power. Unlike most mainstream Christians of their day, many spokespersons for these groups regarded woman as the victim of the curse rather than its perpetrator. Logically, then, for these believers, woman becomes an instrument of human redemption from the curse.

As with the specifics of gender unity through celibacy described in the last chapter, the approaches of the three groups to gender equality and redemptive female celibacy differ. Those approaches reflect their varying opinions about gender difference and androgyny, as well as their varying beliefs about the gender identity of God and Christ. As will become clear in this chapter, concepts of female spiritual or redemptive power may emanate from a symbolic link between human females and a divine female model, but such an explicit link is neither a necessary nor a sufficient condition for female empowerment. Those concepts can also emerge from the investment of the female celibate herself with God-like powers.

THE SHAKERS

More of life and less of fashion,
More of love and less of passion;
That will make us good and great.[1]

In the female order a stone was prepar'd,
A woman cut out and redeemed from the fall,
To stand in her order, the MOTHER of all.[2]

And then what must we women say?

126

"In all things I will thee obey."
Thus take our counterpart on trust—
Become a slave to lordly lust—
To come and go as he may choose—
To wash his feet or tie his shoes.
We cannot be among the ris'n
But soul and body both are his'n
Thus 'fixed to one peculiar spot
We only propagate and rot.[3]

Although Shaker texts of the late nineteenth century recognized differences in the symbolism of maleness and femaleness, they did not necessarily concede that such difference implies sexual hierarchy. Rather, Shaker texts tended to suggest that sexual difference can coexist with concepts of sexual equality. Further, some writers reversed the mainstream concept of gender hierarchy by describing a special redemptive power for the female celibate.

Key to these suggestions is a reinterpretation of Genesis as a text supportive of both sexual equality and female redemptive power. Instead of judging Eve's admittedly second place in creation as a sign of her lesser importance, some writers explained that she completed Creation by supplementing maleness and rounding out the natural human family. This transposition of the Genesis story matches Shaker views of a bisexual God and Christ Spirit, for in both divine models believers saw a female essence as the fulfillment of a promise only begun by maleness. Furthermore, such writers explained that gender equality in the divine models demands gender equality among human mortals.[4] In acknowledgment of the progressive nature of these views of sexual equality, Anna White wrote in 1891, "Already the glorious revelation of divine truth has . . . brought forth an order of people whose central idea is equality; men and women who have . . . come up to the higher plane [and] have recognized in each other capabilities and powers, each supplementing the other's deficiencies."[5]

Divine Bisexuality and Sexual Equality

Such views characterized Shaker beliefs even in the group's earliest days. In a text of 1819, an anonymous believer wrote, "In the deity there [has] existed from everlasting the twofold character or property of male and female." Maleness is the "first great cause," the writer continued, "the creator of all things." And femaleness is the second great cause as that which gives "birth and existence to any created object." Rather than seeing this distinction as a sign of female inferiority, however, the writer explained that humanity was created in God's image, male and female, to represent "the unity and perfection of God." Woman is the "finishing part of the work of God."[6] Later beliefs, such as those of Hester Poole, echo that early text. Pool explained that human beings reflect the "Deific Essence," in which distinction does not negate equality.[7] Later writers also shared the earlier believer's opinion of the female sex, at least in its celibate, redeemed state. Using Mother Ann as a model, they described the celibate female as the crown of creation rather than its consolation prize.

Shakers defended their deviant interpretation of God's bisexuality on the grounds of its progressiveness. Hester Poole explained in 1887, for example, that it took seventeen centuries for churchmen to understand "that the Jewish Jehovah and the Christian God [is] forceful, revengeful and on occasion hateful" and is therefore a "one-sided Creator [who] lacks all that sweet plentitude of womanly love." The churchmen cannot be blamed, however, because they pre-date Ann Lee's revelation of a God who, in combining womanliness "with a manhood of corresponding wisdom, [is] worthy of reverence."[8] Alonzo Hollister also forgave prior ignorance on this subject. "The things concerning the Father were all they had received in all previous dispensations," he wrote in 1887; "the things relating to Mother, were yet to be revealed."[9]

On the other hand, based on their sense of Shakerism's roots in Christian practice of previous eras, writers also explained their interpretation of the bisexual divine essence in terms of familiar biblical prophecies and precedents. Writing in 1867, Chauncey Sears explained that these prophecies have always been present in the gospel but have been hidden from the unenlightened. He found examples in Romans 1:20, which explains that the best understanding of the Deity emerges from an examination of Creation itself. Because male and female forms abound in Creation, Sears concluded that God also embodies two sexes and represents the interplay of two sets of gender symbols. Sears also noted references in Matthew (11:19) and Luke (7:35) to Wisdom, an identity of God, who is "justified of all *her* children."[10] Using Jerome's translation of a passage quoted by Origen, William Bussell recalled in 1872 that Jesus called the Holy Spirit "My Mother" and concluded from the passage "that there are in the Divine nature both masculine and feminine principles necessary complements of each other."[11]

J. M. Washburn, a non-Shaker whose work was published in Shaker periodicals, found evidence of God's dual sex, accompanied by a duality of gender associations, in both the Old and New Testaments. "In the text," he wrote in 1889, "God is Love. 'O *Theos agapa esti*,' love is in the feminine gender though Theos is masculine." In the Hebrew Bible, he continued, "God is called Elohim all through the first chapter of Genesis, because the Truth is represented as acting." In the second chapter, when "Truth [is] united to Love," however, God "is called Jehovah. . . . Here love, the female element, is considered in relation to truth." Formed in the image of such a God, Washburn concluded, "there is a *male* man and a *female* man."[12]

Anna White and Lelia Taylor also found clues to God's dual gender identities in the Hebrew Bible. Writing in 1904, they explained that "the very name God, Almighty, in its original Hebrew form, El Shaddai, reveals the [duality]. El, God, its first meaning, Strength; Shaddai, the plural whose singular Shad, signifies a Breast and is feminine." Like Sears, the two women interpreted wisdom as one of God's feminine qualities.[13] Alonzo Hollister observed that "the Holy Spirit is feminine in Hebrew, and in the Syriac, which they spoke."[14]

Such analyses of God's dual gender served primarily to explain the more controversial Shaker belief in sexual duality in the Christ Spirit.[15] As in their arguments about God, several writers attempted to prove both the progressiveness of the concept of a female Christ and its consistency with biblical prophecy. A favorite New Testament prophetic passage for such writers was John's reference to Jesus as the bridegroom accompanied by the bride. Many Shakers of the period interpreted the bride as Ann Lee. "[Jesus] already *hath the Bride*," wrote Leonard in 1853, but the "*Bride* had yet to be manifested in a chosen vessel of her own order—a female."[16] Hollister described the bride as the agent of "complete . . . redemption" who will fulfill the promise of Jesus. "We accept Ann Lee as the holy Bride and first virgin Mother in the New Creation," he wrote. She alone presents the "power and spiritual gifts which no other person or church . . . could impart. Power over sin; to subdue our passions, and crucify the lusts and desires of the world within; power to cleanse the heart and to imitate the pattern set by the first born Son of God." Hollister also identified Lee as Jesus's successor because of the latter's promise that " 'I will not leave you orphans. I will ask the Father and he will send you another Comforter, even the spirit of truth whom the world cannot receive, because it sees her not, neither knows her.' "[17]

W. Watson Andrews, writing in 1893, explained that the second coming of the Christ Spirit in the female line is the logical result of the pattern of prophecy in the New Testament. "[We] believe Jesus . . . to be the anointed Savior in the male line, because his advent was foretold by ancient prophets and typified by numerous symbolic representations . . . so we believe Ann Lee . . . to be the anointed Savior in the female line."[18]

Other writers emphasized Old Testament antecedents for Lee's coming. Some saw the strong Hebrew women as her foremothers. Henry Blinn wrote in 1896 that God favored several women in Israel, and he wondered why the Deity would not again "raise up another daughter as a witness of his word."[19] White and Taylor cited Deborah as a "Mother in Israel," and interpreted the words of Jeremiah ("Behold the Lord hath created a new thing in the earth, a woman that compassed a man") as evidence of God's plan for a second, female Christ to fulfill and supersede the mission of the first.[20] In a text of 1879, Harvey Eads interpreted Jeremiah's use of the term *prophet* in reference to the daughters of God (as in " 'This is the name [prophet] whereby *she* shall be called.' Jer. xxxiii, 16") to justify the Shaker claim "that the son [Jesus] and daughter [Ann] already named now stand at the head of the new creation of God."[21]

William Bussell, writing in 1872, even translated a portion of the Hebrew text, in which the temple is named, as "Ann Lee." He explained that the temple name, usually translated as "Grace to it," actually includes "the Hebrew word . . . from which we have derived our proper name Ann" as well as a phrase (usually "translated [as] 'to it' ") that can mean "Lee." He defended his translation by saying that "any one . . . who is familiar with the Hebrew" will agree.[22]

Several writers also found figures in biblical texts that they interpreted as prophetic of the Second Coming in the female line because the language in the texts requires complementary gender symbolism for its completion, either theologically or rhetorically. The most popular of these figures occurs in the story of Genesis, which provided several writers with evidence both of the link of Shakerism to previous religious eras and of the progressive nature of Shaker theories of the Savior's dual sex. First, some writers explained that the masculine identity of both the first and second Adam (Jesus) presupposes the femininity of both the first and the second Eve (Ann Lee). William Leonard offered a slight variation on this argument:

> The *first* Adam made his *second appearing* in Eve, the mother of all living. The second Adam must needs do the same, by appearing the second time in a SECOND EVE, the *Mother of all living in the new creation;* or evidently the figure would not be fulfilled. . . . Therefore it is our province to testify to mankind, that Christ has made his *second* appearance, *in and through the female order,* without sin unto salvation, to those who look for him, as assuredly as he ever made his *first appearance in and through the male order* eighteen centuries ago.[23]

Leonard further explained that the Christ essence "first descended in the form of a dove from heaven and lighted upon Jesus."[24] Such a descent did not limit the Christ essence to that male being, however. Further, argued Ruth Webster, "If the second Adam was the representative of the Eternal Father, there should be a second Eve to represent the Eternal Mother."[25] Henry Blinn reasoned in 1896, "If a man is to be called, 'The Lord our Righteousness,' because of a special anointing, then with equal justice a woman should receive the same title, and the same special anointing, as they are said to be one in the Lord."[26]

As with Adam and Eve, the Shakers maintained that the first advent of the Christ Spirit is not necessarily to be understood as the most important. Rather, they believed that neither advent can be seen as complete without the other. Although earlier writers interpreted the order of creation as a hierarchy, with femaleness (Ann Lee) subordinated to and dependent upon maleness (Jesus), later writers had other ideas. Frederick Evans was one of these. Evans quoted Lee as saying that " 'in nature it requires a man and a woman to produce children, the man is first and the woman second. . . .' " The family analogy only appears to reflect the subordinate status of woman; actually it represents the line of succession in God's plan and justifies Lee's identity as an anointed one according to that plan. "He is the father, and she is the mother . . . ," the quote continues, "and when the man is gone, the right of government does not belong to the children, but to the *woman: so is the family of Christ*."[27] Because of the order of succession, Lee inherits not a lesser power but the same power, in her turn, from her male predecessor.

In sum, to such writers the coming of the Christ Spirit in the female line completes the figures of scripture and advances the essence of the Christian revelation to include sexual equality as a principle of divinity. The female incarnation of the Christ Spirit continues Jesus's work and modernizes his message. Ann Lee's celibacy is a critical link with Jesus as well as a crucial symbol of her association with divine sexual equality. Blinn explained that "all that may be drawn from these Scriptures in reference to the man who is anointed Christ, may as readily be drawn from the same source in reference to the woman, who is to be anointed the Christ . . . . Her Christian mission will run parallel with that of the man Christ, or the testimony of the Prophet is a dead letter."[28]

Human Sexual Equality

Several Shaker writers of the period also claimed biblical precedent for the ideal of human sexual equality. Some interpreted Paul's statement in First Corinthians 11:11 — that in the Lord " 'neither is the man without the woman [nor] the woman without the man' " — as evidence of the fact that sexual equality is a basic tenet of Christianity. That tenet, they suggested, had either lain dormant or had been sabotaged by the incomplete redemption from the sexual sin achieved in the first advent. Henry Blinn asserted in 1896 that the Apostle Paul actually supported equality between the sexes when he said that "there is no perfected system, either in the natural or spiritual orders that are formed in society, unless there is an equal representation of both man and woman."[29]

Likewise, the Creation story was seen by some as evidence not only of divine sexual duality, but also of human sexual equality. William Leonard explained that "Adam" is a generic term: " 'Their name was called *Adam* before the woman was separated.' "[30] J. M.

Washburn also explained that, "In the original, the race name of Adam is given to the male and female, which constitutes the race. *Ish* is the name for *a* man, *Isha* is the name for *a* woman, but *Adam* is the name of the race, constituted of male and female."[31] Both writers suggested that the privileges and qualities granted to Adam were originally granted equally to both sexes. Chauncey Sears also interpreted Genesis 1:26-27 as an expression of the equality of male and female principles in the undivided Adam.[32]

Such believers were proud of the Shaker mission to return humanity to the original status of equality between the sexes through their understanding of the complementary nature and interdependence of symbolic gender. The period between the sin of Eden and the coming of Jesus was a cursed one. It required female subordination and male dominance. Jesus began the process of liberation from the curse, but even he warned that the ultimate fulfillment of his redemptive mission must await the second advent. Thus, many Shakers considered Ann Lee to be the fulfillment of that promise, partly because she represents, in W. Watson Andrews's terms, the "quickening into life [of] the female nature, in humanity, as the male had been in the first advent."[33] Ruth Webster explained, "In Christ's first appearing woman was not redeemed from the curse, but was required to be silent in the church and to obey her husband . . . but it was said that his second coming should be 'without sin unto salvation.' "[34] As the second incarnation of the Christ Spirit, Ann Lee symbolizes female sinlessness and salvation, the perfect redeemer of humanity from the sin of inequality. In Shakerism, if nowhere else, the divine logic of sexual equality can prevail. "The knowledge that woman is represented in Deity, will yet place her in the true position upon earth, in the natural family," wrote Chauncy, "even as she enjoys it now with those [i.e., the Shakers] who have chosen to live on earth as the angels do in heaven."[35]

Equality does not require identity in the Shaker system, however. Because differences in male and female do not reflect stratified domains, differentiation between the sexes does not imply unequal status in Shaker thought. In the words of J. M. Washburn, "each [sex] is the equal of the other by virtue of the sex-constitution. Woman, as such, acts from *love* and truth; and man, as such, acts from *truth* and love; while the two things are so adjusted as to make male and female exact equals as images of God."[36] Those who exploit such differences in order to exercise tyranny over others violate the Shaker principle of radical equality. "It is the faith of the Society," explained Green and Wells in 1879, "that the operations of the divine light are unlimited. All are at liberty to improve their talents and exercise their gifts."[37] In 1871, another writer explained that Christian equality banishes all "distinctions created and fostered by human pride" and eliminates "that selfish abuse of God's gifts, by which a few appropriate to themselves that which belongs to the many."[38]

In short, although the Shakers of the late nineteenth century saw many of the same constitutional differences between the sexes as did their mainstream counterparts, most insisted that gender differences, even those that promote the separation of the sexes, do not obviate the belief that "equal rights, justice, equity and privileges be awarded to both sexes," in Washburn's words. "Less than this is not Christian, is not justice, is contrary to natural rights and to the equity that is called conscience." Shaker texts express no concern that equality might obscure God-given differences between the sexes. Crediting woman with more moral judgment than most of his contemporaries, Washburn concluded, "Give [woman] her axiomatic rights, and let her use the rights for the good of her sex and for the elevation of the race as she deems best."[39]

Although Shakers of the late nineteenth century considered their support of sexual equality as a sign of their religious progressivism, they also forgave ignorance of this principle among both their peers and their predecessors. In fact, several writers regarded such ignorance as the best justification for the Shaker remedy. "[Other] people will never know the Truth, until they learn to recognize the free, Godlike woman as quite important a factor in the role of man's redemption from error and folly, as is the Godlike man," wrote Hollister in 1904.[40] White and Taylor likewise expressed no surprise "that woman should have been driven from her legitimate position by the dominant spirit of man" in pre-Shaker Christianity; after all, "the race to a large extent has considered that might is right in all affairs of life."[41]

Blinn observed that male authority might have made some sense at a time when every woman could have a husband, but he realized in the postwar world of 1896 that "it presents a very different phase in the present day when one of the states of the union has some

40 or 50,000 more women than men."[42] Mainstream society has seldom recognized that women have frequently outnumbered men in American society, nor, as a consequence of that fact, has it modified its expectation that every woman will marry and be economically and emotionally dependent on a man. Certain Shakers recognized the folly of this exercise in impossible pairing, however, and they were determined to institute alternatives that allowed persons to exist outside of the traditional mode.

Extending the Shaker scenario of progress and change to secular history, some writers of the period, such as Henry Blinn, considered sexual equality to be a stage in human development inspired by Shaker doctrine. "It is worthy of note," he wrote, "that coincident with the declaration of American Independence, came the joyful tidings of the emancipation of woman, proclaimed by this heaven ordained messenger [Ann Lee]."[43]

The key to the achievement of sexual equality in Shaker documents of this period, like the key to unity, is celibacy. Only celibacy attacks the root cause of sexual inequality—sexual desire. The texts identify woman's desire as a catalyst for the sins of sexual dominance and lust in man, but this identification is not the equivalent of blaming woman for original sin or for the Fall. Rather, in contrast to mainstream beliefs in the primary guilt of Eve and all her daughters, Shaker writers of this period considered woman's sexual desire and male dominance linked to God's curse rather than to the innate natures of each sex. Sexual desire afflicts both men and women when they are in a cursed state. They simply enact that desire differently and suffer different consequences for it. In a 1901 reprint of his 1846 analysis, Hollister explained the ill effects upon humankind, especially woman, of the vicious circle of that curse:

> to usurp control to gratify libidinous passion, is violating Divine law—is shocking to all refined sensibility—is an insult to woman and to intelligence and is not less than rape. Why will men and women of clear heads and fine intelligence consent to serve this hypnotizer, this destroyer and murderer of innocence, this breeder of hate, shame and confusion, any longer, why wear out your lives doctoring effects and experimenting with theoretic remedies while leaving the cause untouched?[44]

Because celibacy rings the death knell for lust, it also signifies the

elimination of the many social problems that lust and male dominance have wrought upon the earth. Evans, who blamed sex and
lust for war, the class system, as well as for competitive, capitalistic
business practices, also suggested that the gender equality resulting
from celibacy has the power to reform those ills in the social system.
In fact, he hypothesized in 1890, "if women had been citizens and
all citizens freeholders, as in Judea, there had been no antagonistic
classes and no great cities in our country, where people are 'piled
upon one another'. . . ." Evans also saw woman's victimization as a
metaphor for all human victimization, and he believed equal education, peace, and freedom for all races to be the inevitable result
of women's political and social equality.[45] Chauncy, writing in 1871,
blamed the injustices of society upon the "peculiar philosophy" in
mainstream religion that attempts "to balance the incongruity of a
home without a Mother, as well it may! Here we have the reason,"
he continued, "of female misrepresentation in the nations, and the
denial of her individual rights."[46]

The Redemptive, Celibate Spiritual Mother

Shaker views of a female role in the redemption of humanity from
the curse also contradict traditional views of woman as the first in
sin. Several Shaker writers followed this logic and defined a form
of female redemptive power through celibacy for a world they saw
as poisoned by lust and male dominance.

An important metaphor of the celibate woman's redemptive function in several texts is spiritual motherhood, an image that connects
the celibate woman with Ann Lee as the spiritual mother of the
Shakers. Lee's spiritual motherhood is, in turn, an extension of the
divine "infinite mother," or Holy Mother, to whom writers in many
periods alluded. According to Aurelia Mace, Mother God is the
creator of "the beautiful things."[47] Anna White defined the maternal
spirit as a force for unifying the "spiritual, intellectual and human-
itarian" elements of the universe and for instilling sensitivity, tact,
sympathy, and spirituality in the daily lives of her children.[48] Some
writers saw the Divine Mother as the embodiment of divine love;[49]
others saw her as the embodiment of divine wisdom.[50] Some saw a
darker, more powerful side to the Divine Mother as well as a
nurturing, loving side. In 1889, Catherine Allen wrote of "Mother's

Love" as a "two edged sword that wounds, —/And then the balm that soothes and heals; —/It is the fire that sin consumes, —/And light that endless life reveals."[51] Henry Blinn wrote of her as the spirit who can "raise the dead" and "break in pieces many peoples and devote all that they may possess to the Lord of the whole earth."[52]

In reflection of the nurturing images of God's motherhood, Ann Lee represented to many believers what Blinn called in 1896, "the maternal principle which so intuitively accorded to her the title of Mother . . . manifesting itself in her love, care and interest for [her] children."[53] Sarah Lucas conceptualized Lee's motherhood function as a delivery of believers "from the fetal condition of our natural and worldly life" and a birthing of their souls "out of the world state into the Christ state."[54]

In these images, Lee (as a reflection of the divine mother) appears to represent a degree of control over the process of spiritual rebirth generally dissociated from female powers of reproduction in mainstream Christianity. The Shaker metaphor of spiritual motherhood builds upon, but transcends, the traditional source of female power— the ability to give birth—by translating biological (or natural) motherhood into spiritual (cultural) terms. The metaphor invests Lee's female followers with a similar power, providing they incorporate the key symbol of celibacy into their gender identities. This symbol anchors woman in her original role in human culture, as well as in religion, a role historically distorted by the curse.

In the 1904 text, Alonzo Hollister wrote that "woman's most important office [in the cursed era] . . . was to produce and rear children, to multiply the seed of Abraham." Yet, despite pressures upon her to fulfill this office, biological motherhood always "pertained to an inferior line of conduct" and contributed to woman's unfair identification with her sexuality. Hollister noted that the ancient way to overcome this degradation was for woman to achieve a position "above the position of wifehood" through celibacy or virginity. Only then could she "teach, prophesy, and exhort."[55] The metaphor of spiritual motherhood reverses the traditional association of women's reproductive function with an excessive form of carnality (and nature) by emphasizing her spiritual (or cultural) rather than her physical prowess.

In greatest need of the celibate female's spiritual powers, according to Shaker belief, are men. Even the celibate male has shared in the general male symbolic association with lust and privilege. He was seen therefore as handicapped in effecting either his own salvation or social reform. The celibate female, on the other hand, was seen as doubly dissociated from lust—first as a female and second as a celibate. She was therefore considered better able to "comprehend [man's] lost and captive state, the causes which brought him into it, and compass him with wisdom and knowledge to rise out of it," in Hollister's words of 1887.[56] As the celibate female stands "erect, according to the design of the master-builder," continued Hollister, "she must work to roll back the flood of sensuality—the giant sin of our time, which finds its way into all ranks of society."[57]

Washburn recognized that a celibate woman's ability to act from her symbolic strengths depends upon the principle of sexual equality. He implored man to "give woman the opportunity of mere naked justice, and let her have a word to say where man has signally failed. . . . Cease to withhold in the grasp of the tyrant her clearest rights and let time afford results. No man of thought and heart can or will fear the consequences," he concluded.[58]

Anna White summarized the redemptive aspect of spiritual motherhood when she wrote in 1891 that "it is in the providence of God that redemptive agencies are given through the female for the emancipation of the race from the bondage of the flesh. The Maternal Spirit will not rest; it is operating in a wonderful manner upon the daughters of men. . . . Aye, woman stands upon the threshold of a new existence: The Times are full ripe for her advent."[59]

The metaphor of spiritual motherhood is a positive symbol for woman because it transforms qualities that have been perceived as liabilities of female gender symbolism into strengths. The same qualities that confine her to the natural realm in the mainstream deliver her to the spiritual/cultural realm in Shakerism. The metaphor of spiritual motherhood reveals the cultural value hidden in traditional female characteristics, personalities, and experiences.

The metaphor of spiritual motherhood also links the celibate female with God and the Christ Spirit. Because those spirits also embody maleness, however, they suggest the potential benefits of spiritual motherhood for celibate men. Men who, in the 1872 words of Harriet Bullard, are "not seeking the spoliation of the angel virtue in woman," can improve through the influence of their sisters.[60] The cooperation by celibate men with female spiritual leadership does not reverse gender hierarchy in Shaker thought or substitute a domineering female deity for a male God. Rather, the celibate female's superordinate position simply permits a return for all to God's plan of equality and justice. Antoinette Doolittle explained in her 1880 autobiography that the Shaker sister of the nineteenth century wanted merely to become "a co-worker with her brother man in every department of life . . . working in harmonious relations together."[61]

The Spiritual Mother Gives Birth to Herself

Several Shakers who discussed Ann Lee's spiritual motherhood also noted the potential within the metaphor for the enhancement of female self-esteem. Such writers understood that freedom from male-dominated institutions could promote a new self-concept for women; as spiritual mothers, women could achieve a greater sense of freedom and self-determination while retaining their sense of a female identity.

Ann Lee also symbolizes this aspect of the metaphor. Like many Shaker women, Ann Lee came to celibacy and spiritual motherhood after having experienced both sexual relations and biological motherhood. Unlike most of her followers, however, Lee had opposed all sex and reproduction from early childhood. According to Shaker legend, she even tried to dissuade her parents from having sexual relations when she was only a child. Her efforts were predictably unwelcome, however, and resulted in physical abuse from her father.[62] Unlike many later converts, she was coerced into marriage (to Abraham Stanley), and she experienced not only the ordinary pain of childbirth, but also the profound grief of losing all four of her children, three in infancy and one at the age of six.[63]

Some scholars have suggested that Lee's "unnatural" aversion to sex and her unfortunate motherhood experiences caused her commitment to celibacy and thus to spiritual, rather than biological, motherhood. Her followers did not recognize such a cause, however. Rather, they tended to explain Lee's conversion from biological to spiritual motherhood as a deliberate act of spiritual and cultural reform, as well as a personal revolution in which she, as a woman, escaped from and rejected her male-dominated past. In Anna White's view, Lee's commitment to celibacy allowed her to escape the "fathers of church and creed and covenant, old relationships of blood, old ties and bonds of ideas, customs and conformity." Lee was willing to "[forsake] her own people and her father's house," and to work "out her own salvation thru [sic] suffering of spirit." Only "thru supreme toil and anguish [did she come] to the heritage of spiritual Motherhood," White concluded.[64]

The language of White's analysis suggests the potential for personal rebirth within the metaphor of celibate spiritual motherhood. By rejecting the fathers and the blood ties in a patriarchal society, the Shaker female celibate symbolizes self-determined rebirth. Fathers, along with their creeds and covenants, represent limits both on female social roles and on female consciousness. Celibacy gives woman a sense of herself outside of male definitions. Celibacy also reduces the efficacy of male authority by eliminating woman's need to comply with it. In celibacy there need be no fathers or husbands—the key players in the drama of female limitation. The celibate woman gains authority over herself as she seeks a new life according to God's true plan.

The self-mothering, liberating component of symbolic spiritual motherhood was a factor in nineteenth-century Shaker support of female suffrage and other public and governmental roles for women in spite of the general Shaker prohibition against civic involvement. Catherine Allen explained in the 1880s that woman's equality must be accompanied by the right to "frame the laws by which she is governed" so that "the blackened waters of sensuality and intemperance will give place to the crystal river of purity and peace . . . throughout all the avenues of society." Allen believed that many changes, from the conservation of natural resources to world peace, could be effected by the "cleansing tide" of the self-determined woman with civic rights.[65]

One can conclude that the metaphor of spiritual motherhood in these Shaker texts promotes redemption through female celibacy in two ways. First, spiritual motherhood is a force for the redemption of society. The reliance of human redemption upon female celibacy eradicates the dominance and lust in men's hearts and the evils that have resulted from those sins in social institutions. Second, spiritual motherhood redeems woman's gender identity from its degraded history in a sexual and reproductive world. The metaphor gives woman a symbolic connection with the freedom and self-determination lost to her in the curse, and it allows her to reclaim those qualities as she presents herself to God. The celibate Shaker woman thereby achieves a social and spiritual status independent of paternalism or male protection. Her role as spiritual mother—even if it entails the care of children, as it did in Shaker communities—implies less her association with children than her association with the nurturing elements of God. The spiritual mother is symbolically removed from the domestic/natural realm and elevated to the cultural/spiritual realm. This transformation is supported by the symbolism of the combined family/work domain. The spiritual mother's healing influence also extends to herself. Through spiritual motherhood, the celibate female becomes an effective adult, equal to man, and a spiritual guide for them both.

The spiritual mother metaphor may have developed because of its importance to Shaker communal goals. The transformation of woman's natural symbolic associations to cultural ones helped to facilitate the transformation of the entire community from a merely private, domestic, natural structure to a celibate/communal, cultural structure. If woman were left, symbolically, in the natural realm, she would be a hindrance to the communal goals of the Society. Spiritual motherhood symbolizes values essential to the Society, as well as to woman's status. The metaphor is not a mere trick designed to keep women "feminine," however. Rather, several writers recognized the Society's continuing need to embrace female symbolism for the survival of the community. Evans expressed such a view when he wrote, "Woman must be as potent a factor in founding the second cycle as she was in founding the first."[66]

THE KORESHANS

The subjection of woman and interference with her liberty of person and of conscience, are the principle causes which have sapped the foundation of existence.[67]

Woman . . . is the environment of the sanctuary of reproductive energy and formulation, and without the liberty to guard this most holy domain from the encroachments of carnal aggression, she is made to entail upon the unhallowed product of her divinest natural function all the evils of a desecrated sacrament.[68]

"Thy seed," take note, the *woman's* seed,
"Thy seed shall crush the serpent's head";

By her enslaved—by woman freed!
Mankind to life e'er lasting led.[69]

In Koreshan texts, notions of both sexual equality and female spiritual power emerge, ironically perhaps, from the figure of the ideal, biune androgyne in whom even physical sexual characteristics have disappeared. Until the happy day when the biune being becomes a reality, Koreshan writers gave to the symbolic celibate female two important roles. First, she was to be the primary facilitator of spiritual reproduction. Second, she was to serve as redeemer of a cursed, male-dominated world. These roles resemble those of the Shaker female celibate, but in Koreshanity they are shared by the male messiah, Koresh. That factor mitigates the impact of female spiritual power on the celibate female, although it contributes to her spiritual—and therefore cultural—symbolic identity.

Sexual Equality: Biunity in God and Christ

Like many Shaker writers, Koreshans based their belief in the equality of males and females upon their view of God. Koresh carefully distinguished between his and the Shaker view of divine bisexuality, however. He commented in 1892, for example, that Koreshans saw not "two persons of the one Godhead [like the Shakers] but two forms of the identical person." The genders of God alternate, he explained: "God as man in one presentiment of himself to his people, then as woman in her tangible presentiment."[70] When "the masculine is visible the feminine is [simply] invisible."[71] Koresh considered the two genders in deity to be of equal stature. "When the Lord is manifest as the God-Man," Koresh explained in a letter to Shaker Daniel Offord, "it is He, the Lord our Righteousness, and when the Lord is manifest as the God-Woman 'She shall be called Lord our Righteousness.' "[72]

Koresh agreed with the Shaker idea that the existence of one sex in God presages and presupposes the existence of the other; to the extent that God is male, it must also be female. Reflecting the Shaker view of the progressive order of creation, Koresh explained that the "masculine energies" of God the Father "[bring] into manifestation and form the materialized Motherhood of Deity, not as another personality, but the same Godhood and Godhead . . . the biune

Mother in whom the Father is hidden."[73] With reproductive overtones not evident in the Shaker view, however, Koreshans considered God to be a kind of divine hermaphrodite, able to reproduce within itself the energies associated with each sex.[74]

Although both the Shaker and the Koreshan systems acknowledge the existence of divine femaleness, the Koreshan system ultimately reduces the importance of the divine model to the human celibate female. On the one hand, Koresh considered the female presentiment of God indicative of God's nurturing and purifying functions, and he translated those functions into the human female celibate's purifying role in spiritual reproduction. On the other hand, because Koresh himself was the only witness of God's motherly functions— they were, he explained, "yet to be manifest" throughout the world— he also considered himself to be their primary agent on earth.[75] Therefore, Koreshanity promotes a male, rather than a female, earthly model of God's female identity.

Although less exacting than the Shakers, Koresh also maintained that both scriptural sources and the nature of Creation give support to the notion of the bisexual God. "We need not resort to scripture for the corroboration of the conviction that, inherent in the cause of being, there obtain both the elements and principles of masculinity and femininity, yet we are glad to be able to say that all the teachings of the Bible are explicit as to the bisexual character of God," he wrote. In 1892, he observed that "the very fact that the term wife is coupled with that of Lamb would indicate that the Lamb, as symbolizing an attribute of the Divine character, meant the begetting principle of Deity, which is called Father." The wife can thus be seen as the Mother principle in God. "The cause of . . . male and female life" as it exists on earth, he reasoned, "is also male and female."[76]

The symbolism of femaleness in a bisexual Christ Spirit was a trickier matter for Koresh than for Shakers, who identified Ann Lee as the female Christ Spirit. Koresh wished to justify his own identity as messiah and religious leader while simultaneously asserting his association with divine female characteristics. He joined his two purposes by defining his own powers of theocrasis as female in nature. In his writings, he provided two explanations for that definition. First, because of his alleged talents in alchemy, he considered himself capable of transforming biological forces into spiritual forces.

He then identified the powers of spiritual transformation in God as female. While he attributed similar transformative powers to the celibate human female, he also associated his own powers with God's femaleness. He wrote of himself in 1900 as a "spiritous essence . . . the quickener and vivifier of the supreme feminine potency." Second, as the only witness of Mother God, Koresh concluded that he had been selected to represent Her female essence to others. On such grounds, he claimed to be both a male and a female messiah, the androgynous fulfillment of Jeremiah's prophecy that " 'a woman shall compass a man.' "[77]

Because he respected the Shakers, Koresh occasionally associated himself with Ann Lee. On such occasions, he explained that they had both been anointed by the Christ Spirit and told of their messianic roles through divine revelation. He even attributed his spiritual authority, in part, to the Shakers' acceptance of him. Shakers "regard me as called of God to preach the gospel of purity," he reminded Shaker Daniel Offord in 1893. (The Shakers were polite to him, but they considered him somewhat bizarre.)[78] Koresh ultimately considered his own female spiritual identity to be more developed than Lee's, however. Although he explained that Koreshans "hold that [Lee] was the chosen Christ of God's Motherhood, as far above the ordinary reformer as virtue is above profanation, and that she moves in the median line of reincarnation to her perfect state as the Mother Lord," he concluded that "she only reached her partial state of perfection." He, presumably, had surpassed that state.[79]

Human Sexual Equality

The Koreshan understanding of God's bisexuality has two consequences for Koreshan theories of human sexual equality. First, like the Shakers, Koresh saw the biunity of God—and the equality of the two sexes in the Godhead—as supportive of equality in human beings. "As femininity [in God] is as much an attribute or principle as the opposite," wrote Koresh in 1892, "woman may assert and proclaim her inalienable right to life, liberty, and the pursuit of happiness as ordained by the great cause of her being."[80] Second, in Koresh's view, the equal coexistence of two sexes in God reduces the ultimate importance of divine sex differentiation and, therefore, of human sex differentiation. Why discriminate on the basis of sex if it is ultimately a trivial distinction, he reasoned. Lucie Page Borden explained in 1898 that "every person masculine externally is feminine as to his interior nature, and vice versa, while the perfect being, the archetype of creation, is biune, two-in-one, a state which as it was man's origin, will be his destiny."[81] Therefore, since Koreshanity sought the "unity and blending of the two sex principles with their forms into one organic structure, form and life, constituting that life the neuter life," their theory of sexual equality implies a theory of sexual insignificance. Only sex neutrality can "restore man to his original paradise in God."[82]

Like many of their Shaker counterparts, however, Koreshans realized that human history had been cursed with sexual inequality and hierarchy. Thus, they reasoned, the road to the neuter being, or a balance of male and female, must be paved with women's rights. Only after a concerted effort to gain that which she has been denied can the female march into the future beside rather than behind her brother. Koresh explained in 1900 that women must seize their rights rather than "degrade [their] womanhood by cringingly imploring that which man, the usurper, has no right to bestow."[83] Even though Borden considered the "woman question" to be "practically a misnomer, for a woman is first of all a human being who was very possibly masculine in a previous incarnation, and may again find expression in the same form before the cycle of segregative existence reaches its terminus," she realized that restitution must be made before gender issues could be discarded.[84] The franchise was considered an important step in gender reparations. Annie Ordway suggested in 1887 that "woman's restoration to [the] perfect state is through enfranchisement," whereas man's "is through unity with woman."[85]

Women's rights were also seen by Koreshan writers as a way to counteract the social effects of male dominance. Thus, Koreshan arguments for woman suffrage, equal wages, and a single standard of morality emphasize the benefits of such reforms for both sexes.[86] The world would be a better place, Koresh argued, if both sexes were represented in both the national government and in the Koreshan governance structure. To that end, Koresh promised in 1896 that the executive power of the Koreshan Unity would be "vested in a permanent female head."[87]

145

Female Celibacy and Human Redemption

In spite of their failure to associate female roles with functions that have cultural rather than natural status, Koreshan texts do suggest the highest spiritual role, albeit a temporary one, for the female celibate. Like the Shaker spiritual mother, the Koreshan female celibate has the power to redeem a fallen race, mired as it has been in sexual inequality and lust. In fact, in defining this role, Koreshans evidently relied upon Shaker theory. In an article reprinted in *The Flaming Sword* in 1892, the Shaker Catherine Allen elucidated that redemptive role based in celibacy in a way the Koreshans evidently approved: "the real cause of all intemperance in food, drink, and property is the false and corrupt relations of the sexes.... When woman becomes fully emancipated [from those false relations], a just system of commerce will be the natural sequence, and the whole fabric of society will be so reconstructed as to render unnecessary all the efforts as patchwork now manifest in fragmentary reforms too numerous to even mention individually."[88]

Koresh wrote in the same year that "CHURCH COMMERCE, SEXUAL COMMERCE AND SECULAR COMMERCE are inseparable, but sexual commerce is the central sphere of the three."[89] As in Shakerism, the celibate female in Koreshanity has special power in sexual commerce because she has been less corrupted by the history of lust than the male. Even the male's conversion to celibacy cannot completely counteract his longstanding symbolic association with privilege, lust, and dominance. Rather, as Lucie Borden explained in 1898, the choice of celibacy by woman is "the balancing power to counteract the evils of license ... to stem the surging tide of evil and deliver woman from the curse of subjection."[90]

As A. M. Miller explained, female celibacy also restores woman to a personal status that sexuality has denied her, that is, her "inherent right to have full control of her own person." That right, she concluded, has even "more vital bearing on the interior life and character of woman, and of the race, than the right of franchise."[91] Thus, as for Shakers of the period, celibacy was seen by Koreshans as restoring woman, and, through her, man, to a state of equality intended by God.

Celibacy was credited in Koreshan texts with the power to return woman to her innate purity, a mainstream view of woman adopted and expanded by the Shakers as well. That purity, once restored through celibacy, forms an appropriate basis for female redemptive power. A. M. Miller explained that "when we consider the difference between moral standards of man and woman, we can see easily [that attempting to encourage purity] would be more 'making a virtue of necessity,' more slow of development, in man than in woman. So that in this he must be led, if not compelled."[92] In 1892, Koresh also recommended celibacy to women as a way to combat "the habit of obedience to authority, concomitant of man's usurpation," and therefore of restoring woman's self-reliance and self-esteem. Obedience, he explained, has promoted woman's "perpetual dese-cration."[93]

From his belief in innate female sexual purity, Koresh slid easily into another mainstream assumption — the belief in woman's moral superiority to man. "It is an uncontestable fact," he wrote, "that woman is ethically infinitely superior to man; her moral perceptions are firmer and stronger, her usefulness far greater, her spiritual nature deeper and richer than that of her brothers."[94] An association with celibacy restores her and reaffirms the "innate sense of protection and purity native to her soul progress, and operative till brought under the sensualism of masculine perversion."[95]

Miller explained that women's history also contributes to the different male and female motivations for embracing celibacy. "Woman in coming down the ages under man's dominance, a slave, is fitted to look for a deliverer from this bondage, and to recognize that deliverer if he comes. . . . man, who feels not himself the gall of the bonds . . . is not seeking deliverance in that line, so he is not inclined to adopt her stand," she wrote in 1892.[96]

Having reclaimed her lost purity, wrote Koresh in 1900, the female celibate can "declare her liberty and, from a renewed religious zeal begotten from an impulse of the refining purification of virginal fire . . . expurgate the final vestige and relic of the curse: 'Thy desire shall be to thy husband and he shall rule over thee.' "[97] Then woman can lead humanity in eradicating sensuality and all the ills it has produced. "Woman will evolve or advance through the . . . law of chastity, whereby she is enabled to comprehend all that chaste life can bring to her and to the race through her," predicted A. M. Miller in 1892.[98] Thus, in the Koreshan as in the Shaker view, human liberation depends upon the restoration of woman to her lost symbolic stature. Both forms of liberation, in turn, depend upon female celibacy.

Koreshan Spiritual Motherhood

Like Shakers of the period, several Koreshan writers employed a metaphor of spiritual motherhood to represent the redemptive powers of female celibacy. Through her identity with Koresh's own putatively female powers of theocrasis, the female celibate shares his power to transform biological substances into the substances of spiritual reproduction. The celibate female represents, in Miller's words of 1892, an "exalted maternity," modeled on the motherhood of God.[99] In the purely virginal woman there are "fitting channels of the descent of the Divine Spirit into humanity."[100] Woman's decision "that she will no longer submit" to male lust, wrote another Koreshan, completes the "transmorphosis of male and female" into a single being.[101] Therefore, as noted earlier, woman's power of spiritual reproduction serves ultimately to obliterate sexual distinctions, including the distinction that provides her with her important role.

Before the obliteration of her sex, however, the Koreshan spiritual mother, like the Shaker version, does enjoy the spiritual/cultural power of effecting spiritual birth and rebirth, a function usually dissociated in Christian doctrine from female reproductive powers. Annie Ordway, writing under her Koreshan name of Victoria Gratia in 1898, explained the celibate female's role in producing the biune being:

> [Female celibacy will] constitute the vitalization of the material womanhood. It will constitute her transformation from the mortal and degenerate state to the divine natural Motherhood. It is the literal creation of the Goddess, so forming and vitalizing her maternity as to prepare her for the influx of the spirit which has been produced by the conflagration of the thousands who have been dissolved. She becomes the nucleus of inflow, and therefore the materializer of the sons of God who she will project from herself as full grown, materialized forms. These are the biune, virgin men . . . because to produce them there will have been formed at this centre the biune nucleus. . . . [male and female] energies will have merged together into the one recreative centre, from which

they will project as the two-in-one, biune sons of God. . . . it is
the central pole of masculinity and femininity united in the primate
biunity.[102]

According to A. M. Miller, the progeny produced by this process
are "superior offspring, sons and daughters of love and chaste desire,
instead of lust and misbegotten accident."[103]

In the end, the role of the Koreshan spiritual mother is short-
lived. "Woman will carry man through this practical purity of progression, into the celestial domain, when both shall become united
to constitute the Son of God," explained Annie Ordway.[104] Such
observations, particularly the use of the term *son*, suggest the ultimate
loss of female distinction, as well as the subsumption of female
capacities, by a being identified with the generic male pronoun.
Granted, nonsexist language would be a hundred years in coming,
but a self-consciously egalitarian society might have been more careful with language. The loss of female identity in the spiritual birthing
process resembles the symbolic loss of female status in the mainstream biological birthing process within the nuclear family. In both
cases, female characteristics serve cultural systems that either dis-
parage or usurp their powers. Unlike the Shaker spiritual mother,
whose specifically female gender identity has cultural/economic significance beyond the act of reproduction, the Koreshan female re-
linquishes her gender identity after contributing its uniqueness to
the Koreshan cause.

Koreshan Female Spiritual Power: An Overview

The Koreshan spiritual mother resembles the Shaker version of the
metaphor to some extent. Through celibacy she, like her Shaker
counterpart, exploits the nineteenth-century image of female purity
into a strength through which she alone can redeem a cursed sexual
culture. She also achieves a spiritual status that transforms female
natural symbolism into cultural value. The Koreshan theory of female
redemptive power, however, lacks the symbolic impact of the Shaker
version of the metaphor because the identification of female spiritual
qualities receives little support in other domains, particularly the
domain of work. In addition, Koreshan spiritual motherhood ultimately extinguishes sex distinction and thus ends the woman's privileged role. The language used to describe the biune progeny of the

spiritual mother contributes to this effect, the biune being is defined as if it were male. Finally, Koresh's role in spiritual motherhood— as a male who embodies female reproductive powers—dilutes the celibate female's association with female spiritual powers.

Underscoring the limitations of Koreshan spiritual motherhood, A. M. Miller identified female sexuality—not her redemptive powers—as woman's "highest energy, from which (when recognized as such) power could go out to all the circumferences of her work."[105] Thus the Koreshan woman continued to be defined by her sexuality and reproductive functions, like her mainstream counterparts. Therefore, she remains in closer association than the Shaker female with the natural domain.

THE SANCTIFICATIONISTS

> God made man and woman equal, and to woman in these last few days he has revealed his will concerning his own elect few.[106]

> The women have no politics and do not pretend to be reformers. Nor do they interfere in any manner with the outside world.[107]

The Woman's Commonwealth offers another model of sexual equality and female spiritual power through celibacy. After her sanctification and commitment to celibacy, McWhirter declared that "God made man and woman equal." That axiom served as a basic principle of the group's approach to family, work, and religious life. To the Sanctificationists, sexual equality, like sexual unity, implied the incorporation of male and female symbolic qualities within an ideal being who retains a specifically female identity. Their maintenance of that female identity, even as they sought male-identified rights, is evidence of their dedication to sexual equality. The sisters did not wish to become men or to be perceived as men. When adopting male characteristics, the sisters modified them to suit their female values. They eschewed personal gain and competition among themselves even while they embraced the business activities usually associated with those values. Further, there is evidence that the Commonwealth sisters, like some of their Shaker counterparts, supported the suffragist movement and other struggles for women's rights.

Although the Sanctificationists conducted their spiritual lives as if they were messengers of a traditional God, they retained their female identities in that practice as well, thus contributing to female spiritual power in their community. The Sanctificationists credited themselves as women—their own unconscious minds and decision-making power—with spiritual authority. Unlike the other two groups, however, they found no prototype for female spiritual power in a bisexual God or Christ.

Sexual Equality in the Symbolic System of the Commonwealth

Essential to establishing a balance of male and female traits was the discipline of celibacy, a discipline with female associations in the Commonwealth experience. First, by annulling the marriage bond, celibacy wiped clean the symbolic slate of womanhood, allowing the sisters to redefine it in their own way.[108] As borne out in the lives of celibate women in early Christianity, the dissolution of the marriage bond placed the sisters in an anomalous position, not quite female but not quite male, either. In their case, such deviance probably contributed to social ostracism in Belton. On the one hand, Sanctificationist celibacy made possible the sisters' acceptability as business owners; on the other hand, it created socially threatening loose women.

As sexual anomalies, the women were subject to the jibes of their contemporaries who assumed that the sisters' incorporation of male economic symbolism also implied their incorporation of male sexual values. Completely misunderstanding the circumstances of the case, a reporter assumed that the women must be sex-starved when he reported the defection of community member Ada Pratt with the headline: "She married the first man she met."[109] (The interview reveals not desperation but infatuation with a particular man.) For Pratt and the other women of the Commonwealth, however, there is little evidence of a sense of sexual discontent. In fact, according to the testimony of Martha Scheble, the last survivor of the group, many forays outside the community resulted not in marriage but in the return of the adventurer to the fold.[110] Those who were married before joining the community appear to have been especially content with their celibate lot, suggesting that the best training ground for a celibate life may have been married sex, as well as the unfair economic bargain of nineteenth-century marriage.

Because the commitment to celibacy resembles the traditional nineteenth-century value of female sexual purity, which even feminists of the day tended to favor, women were more easily able both to adhere to its disciplines and to feel fulfilled through sexual abstinence. For the Sanctificationists in particular, celibacy itself, therefore, represents a specifically female value that balances the male-identified values of achievement and economic independence in their androgynous ideal.

In achieving balance and equality in male and female symbolism, the women temporarily lost cultural status in terms of social class. Celibacy reversed the economic status the women had enjoyed in marriage. As married women, most of them had lived middle-class lives. As independent breadwinners, at least initially, they entered the working class. The women effectively transformed class identity from a male-identified trait, conferred by a man on a woman, to a female-identified trait, earned by a woman on her own. Because of that symbolic transformation, the sisters ultimately preferred their lower-class status. Although some felt shame at the loss of prestige, particularly when they went as maids into the homes of their friends, such feelings quickly turned to a sense of satisfaction and pride. The sisters reported new levels of self-esteem from the discipline and integrity of their menial but independent work.[111]

In a few years, of course, the sisters' business success produced upward mobility, and they eventually earned middle-class and even leisure-class status on their own merits. Like good entrepreneurs, the women gained control over the profits of their labor and, ultimately, the respect of their fellow citizens. In 1894, McWhirter was even asked to serve as the first woman member of the Belton Board of Trade.[112] Finally, through the regulation of work, they even earned the right to leisure time. They eventually transformed the traditional woman's day of work from an endless round of ill-defined tasks to a four-hour workday in which tasks were defined, professionalized, and rotated. Outside of those specified hours, a woman's time became her own.[113] Their collective efforts enabled them to travel extensively, in small groups while continuing to run their profitable businesses.

Female identification apparently turned to feminist identification in the Commonwealth. Whenever they encountered barriers to their goals, the sisters advocated not only their own but all women's rights and fought for them deliberately. McWhirter paid dues to the National American Woman Suffrage Association throughout the 1890s and until her death in 1904. The women's efforts to claim rights to property that was due them, morally if not legally, occasionally led to outright battles. On one occasion, in 1882, the sisters attempted to establish a commercial laundry on the corner of a lot jointly owned by Sister Margaret Henry and her husband. Mr. Henry objected and confronted the women, breaking his wife's arm and calling the police. He had several of the women, including his wife, arrested. Each woman, including his wife, was fined $20 for trespassing.[114] Such confrontations and disappointments drove McWhirter to draft a bill to the Texas legislature in 1892, asking for the repeal of laws limiting the rights of married women.[115]

The balanced gender identities of the sisters paid off. While fighting for women's rights, the women were achieving and earning like men. By the turn of the century, the group had assets estimated at between $100,000[116] and $500,000.[117] Investments included a 120-acre farm in Montgomery County, Maryland, which was purchased shortly after the move to the Washington, D.C. area in 1898.[118] Moreover, in what may be cosmic justice, many of the women, including Margaret Henry, outlived their husbands. Many eventually inherited and controlled the property denied to them during their marriages.[119]

The gender-balanced celibate female also achieved a level of personal freedom that was unusual for nineteenth-century women. While still living in Belton, the women made trips to Mexico City (where they met President and Mrs. Diaz), as well as to Chicago, New York City, Washington, D.C., Florida, and Colorado. The trips were ostensibly devoted to the search for a new home, but they also offered a chance for adventure.[120]

The decision, made early in 1898, to move to Washington, D.C., also represents an unusual level of freedom for formerly married women. Although many of the sisters, including McWhirter, had followed fathers or husbands to the Texas frontier, they required no male leadership for the return to the East Coast. The move was carefully planned and executed gradually to ease the transition. Still, such a move required the women to abandon a small, familiar town where most of them had spent at least their adult lives for an unfamiliar metropolis. They left behind familiar surroundings and challenged themselves to live by their wits and talents rather than by established contacts or small-town benevolence.[121] Contemporaries observed that the women experienced little difficulty making the transition implied in this daring move. Once settled in their new home, the sisters took full advantage of the cultural opportunities offered by the capital city.[122]

Even in the early days as a community, the women balanced such independence and adventure with a concern for women's lot. McWhirter was especially troubled by the double standard of morality that existed for men and women: "how a man could be the lowest of the low in sensuality yet still retain the esteem of society. . . while the woman was thrust out, insulted and abused." Determined that "this outrage should not be permitted at the Central," she encouraged the sisters to ignore vicious gossip and to admit women to their hotel on the same basis as they admitted men. Everyone, including the townsmen, learned a lesson from their insistence on a single standard of morality.[123] Such actions and values demonstrate that the Sanctificationist incorporation of traditionally male traits—such as property rights, personal freedom, and the right to moral self-determination—is balanced by an awareness of women's concerns and by a conscious identification with the female sex.

Pragmatic Motherhood

Despite its strongly female symbolism, the Sanctificationist androgynous ideal does not incorporate the metaphor of spiritual motherhood evident in the symbolic systems of the other two groups. This omission is puzzling in light of both the strong female and feminist symbolism in the ideal and the actual motherhood of so many group members. Records suggest, however, that the women interpreted celibacy as irrelevant to their actual and apparently comfortable and positive roles as mothers, at least for the children who accompanied them into the community. The sisters dissociated themselves from the nurturing or birthing symbolism of motherhood, if not from its day-to-day duties.

Such dissociation may reflect in part the tragic facts of motherly life, at least for the group's founder. Like Ann Lee, Martha McWhirter had lost many children—two of her twelve died shortly before her sanctification in 1866. Her favorite daughter, Ada McWhirter Haymond, who was a member of the community, died in 1898, six years before McWhirter's own death.[124] Therefore, even more than Lee, McWhirter was continually reminded of the fragility of the mother-child bond. Also, McWhirter knew the difficulties of raising children into adulthood and of managing a large family. Because of her powerful role in the community, her tragic experiences may have influenced the imagery of the group.

Whatever the reason, what actually emerges from the group's constitution is a model of parenthood that combines symbolic elements of mainstream fatherhood and motherhood. After the physical act of procreation, the biological mothers among them apparently had no greater nurturing responsibilities than other sisters. Members shared in childcare; various sisters acted as teachers and nurturers for the smaller children. In addition, no distinctions between mothers and nonmothers appear in documents describing the Commonwealth economic system. Everyone engaged in productive work; mothering and teaching duties did not preclude economically productive activity. This model of parenthood is both consistent with the balanced gender identity of the sanctified androgyne and inconsistent with a metaphor of spiritual motherhood. If motherhood symbolism interferes with female economic independence, women's rights, and the conduct of business, then why utilize it in the promotion of such values?

Even in the key scenario of sanctification no spiritual motherhood imagery appears. Women are not seen as giving spiritual birth to themselves or as facilitating the rebirths of others. The sisters' view of sanctification emphasizes direct individual conversion without mediation. Lacking such spiritual rebirth imagery, however, the community system also lacks a strategy for promoting conversion and ensuring future generations of believers. Instead of seeking converts to their beliefs, the Sanctificationists concentrated on improving those already "born" into their system. In them would shine "the light which ever glorifies the mountains of the ideal."[125]

Female Spiritual Authority

Without the metaphor of spiritual motherhood and without a model for female authority in God or Christ, the Commonwealth system appears on the surface to lack a theoretical basis for establishing female spiritual power. Yet a closer look reveals that such a basis does exist, and it derives from the sisters' original understanding of sanctification. In fact, that understanding includes two elements that support female spiritual power. First, although available to all, true and lasting celibate sanctification was ultimately achieved only by women. Second, sanctification endows believers with the right to interpret God and to act in His name. Together, those features of sanctification resulted in the establishment of religious authority in the minds of an exclusive group of female celibates.

Testimony of sanctification was a prerequisite for Commonwealth membership. All applicants were required to reveal their direct experience of God before being admitted.[126] The power of direct revelation was kept alive through the group's decision-making process, which frequently depended on the collective interpretation of members' dreams. Because of her acknowledged wisdom and judgment, McWhirter was the primary authority for dream interpretation, but, as she testified in 1887, "any of us have about as clear an understanding of our revelations as the other."[127]

Dream interpretation can be seen as a form of spiritual self-reliance, reminiscent of other manifestions of self-reliance in the Commonwealth system. Because dreams were seen as messages from God, their recitation and interpretation eventually replaced other forms of religious observance in the community. After their experience with male-dominated mainstream religion in Belton, the sisters may have preferred their own authority to any inevitably male authority they might have chosen.

The move toward spiritual self-reliance was gradual. In the early years, members were allowed to attend any church they chose, or none at all. Soon services within the community replaced attendance at outside church services.[128] Finally, even services within the community were eliminated. By 1891, McWhirter reportedly prohibited religious discussions and offered no religious rituals in the group.[129] In about 1901, McWhirter dismissed organized religion entirely by proclaiming that "theologians are to blame for much of the evil and unhappiness from which people suffer in this world."[130]

Consistent with their spiritual self-reliance, Commonwealth members were also apparently permitted intellectual autonomy. Garrison noted that the group's library included the works of Tolstoi and Bellamy and that the women subscribed to many magazines of the period, including the Koreshan publication, *The Flaming Sword*. They read extensively about other communal societies, including the Shakers and the Koreshans, and they regularly received suffrage literature. Probably to facilitate family harmony, however, Mc-Whirter discouraged discussions of political issues in the community.[131]

Gradually, then, celibate sanctification came to symbolize female spiritual as well as secular authority. In contrast to the other two groups, the religious motivation for celibacy was eventually supplanted by the group's secular experience. Religion drove the women to celibacy, which, in turn, promoted their separation from men, family, and other institutions of mainstream American life. That separation promoted the values of self-reliance, sisterhood, and a powerful female gender identity enriched by the traditional male symbols available to the women because of celibacy. Even the group's temporary ostracism by Belton townspeople probably helped to solidify these values by encouraging solidarity, independence, and autonomy.

Finally, however, having served its purpose, religion faded away. Celibacy rose in symbolic importance over the religious beliefs that had spawned it. Sanctified spiritual power was reinforced by female secular efficacy. Any group of women who could succeed and prosper as they had done must be in tune with divine will, the sisters reasoned. Thus they crowned their cultural identities as independent and autonomous female beings with the highest cultural symbol of all, authority in the spiritual domain.

In the end, the Sanctificationist cultural system is a good example of religion's symbolic usefulness for female empowerment. Religion can facilitate secular goals when those goals are defined as signs of God's approval, as they were in Calvinism. Eventually, secular and religious power can blend, and persons endowed with one form of power are also credited with embodying the other. If women can involve their feminist goals in this process, religion can serve their needs, as it so often has for men. Commonwealth women learned to give less service to male religious institutions and more service to their own spiritual/secular ideals.

FEMALE CELIBACY: EQUALITY AND REDEMPTION

The key symbol of celibacy in the idea systems that emerge from the late-nineteenth-century texts of the three groups reverses the sexual hierarchy of mainstream heterosexual culture. Shaker and Koreshan writers of the period redefined the biblical origins of such hierarchy by seeing female sexual desire as a curse. That desire has its origins in God's admonition to Eve that her desire should be for her husband and that he should, therefore, rule over her. It is not a quality intrinsic to womanhood. Thus, they identified the curse, rather than female nature, as the real source of woman's subordination. Shakers and Koreshans of the period proclaimed celibacy as the key to the emancipation of woman from that curse. They thought that her subordination to man would end when she was freed from her desire. She would then have no further need to comply with the parallel tenet of the curse—male domination.

Further, writers in both groups also credited celibate womanhood with the power to redeem all humanity from the cursed state. They reversed the usual identity of woman as the first in sin by identifying her as the first in redemption. Female celibacy, they claimed, would also eradicate the evil influence of male dominance on men and on the decadent social institutions created by men in their cursed state.

Texts of the two groups also share the metaphor of spiritual motherhood. Uses of the metaphor in both Shaker and Koreshan documents elevate the status of uniquely female reproductive capacities to a spiritual level which, in a Christian context, has prestigious cultural associations. Analysis reveals, however, that the Koreshan failure to support the metaphor with other culturally valued roles, as in work, diminishes its usefulness in the transformation of female characteristics from the natural, domestic domain to the more prestigious cultural domain.

Sanctificationists looked less to the personages of the divine realm in their justification for sexual equality than did the other two groups. Rather, they based the equality of the sexes upon revealed divine logic. "God made man and woman equal," according to McWhirter.[132] Having encountered cultural barriers to the realization of God's intention, however, the sisters created a new system, combining male and female (cultural and natural) symbolism in a proud,

158

woman-identified persona. They also created the spiritual authority necessary to legitimate their independent economic and social life.

NOTES

1. "Life's True Significance," *The Shaker Manifesto* 18 (July 1880): 165.

2. Quoted from "Millennial Praises," 1812, in Anna White and Lelia S. Taylor, *Shakerism: Its Meaning and Message* (Columbus, Ohio: Press of Fred G. Herr, 1904), p. 11. This quotation is early for the current study, but it does demonstrate the roots of later expressions of a female spiritual role.

3. Lizzie Morton, "Open Letter," *The Shaker Manifesto* 10 (April 1880): 83.

4. Like many Shaker beliefs, the belief in a bisexual God and Christ Spirit evolved over time. The doctrine of a dual-sex God first appears in writing in Benjamin Seth Youngs's *Testimony of Christ's Second Appearing* (Lebanon, Ohio: John MacClean) in 1808. What relationship the doctrine had to leadership practices is unclear. The institution of dual-sex leadership preceded that publication date by many years. Just because there is no earlier record of the doctrine does not, of course, mean that it did not exist. There are very few community records before the 1808 work. It is also difficult to tell when the belief in Mother Ann as the female incarnation of Christ began. Youngs's 1808 *Testimony* does suggest such a belief, but the 1816 *Testimonies Concerning the Life, Character, Revelations, and Doctrines of our Ever Blessed Mother. . . .* (Hancock, Mass.: J. Talcott and J. Deming, Jrs.) describes Lee as Jesus's wife as well as the second Eve. In that work, Lee is also quoted as comparing herself to Jesus. The controversy implicit in the two sources does, at the very least, indicate the association of Lee and Jesus from an early date, even if the exact nature of that association is unclear. Lee was called "Mother" in her lifetime, as well as later, and that title certainly suggests a parallel to the Father God concept. As opposed to Marjorie Procter-Smith's suggestion that mother imagery is less precise than father imagery in early texts and hymns, I find neither figure very well developed — Mother God no less than Father God. See Marjorie Procter-Smith, *Women in Shaker Community and Worship: A Feminist Analysis of the Uses of Religious Symbolism,* vol. 16, Studies in Women and Religion (Lewiston, N.Y.: Edwin Mellen Press, 1985), pp. fvii, 100-3, 145-48, 155-56.

5. Anna White, "Woman's Mission," *The Manifesto* 21 (January 1891): 4.

6. *Mother's Gospel: The Last Dispensation of God to Man* (New Lebanon, N.Y., 1819), pp. 16-17.

7. Hester Poole, *Shakers and Shakerism* ([Chicago, 1887]), p. 4. Earlier texts, notably Seth Y. Wells's 1813 *Millennial Praises* (Hancock, Mass.: Josiah Talcott, Jr.) emphasized Eve's sin—and the secondary status of her daughters—in order to set the stage for Ann Lee's and celibate women's sinlessness. There are contradictions in other works about the meaning of woman's second place in creation. See Procter-Smith, *Women in Shaker Community and Worship*, pp. 149-54. In order to understand the point being made in the later works considered in this book, however, Shaker views of men and women living under the influence of the curse must be distinguished from their views of men and women who have reversed the tenets of the curse by rejecting sexuality. Thus, the view of Eve's daughters and the view of Ann's daughters are not the same. Celibate woman is not subject to the degradation, dependence, and sin that sexual woman has been. Shaker writers seem fairly clear on two points: before the sin of lust, men and women were equal; Shakerism is designed to restore the sexes to that original equality through celibacy.

8. Proctor-Smith, *Women in Shaker Community and Worship*, pp. 149-54.

9. A[lonzo] G. Hollister, *Heaven Anointed Woman* ([Mt. Lebanon, N.Y.?, 1887]).

10. Chauncey Edward Sears, *Shakers: Duality of the Deity; or, God Father and Mother. . . .* (Rochester, N.Y.: Daily Democrat Steam Printing House, 1867), p. 7.

11. William H. Bussell, "Mother," *The Shaker* 2 (June 1872): 45.

12. J. M. Washburn, "The Male and Female Principles in Deity," *The Manifesto* 19 (October 1889): 227. Washburn's article bore his name and the designation, "Terrell, Texas." Because there were no Shaker communities in Texas, and the article was clearly a letter to the *Methodist Recorder*, it is probable that Washburn was a non-Shaker whose work caught the eye of the editors of the *Shaker Manifesto*.

13. White and Taylor, *Shakerism*, p. 257.

14. A[lonzo] G. Hollister, "The Free Woman," in "Calvin's Confession," ed. J. Lafume, printed in *Progressive Thinker* (New Lebanon, N.Y., 1904), pp. 19-20.

15. For examples of the verbal and physical persecutions suffered by early Shaker founders because of their beliefs in Ann Lee as both the female Christ and a religious leader, see especially Edward R. Horgan,

The Shaker Holy Land: A Community Portrait (Harvard, Mass.: Harvard Common Press, 1982), pp. 25-27, and Clara Endicott Sears, *Gleanings from Old Shaker Journals* (Boston: Houghton Mifflin, 1916), passim. Interviews with living Shaker sisters reveal that the importance of the female in God has diminished over the years. Eldress Bertha Lindsay of Canterbury explained that she never thinks about the gender of God in her prayers, for example. Living Shakers still regard Ann as the anointed of the Christ Spirit, however, just as their predecessors did. Interview with Eldress Bertha Lindsay, Canterbury Shaker Community, Canterbury, N.H., July 30, 1983.

16. William Leonard, *A Disclosure on the Order and Propriety of Divine Inspiration and Revelation, Showing the Necessity Thereof, in All Ages, to Know the Will of God. Also, a Discourse on the Second Appearing of Christ, in and Through the Order of the Female. And a Discourse on the Propriety and Necessity of a United Inheritance in All Things, in Order to Support a True Christian Community....* (Harvard, Mass.: United Society, 1853), p. 61.

17. Hollister, *Heaven Anointed Woman*, n.p.n. Procter-Smith interprets the Bride imagery of Ann Lee in the hymns in *Millennial Praises* (1813) as signs of Lee's subordination to Jesus. Without her assumption that sequence in time is analogous to sequence in importance, however, there is no real reason to interpret her examples as illustrative of subordination rather than of progression. See Procter-Smith, *Women in Shaker Community and Worship*, pp. 151-53. In any case, the imagery she cites far predates the period under consideration here.

18. W. Watson Andrews, "Second Appearing of Christ," *The Manifesto* 23 (August 1893): 185.

19. Henry Clay Blinn, *The Advent of Christ in Man and Woman* ([East Canterbury, N.H., 1896]), p. 5.

20. White and Taylor, *Shakerism*, p. 266.

21. Harvey L. Eads, *Shaker Sermons: Scripto-Rational. Containing the Substance of Shaker Theology. Together with Replies and Criticisms Logically and Clearly Set Forth....* (Shakers [Watervliet], N.Y.: *The Shaker Manifesto* [Albany, N.Y.: Printed by Weed, Parsons, 1879), pp. 5-6.

22. Bussell, "Mother," p. 45.

23. Leonard, *Disclosure*, pp. 61-62.

24. Ibid., p. 61.

25. Ruth Webster, "The Second Eve," in N[icholas A.] Briggs, *God, — Dual* ([East Canturbury, N.H., n.d.]), p. 6.

26. Blinn, Advent of Christ, pp. 8-10.

27. Frederick W. Evans et al., *Shakers: Compendium of the Origin,*

History, Principles, Rules and Regulations, Government and Doctrine of the United Society of Believers in Christ's Second Appearing (New York: D. Appleton, 1859), p. 146.

28. Blinn, *Advent of Christ*, pp. 8-10. Although some might interpret any family analogy in Shaker texts in light of nuclear family values, Shaker belief really requires one to remember the new family form of their communities and to exercise caution in interpreting all references to family in a negative light. Attention should also be paid to the fact that the man in the reference (Jesus) is gone; the leadership now belongs to the woman (Lee).

29. Ibid., p. 6.

30. Leonard, *Disclosure*, p. 61.

31. Washburn, "Male and Female Principles in Deity," p. 227. This interpretation of the Hebrew language and syntax has recently been discussed in contemporary feminist sources. See, for example, Phyllis Trible's "Eve and Adam: Genesis 2-3 Reread," in *Womanspirit Rising: A Feminist Reader in Religion,* ed. Carol P. Christ and Judith Plaskow (San Francisco: Harper and Row, 1979), pp. 74-83. Trible was apparently unaware of the Shaker texts as precedents for this interpretation when she explained that she found virtually no historical support for an androgynous interpretation of "adham from (male) biblical scholars" (p. 82n).

32. Sears, *Shakers,* p. 7.

33. Andrews, "Second Appearing of Christ," p. 185.

34. Webster, "The Second Eve," p. 6.

35. Chauncy [Chauncey Edward Sears?], "God My Father and Mother," *The Shaker* 1 (July 1871): 51.

36. Washburn, "Male and Female Principles in Deity," p. 228.

37. Calvin Green and Seth Y. Wells, *A Brief Exposition of the Established Principles and Regulations of the United Society of Believers Called Shakers* (New York: E. S. Dodge Printing, 1879), p. 11.

38. "Christian Equality," *The Shaker* 1 (December 1871): 90.

39. Washburn, "Male and Female Principles in Deity," p. 228.

40. Hollister, "The Free Woman," p. 19.

41. White and Taylor, *Shakerism,* p. 266.

42. Blinn, *Advent of Christ,* pp. 9, 13.

43. Ibid.

44. A[lonzo] G. Hollister, "Appeal to Loyal Workers," in Calvin Green, *The Law of Life* (1841; repr., Mt. Lebanon, N.Y., n.p. 1901), pp. 11-15.

45. Frederick W. Evans, *Two Orders: Shakerism and Repubicanism. The American Church and American Civil Government, Coequal and*

162

Separate. The New Heavens and Earth (Pittsfield, [Mass.]: Press of the Sun Printing, 1890), p. 7.

46. Chauncy, "God, My Father and Mother," p. 51.

47. Aurelia J. Mace, "The Mission and Testimony of the Shakers of the 20th Century to the World" (a lecture delivered at Greenacre, Eliot, Maine, July 9, 1904), p. 13. Texts defining the qualities of Mother God are rare, even in the late period, as Procter-Smith points out. However, texts defining the qualities of Father God are equally scarce. It is also sometimes confusing whether "Mother" refers to Mother Ann or Mother God. See Procter-Smith, *Women in Shaker Community and Worship,* p. 154.

48. [Anna White], *The Motherhood of God* ([Canaan Four Corners, N.Y.: Press of Berkshire Industrial Farm, 1903]), pp. 21-22.

49. Frederick W. Evans, "Shakerism," *The Shaker Manifesto* 9 (May 1879): 106; Washburn, "Male and Female Principles in Deity," p. 227.

50. Sears, *Shakers,* p. 7; Leonard, *Disclosure,* p. 64.

51. Catherine Allen, "A Mother's Love" (poem), *The Manifesto* 19 (February 1889): 39.

52. Blinn, *Advent of Christ,* p. 9.

53. Ibid., p. 19. This is a rare reference to Lee's love of children. Its rarity suggests that the term *children* refers more to her spiritual off-spring — Shaker believers — than to youngsters in general.

54. [Mary Frances Carr], *Shakers. Correspondence between Mary F. C[arr] of Mt. Holly City and a Shaker Sister Sarah L[ucas] of Union Village,* ed. R. W. Pelham ([Union Village, Ohio?], 1868), p. 13.

55. Hollister, "The Free Woman," pp. 24-25.

56. A[lonzo] G. Hollister, *Divine Motherhood* ([Mt. Lebanon, N.Y.?, 1887]).

57. "God's Spiritual House; or, the Perfected Latter Day Temple," *The Shaker* 1 (March 1871): 20.

58. Washburn, "Male and Female Principles in Deity," p. 228.

59. Anna White, "Woman's Mission," *The Manifesto* 21 (January 1891): 4.

60. Harriet Bullard, quoted in White and Taylor, *Shakerism,* p. 391.

61. Mary Antoinette Doolittle, *Autobiography of Mary Antoinette Doolittle: History of Early Life Prior to Becoming a Member of the Shaker Community. . . .* (Mt. Lebanon, N.Y., 1880), p. 36.

62. Horgan, *Shaker Holy Land,* pp. 8-9.

63. Horgan reports that the fourth daughter died in 1766. Ibid., p. 10. He and others have concluded that Lee believed the deaths of the children to be a punishment for her sexual indulgence. Henri Desroche concludes that, because Lee joined the Wardleys' group just two years

after the death of her last child in 1766, she chose celibacy as a palliative for her grief. Henri Desroche, *The American Shakers: From Neo-Christianity to Presocialism*, trans. John K. Savacool (Amherst: University of Massachusetts Press, 1971), p. 29. Desroche, in fact, seems to believe that her religious commitment rested almost entirely on an unnatural aversion to sexuality. There is little evidence, however, that other Shakers felt revulsion at the thought of sexual relations. They simply found celibacy to be the path toward spiritual perfection and the other goals described herein. Many wrote sympathetically about married people, particularly in the later decades of the nineteenth century. A close reading of the texts under consideration here reduces the plausibility of Desroche's analysis as an explanation of the enduring principle of Shaker celibacy.

64. [White], *Motherhood of God*, p. 20.

65. Catherine Allen, *The Questions of the Day* ([Mt. Lebanon, N.Y., 188-?]), p. 5.

66. Frederick W. Evans, quoted in White and Taylor, *Shakerism*, p. 392.

67. "The Celibate Life," *The Guiding Star* 1 (February 1, 1887): 4.

68. Annie Ordway, "Woman's Restoration to Her Rightful Dominion and Her Relation to Koreshism: Address Before the Koreshan Convention, at Central Music Hall," reprinted in *The Guiding Star* 2 (September 1888): 321.

69. Julia A. Macdonald, "One Phase of the Divine Mission of Woman," *The Flaming Sword* 3 (March 5, 1892): 7.

70. Koresh [Cyrus R. Teed], "The Biune Genus," *The Flaming Sword* 3 (May 7, 1892): 2.

71. Koresh [Cyrus R. Teed], "The Femininity of God: Excerpts from Koresh's Lecture to the Woman's Mission, January 22, 1892," *The Flaming Sword* 3 (February 20, 1892): 6.

72. Koresh [Cyrus R. Teed], *Letter from Daniel Offord, with Reply by Koresh* ([Chicago, 1893]), pp. 7-8.

73. [Koresh?] [Cyrus R. Teed], "A Brief Summary of the Koreshan System," *The Flaming Sword* 3 (April 16, 1892): 15.

74. O. F. L'Amoreaux, "Forbidding to Marry," *The Flaming Sword* 4 (October 1, 1892): 5.

75. Koresh [Cyrus R. Teed], *Judgment* (Chicago: Guiding Star Publishing House, 1900), p. 17.

76. Koresh? [Cyrus R. Teed], "The Wife of God," *The Flaming Sword* 3 (March 26, 1892): 6.

77. Koresh [Cyrus R. Teed], *The Illumination of Koresh. Marvelous*

Experience of the Great Alchemist Thirty Years Ago, at Utica, N.Y. (n.p., [1900]), p. 21.

78. Koresh, *Letter from Daniel Offord,* p. 9.

79. Ibid., pp. 8, 10.

80. Koresh?, "Wife of God," p. 6.

81. Lucie Page Borden, "Current Topics from the Koreshan Standpoint," *The Flaming Sword* 12 (September 30, 1898): 6.

82. Koresh, "Biune Genus," p. 32.

83. Koresh, *Judgment,* p. 9.

84. Borden, "Current Topics," p. 6.

85. Annie Ordway, "The Function of Woman in the Coming Government," *The Guiding Star* 2 (May 1887): 150.

86. [Annie Ordway], "Woman's Rights vs. Woman's Weakness," *The Flaming Sword* 3 (January 9, 1892): 5; Koresh, "Equal Rights and Privileges," *The Flaming Sword* 3 (January 16, 1892): 4.

87. [Koresh] [Cyrus R. Teed], *Response to Inquiries* (n.p., [1896]), pp. 7-8. A gap existed between Koresh's theories on equal representation of the sexes in community leadership and his practice. His writings reveal that he saw the logic of egalitarian leadership in a celibate community, however, and it is that connection that is of interest.

88. Catherine Allen, "Most Important Reforms," in *Fragrance from the Altar of Incense: Shaker Contributions to the "Flaming Sword"* (Mt. Lebanon, N.Y., 1892), pp. 14, 15.

89. Koresh [Cyrus R. Teed], "How Can Social Order Be Established? [Part II]," *The Flaming Sword* 3 (March 5, 1892): 4.

90. Lucie Page Borden, "Mrs. Stanton's Lament," *The Flaming Sword* 12 (April 29, 1898): 6.

91. A. M. Miller, "Foundation of Woman's Rights," *The Flaming Sword* 3 (February 27, 1892): 7.

92. A. M. Miller, "What Does the Woman's Rights Movement Mean?," *The Flaming Sword* 3 (March 5, 1892): 6.

93. Koresh [Cyrus R. Teed], "What Constitutes a Shaker?," *The Flaming Sword* 4 (October 15, 1892): 3.

94. Koresh [Cyrus R. Teed], *The Flaming Sword* 3 (April 30, 1892): 9, 10.

95. Koresh, "What Constitutes a Shaker?," p. 3.

96. A. M. Miller, "Can Woman Adopt Chastity Without Bringing Disaster on the Race?," *The Flaming Sword* 3 (April 30, 1892): 7.

97. Koresh, *Judgment,* pp. 8-9.

98. Miller, "What Does the Woman's Rights Movement Mean?," p. 6.

99. A. M. Miller, "Who Opposes Woman's Progress?," *The Flaming Sword* 3 (January 23, 1892): 6.

100. Koresh?, "Wife of God," p. 7.

101. "God the Lord Alternately Male and Female: The Sons of God, Neuter," *The Flaming Sword* 3 (January 23, 1892): 1.

102. Victoria Gratia [Annie G. Ordway], "The Coming Conflagration and Birth of the Sons of God," *The Flaming Sword* 13 (December 16, 1898): 7.

103. Miller, "Who Opposes Woman's Progress?," p. 6.

104. Ordway, "The Function of Woman," p. 150.

105. Miller, "Foundation of Woman's Rights," p. 7.

106. Martha McWhirter, quoted in Gwendolyn Wright, "The Woman's Commonwealth: Separatism, Self, Sharing," *Architectural Association Quarterly* 6 (Fall-Winter 1974): 37.

107. "Mrs. M'Whirter and Her Community of Celibate Women in Washington: They Migrated from Belton, Texas: How They Work and Prosper in Their New Home," *The Waco Weeky Tribune,* July 20, 1901, George Pierce Garrison Papers, Barker Texas History Center, the General Libraries, the University of Texas at Austin.

108. A. H. Mattox, "The Woman's Commonwealth," *Social Service* 4 (November 1901): 167.

109. Ada Pratt (spelled "Adah" in the article) reported that five women left the community to marry. "Married First Man She Met," Gatesville (Texas) *Star-Messenger,* April 24, 1908, George Pierce Garrison Papers, Barker Texas History Center, the General Libraries, the University of Texas at Austin. Letters concerning Ada Pratt reveal that she had been a troubled member of the community since at least 1898. She had certainly met and known many men by the time of her elopement.

110. I interviewed Martha Scheble, the last Sanctificationist, on June 4, 1983, at the Montgomery County, Maryland, property (then only about two acres). At the time of the interview, Ms. Scheble was 101 years old. She had been raised in the community from the age of eighteen months. She left the community for several years starting in 1901, but she finally decided she "didn't like" the outside world. She returned and remained in the community, outliving all other members. She died November 19, 1983.

111. George Pierce Garrison, "A Woman's Community in Texas," *The Charities Review* 3 (November 1893): 38; Margarita Gerry, "The Woman's Commonwealth of Washington," *Ainslee's Magazine* (September 1902): 135.

112. "The Life and Spiritual Experiences of Martha McWhirter,

Leader and Founder of the Women's Commonwealth," n.p., n.d., p. 23 (typewritten).

113. Garrison, "Woman's Community in Texas," pp. 41-42. Letters reveal that at crisis times, especially during the transition from Belton to Washington, everyone worked much longer hours, but tasks were always well defined.

114. Gatesville (Texas) *Advance,* November 18, 1882; Garrison, "Woman's Community in Texas," p. 36.

115. "Life and Spiritual Experience," p. 13.

116. "A Happy Home without Husbands," (ca.) 1901, George Pierce Garrison Papers, Barker Texas History Center, the General Libraries, the University of Texas at Austin.

117. "Mrs. M'Whirter in Washington."

118. Deed in Trust for Colisville, Maryland, farm, recorded October 5, 1903.

119. "Happy Home without Husbands"; Eleanor James, "The Sanctificationists of Belton," *The American West* 2 (Summer 1965): 69.

120. A. L. Bennett, "The Sanctified Sisters," *The Sunny Slopes of Long Ago,* Publications of the Texas Folklore Society, no. 33 (1966): 143; Garrison, "Woman's Community in Texas," p. 44.

121. "Married First Man She Met."

122. Mattox, "Woman's Commonwealth," p. 167.

123. "Life and Spiritual Experience," p. 13.

124. Garrison, "Woman's Community in Texas," p. 30; "Life and Spiritual Experience," p. 21.

125. Mattox, "Woman's Commonwealth," p. 170.

126. James, "Sanctificationists of Belton," p. 72.

127. Martha McWhirter, "McWhirter's Answers to Interrogatories in B. W. Haymond v. Ada Haymond, #3037, in the District Court of Bell County, Texas, 17 October 1887," interrogatory no. 20.

128. Gerry, "Woman's Commonwealth of Washington," p. 139.

129. Garrison, "Woman's Community in Texas," p. 46. This prohibition did not stop overt criticism of other religions, however.

130. "Mrs. M'Whirter in Washington."

131. Garrison, "Woman's Community in Texas," p. 44. Garrison also reported, however, that the women did not share the beliefs of the Koreshans.

132. Wright, "The Woman's Commonwealth," p. 37.

· 5 ·

FEMALE CELIBACY AND THE POWER
OF SPIRITUAL PERCEPTION

"Loose the shutters, let God's sunlight enter"

The history of enthusiasm is largely a history of female emancipation.[1]

A final factor in the symbolic transformations effected by celibacy
concerns the role of spiritual receptivity in celibate female gender
identity. In varying ways, Shaker, Koreshan, and Sanctificationist
believers associated the celibate female with heightened powers of
spiritual perception, including skills in spiritual communication, receptivity to revelation, intuitive understanding, and prophetic dreams.
Spiritual receptivity is closely related to the spiritual roles already
discussed, but it extends the symbolic transformations of celibacy
in two ways that deserve special emphasis. First, the link between
the celibate female and receptivity to spiritual communications, as
well as to other forms of subconscious or intuitive perception, is
another example of the extension by these groups of rather traditional female symbolic associations into signs of power. Second, the
association of the celibate female with spiritual receptivity goes even
further than the other spiritual powers already discussed to shape
a uniquely female form of authority within the three groups. Therefore, the brief discussion in this chapter will add another facet to
the symbolic reversals and revisions effected by celibacy.

From one perspective, reliance in a religious group on divine
revelation, visions, and other types of spiritual communication hardly
bears mentioning. Receptivity to spiritual messages has often been
the mark of religious organizations and has often been the major
characteristic distinguishing such organizations from their secular

counterparts. American religious history reveals many groups that have engaged in spiritual communication, including some very traditional sects. Somewhat rarer in that history are sects that have attributed special powers of spiritual receptivity to women. Especially rare are groups that have accorded women leadership roles because of their spiritual powers.

In other parts of the world and in the most ecstatic of American religious groups, however, the association of women or other muted or marginal groups with spiritual possession and spirit communication is more common. Such associations democratize religious power by transforming all believers into potential authorities on the word of God. More pragmatically, they endow marginal groups with religious power as compensation for their lack of secular power.[2]

Although the three groups described in this book did not uniformly translate female powers of spiritual reception into secular authority, they did share with ecstatic sects the attribution of such powers to women. In all cases, female associations with spiritual receptivity in the groups enhanced the *symbolic* status of the celibate female, by linking woman with the high-cultural realm of spiritual life in the communities. To the extent that the groups depended on spiritual perception to guide the conduct of daily life, women in the groups also achieved leadership status.

In this, as in other aspects of the symbolic systems of the three groups, celibacy is the key to power. As has been discussed in the metaphors of spiritual motherhood, Shakers and Koreshans endowed not woman, but the celibate woman with redemptive power. In the context of celibacy, both groups agreed with Jeremiah's prediction that, eventually, "woman shall compass man." Although less biblical in their interpretation, the Sanctificationists also believed that celibacy was the key to female spiritual power by endowing their dreams and visions with divine associations.

Central to the attraction of spiritual communication and intuition in Shaker, Koreshan, and Sanctificationist female symbolism is its suggestion that a female trait can supersede maleness. Spiritual receptivity and skills in spiritual communication are characteristics women could easily claim in the nineteenth century. In the context of religious communities, women could also use that claim in order to counter male rule based on allegedly superior rationality. Celibacy may have been the price a woman must pay for the liberation of her mind, as well as of her body, from the oppressive influence of male rule.

Evidence for this aspect of celibate communal theory in the three groups is less plentiful than for other components of their cultural systems. The records of the groups are only rarely explicit on the topic of female spiritual perception. Yet the connection of the celibate female with spiritual perceptual powers is implicit in the texts. Because that connection represents additional evidence of celibacy's symbolic benefit for female believers, the subject merits attention. Exploration of the celibate female's symbolic connection with spiritual communication will, however, be more speculative than in other parts of this book. In order to understand the topic fully in Shaker history, it is also necessary to deviate in this chapter from an emphasis on late-nineteenth-century texts in the discussion of that group.

THE SHAKERS

> Emotion presents to us the beauty of holiness, the peace of righteousness, love to each other, sympathy and tenderness toward the suffering, the glory and perfect splendor of purity, and often opens up a vista of sublimity and glory far-reaching even into the serenest recesses of heaven itself.[3]

Oliver Hampton's ode to emotion in this quotation of 1880 may appear to contradict the Shaker respect for reason discussed in chapter 3. In order to unravel this contradiction and, therefore, to understand the role of spiritual receptivity and intuition in Shaker life, it is necessary to recall two elements of the arguments about reason revealed in the late-nineteenth-century texts. First, Shakers trusted divine reason rather than human reason, which they believed to be inevitably under the influence of traditional (that is, cursed) human culture. Second, they believed that divine reason emanates from the spiritual plane on which unity—including the unities of reason and emotion, heaven and earth, male and female—is a controlling principle. In seeking identification with the unities of the spiritual plane, some Shaker writers posited a connection between divine reason and human emotion which, in Hampton's words, "opens up a vista of sublimity and glory far-reaching even into the serenest recesses of heaven itself."

Thus, the highest form of human reason in the view of such

writers is that which reflects divine influence. "Our world is a world of effects," wrote Daniel Fraser in 1871. Beyond our world are the causes, the "spiritual intelligent forces."[4] Frederick Evans explained in 1879 that human rationality without the influence of that "fountain and source of spiritual knowledge" is only a pale imitation of the divine mind. Only communion with the "denizens of the inner spheres"—the spirits—supplies human thought with the divine influence it needs.[5]

Several writers suggested that a believer's ability to communicate with the spirit world is a mark of true intelligence. Human reason is, in fact, most highly developed when coupled with skill in spiritual communication. John Lyon of Enfield, New Hampshire, wrote in 1844 that "man was endowed with powers and rational faculties" in order to know and receive "the Will of God" and to perform "his agency according to it." Lyon also explained that the intellectual senses (sight, taste, smell, speech, cogitation) and powers (principle, comparison, judgment, determination, memory, choice, affection) are instilled in human beings to permit the soul to receive messages from the "angels or spirits . . . continually . . . before the Throne of God, and in His presence." The more sharply one receives those messages, the more developed one's intelligence must be.[6]

The major manifestations of spiritual perceptual powers evident in the texts of all periods in the nineteenth century are divine revelations, reflecting Ann Lee's revelations, including visions of God, Mother Ann, or Jesus, and visitations by deceased Shakers, including Mother Ann. During the 1830s and 1840s in particular, living believers heard communications from the spirit world—the Holy Father, the Holy Mother, or other deceased Shaker leaders. Such "instruments" believed themselves empowered to record the messages, which they signed and dated. Scores of these documents have survived.[7]

Also during those decades, known as Mother's Work, a good indication of a believer's receptivity to the spirits was her or his display of a spiritual gift, such as the ability to heal, prophesy, speak in tongues, and perform remarkable feats. Such acts were seen as signs of the recipients' "faith, wisdom, knowledge . . . [and] special dispensations from God, [as well as] signs of divine anointment."[8] Some gift recipients could whirl or run at inhuman speeds. Others were driven to sweep away sin with actual brooms, displaying incredible energy and strength. Ecstatic dancing, song writing, and even drawing abilities were also attributed to spirit possession.[9]

Spirituality, Balance, and Unity

The practical purpose of both the spirit messages and the spirit gifts may well have been the reinforcement of certain group values that were periodically unrealized in Shaker communities. Those who represented the spirits' voices and views to other believers tended to advise and admonish backsliders and to encourage a more spiritual direction for community activities.[10] In symbolic terms, however, these messages and gifts can also be seen as reinforcements of other major symbols in the Shaker system, such as the unity of gender symbolism.

In 1880, Oliver Hampton credited the recipients of spiritual messages with achieving an almost divinely "well-balanced mind" in which intellect and emotion, reason and love are brought into equilibrium. Such a mind also reflects the divine balance of maleness and femaleness within the godhead: "In looking around us and into the general structure of the universe, the most palpable and obvious departments we can discover therein are the dual ones of male and female. The origin of these may be traced to the no less palpable principles of wisdom and love, a duality observable in all the dispensations of Divine Providence, and for aught we know to the contrary, a duality constituting the Infinite mind itself."[11] Therefore, the spiritually receptive believer who approximates God's wisdom may also, by association, approximate the balance and equality of God's male and female essences.

Perhaps because the controlling metaphors of the Shaker spiritual plane are unity and balance, in contrast with the metaphors of separation and differentiation necessary on the earthly plane, the divine symbolism discussed by many writers is not consistently associated with God's gender characteristics. That is, in divinity, neither reason nor love, wisdom nor strength is consistently a male or female trait. For example, writers sometimes associated wisdom with Holy Mother,[12] and sometimes with Father.[13] Likewise, they sometimes defined love as a female trait in Deity and sometimes as a male trait.[14] This inconsistency may also suggest that godliness includes not only the balancing of dualities, but also the crossing of boundaries required to keep order on the earthly plane.

Although the earthly plane was generally characterized by separation and distinction, the quality of mind sought by human believers of both sexes balanced dualities. Late in the century, Hampton suggested that the disciplines of reason be tempered by the values of love in human beings: reason builds the "character . . . discipline, self-government, church government, organization, order and regulations, necessary to the existence of self-perpetuating community," he wrote, whereas love supports "the development of the religious sentiment . . . gifts, inspirations, ministrations from the spirit world, prophecies, tongues, healings of disease" and altruism. "Unless these principles of wisdom and love are equally and normally developed in the individual," he warned, "his or her efforts to attain to spiritual perfection must necessarily be abortive . . . . An individual all *intellect* is a monster who needs regenerating to ever become normal. One who is all *emotion* is in the same degree abnormal, and needs reconstructing quite as well. The golden mean between these extremes is a well-balanced mind, under the influence of a thoughtful, serene and unostentatious wisdom . . . imbued with love."[15]

The ideal mind, therefore, shares the potential for unity—or at least perfect balance—possible on the spiritual plane. In short, the mind has the potential to reach spiritual goals. Perhaps this possibility helps to explain the crossing of gender barriers in Shaker worship, particularly during the more frenzied period of Mother's Work. In worship, men and women did not lose gender identity, but they did engage in identical activities, in contrast to their ordinarily complementary activities. Under the influence of spirits, both men and women danced and enacted the sweeping, shaking, or whirling gifts. Through spiritual inspiration, an activity of the mind, believers could glimpse the kind of unity, including gender unity, available on the spiritual plane.[16] Green and Wells suggested this interpretation when they wrote, "As union is the distinguishing characteristic of the true followers of Christ; so it is an essential part of the Worship of God . . . to render this [unity of spirit] the more perfect, a uniformity of exercise is necessary."[17]

If this muting of gender barriers is a feature of Shaker spiritual life, then it is possible that the men who participated in spiritually inspired activities acted not only as men, but also as gender-balanced beings, able to express in worship their own inner female qualities. That is, while stamping, dancing, speaking in tongues, and recording messages under the direction of the spirits, Shaker men may have been symbolically demonstrating their own femininity, as a gesture toward the female symbolic core of their religion. Women's participation in conscious, rational decision making in governance and business may also have been gestures toward the same kind of balance within themselves, as well as an expression of their equality with the men. Both cases may illustrate the blurring of gender barriers in the mind, in emulation of divinity's own gender balance and unity.

Spirituality and the Female

At the same time that the emphasis on spiritual perception may have reinforced the balance and unity of dualities, including the duality of sex, however, the texts tend to associate femaleness more than maleness with spiritual insight. Although both men and women performed the spiritual gifts of Mother's Work, the imagery of such gifts is heavily female in nature. Many gifts emphasize the symbolic connection between spiritual cleansing and the cleaning chores performed by women to provide a tidy and orderly community. Washing and sweeping imagery also dominates the hymns of this period and before.[18] Later periodicals contain many more female than male musings upon spiritual matters and many more poetic expressions of female than of male faith.

Calvin Green, in his biographic memoir, described a distinction that he perceived between the roles of males and females in spiritual work. Referring to the receipt of spirit messages, he explained that female instruments were probably chosen by the spirits because of their suitability "to bring forth an original inspired message," whereas men were called upon to improve the "language and arrangement" of the original message.[19] This difference may reflect general sex roles or different educational levels of males and females, but it also suggests a form of female advantage in Shaker culture because of the role of spiritual communication in the life of the community. The bringing forth of an original inspired message suggests a closer connection to divinity than does the editing role attributed to males.

Witnesses of Shaker worship in the early decades of the nineteenth century, even before the period of Mother's Work, reported a greater involvement by women in Shaker ritual. In his 1822 *Travels: In New England and New York*, Timothy Dwight, then president of Yale University, observed that the sisters came first to the spiritual " 'operations' " and that they danced, whirled, shook, swept, and exercised other gifts with greater zeal than the brethren. The men appeared "very moderate" in their gyrations, while "the gesticulations of the women were violent."[20] The Shaker scholar Edward Andrews has agreed with Dwight's observations, explaining that the women were routinely more involved, their countenances "rapt and pallid, their eyes wild, their bodies thin, their movements nervous, whereas the brethren looked ruddy, cheerful, and healthy."[21]

Furthermore, it appears that women primarily executed the lovely gift drawings produced during the 1840s and 1850s.[22] These drawings can be interpreted as symbolic presentations of various spiritual unities possible in the heavenly plane, including the reconciliation of a variety of troubling earthly contradictions. The drawings' visions of the heavenly sphere are accompanied by words of comfort and guidance from Holy Mother Wisdom and the Heavenly Father. In many instances, divine voices acknowledge, but promise delivery from, a world of conflict and strife. Heaven provides antidotes to earthly disappointment—through hope—and to human pain—through spiritual joy.[23] Even separation of male and female, so necessary on earth, is overcome in the world beyond. The fact that women were the primary conduits of these messages of unity and balance suggests special female skill in communicating with the divine realm. In addition, the symbolic association of the celibate Shaker female with Mother Ann, also evident in the Shaker metaphor of spiritual motherhood, suggests special female powers of communication with the spiritual plane.

Even in later decades, after the Shakers became more subdued in their worship, texts reveal a special relationship between the celibate female and the spiritual plane. Writers like Hampton and Evans described such a connection. Published poems expressed female spiritual pleasure, possibly as an indication of transformed sexual desire. Memoirs, such as the *Autobiography of Rhoda Blake, 1864-1892*, record one woman's concerted effort to develop spiritual powers. Blake wrote, "I plainly saw that I must gain the gift of prayer in order to become spiritual, or be redeemed from a depraved nature of sin. I made a firm resolve that I would gain this gift and I did." Blake also recounts a vision she had in 1837 as an instrument of a spiritual message. The female imagery of her vision, in conjunction with other evidence, suggests a special relationship between the female believer and the spirits: "Listen to the word of a mighty Angel . . . 'I will ride upon the East wind in a Chariot of fire and carry in my arms the Daughters first born.' "[24]

Letters from later periods reveal that women continued to receive visits and inspiration from departed sisters and brethren. In her correspondence with non-Shaker Laura Holloway Langford, Eldress Anna White wrote about such visits as if they were commonplace in her experience. In a letter of 1904, White wrote of seeing Annie Byrdsall, who had been dead for several weeks, walking "upon the lawn opposite, her favorate [sic] resort," and of feeling a pleasant "shock as of electricity" passing through her with the sight.[25] Eldress Bertha Lindsay, still living at Canterbury, reported in a 1983 interview that she and many of the sisters she has known have been visited by the spirits of departed friends.[26]

In combination with the redemptive power attributed to celibate woman in the late-nineteenth-century texts, skill in spiritual receptivity and in the expression of divine will contributes to the symbolic status of the Shaker female by contributing to her association with the spiritual/cultural realm and, thus, to her transcendence of the natural/domestic domain. At certain periods of Shaker history, spirit messages also influenced community activities.[27] The celibate female's role in spiritual perception demonstrates that the Shaker symbol of celibacy not only unlocks the reproductive chains on woman's body, but it also unlocks the chains on the creative, intuitive parts of her mind. The association of the celibate female with powers of spiritual perception also suggests a new interpretation of Shaker insistence on the separation of the sexes and the relegation of women to domestic duties. Although such practices contribute to gender hierarchy in mainstream culture, they may have created the appropriate women's culture in which female spiritual powers could germinate and flourish. Without a female world, the Shaker woman might not have achieved her transcendent religious identity and, therefore, her highest form of cultural status.

THE KORESHANS

I am the Goddess, and the environment of that which thou has become—the inherent psyche and pneuma of my own organic form.[28]

The major forms of spiritual communication apparent in Koreshan texts are divine inspiration and visions. Those forms were experienced primarily, if not exclusively, by Koresh himself. Yet even though the group's major recipient of direct spiritual inspiration was male, Koreshan views of spiritual perception acknowledge an overarching female spiritual essence that empowers the female celibate believer as recipient of that essence from Mother God. Although Koreshan spiritual motherhood ultimately fails to enhance the cultural status of the Koreshan female because it lacks support in other facets of Koreshan life, this female spiritual aura does enhance female symbolic status in Koreshanity.

Mother's Spiritous Essence, the Psyche

In order to comprehend the divine female aura, it is necessary to return to Koresh's 1869 vision of the Divine Mother. That experience convinced Koresh of God's bisexuality—symbolized by the balance of pneuma and psyche, the male and female spiritual reproductive essences in the godhead—and of the equality of gender symbolism within God. Koresh used this divine gender balance as a model for the elimination of barriers between other dualities, such as science and religion, mind and body, and reason and spirit. At the same time, the appearance of God in female form also convinced Koresh that a specifically female divine force was initially necessary for the redemption of a corrupt, sinful, male-dominated, irreligious world. In God, then, femaleness was seen as having a specific use.

The process of spiritual reproduction in Koreshanity reflects the importance of God's female persona. In fact, theocrasis, which allegedly makes physical reproduction possible through spiritual means, is predicated upon the ability to engage in spiritual communication with that female persona. The power of theocratic transformation emanates from Mother God, and Koresh identified the celibate female as the recipient and conduit of that power. Her receptivity enables the female celibate to provide "fitting channels of the descent of the Divine Spirit into humanity."[29] In the creation of those channels, the celibate female is assisted by the powers of the psyche, defined as "soul" and analogous to the spiritual form of the ovum. The male reproductive force, or pneuma, only fertilizes the channels created by the psyche. In order for theocrasis to occur, then, it must be infused with divine femininity or maternity, otherwise the germinal essences will vanish.

Separately, neither the female psyche nor the male pneuma was seen by Koresh as superior to the other. In 1896, he explained that "the female organism collects and conserves the soul or psyche, while it wastes the pneuma." At the same time, "the male organism . . . conserves the pneumic energy, or the spirit, while it wastes the psyche." But once psyche and pneuma are joined within the spiritually reproductive female, the female psyche plays a superior role. It "is enabled to again conserve" the pneuma, and to build "the new structure by the functional ability (inherent only in woman) to reunite the two forces—the soul and the spirit in the new formation she is thus enabled to create."[30] The suggestion that female spiritual "matter" is superior to male spiritual "matter" in its creative power strengthens the metaphor of spiritual motherhood in Koreshanity and mitigates the continued association of female powers with reproduction. Symbolically, if not actually, the spiritual superiority of femaleness links the celibate woman with an advanced spiritual/cultural (rather than natural) status in the Koreshan system. It is through femaleness that human beings can achieve connection with God.

Divine Wisdom

Koresh's characterization of divine wisdom as female further reinforces the superiority of female spiritual symbolism in Koreshanity. In several texts, Koresh undermined the male power of rationality by explaining that the (male) pneuma's association with Logos—the Word or reason—is both inferior and subordinate to the (female) psyche's "immortal physiology," or spiritual reproductive ability. Because female immortal physiology defies all known rules of anatomy and reproduction, it must involve both spiritual and scientific truths, according to Koresh. Spiritual truth can be known through advanced powers of spiritual perception, through minds attuned to the spiritual root of all knowledge, and of the material world.[31] As creators of spirit from matter in theocrasis, Koresh believed that females possess such minds.

Although Koresh frequently usurped feminine spiritual qualities for himself—identifying femaleness as a useful metaphor for his own ability to transcend and merge science, government, economics, and reproduction and to transform them into a spiritual kingdom of his making—he frequently glorified femaleness in symbolic terms. His homage tilts the spiritual if not the earthly balance of Koreshan biunity toward the female, because theocrasis requires that femaleness encompass maleness rather than the other way around. Koresh even suggested that the ultimate manifestation of his own spirit was its female form. "My Motherhood, in thee I dwell," he proclaimed to Mother God; "in thee I find my rest forever." She is, finally, the "compassing form of [his] spiritual entity."[32]

Attributions of spiritual and perceptual powers to the celibate female mitigate the weaknesses of the Koreshan metaphor of spiritual motherhood by transforming the female reproductive powers from the natural to the cultural realm. Koreshanity fails the human female because it provides no earthly, female models of this divine maternity for women to emulate. The lack of support in other domains, such as work, also minimizes the benefits of female spiritual-reproductive powers. Together, these failings exploit female powers so that they contribute to the glorification of a human male—Koresh—and to an androgyne with a male identity. On the spiritual level, however, the roles attributed to the celibate female—domination of spiritual reproduction, redemption of the cursed human species, and conduit for the divine psyche—are potentially powerful symbols.

THE SANCTIFICATIONISTS

We believe in dreams, and that they are generally given to us to make us have more confidence in God, and to let us know that he knows what we are doing and some times we act upon them literally.[33]

McWhirter replied, "The Divine wish will manifest itself at the proper time."[34]

The Sanctificationist approach to female spiritual receptivity is some-what different than the approaches of the Shakers and Koreshans. Except for the initial conversion experiences of the group's founders, there are no records of ecstatic practices; in fact, all religious ritual ultimately disappeared from the community. Rather, in keeping with their progressively secular and individualistic system, the Sanctifi-cationists increasingly equated spiritual communication with indi-vidual, internalized communicative powers. As sanctified believers, each woman of the Commonwealth was presumed capable of re-ceiving God's messages. Discussions of the uses of dreams in group governance suggest that each believer was also presumed capable of integrating those messages into her own psyche in the form of dream imagery. Dreams thus appeared to believers as divinely inspired, and they were used to guide actions in everyday life. In effect, then, the women's trust in dreams and other forms of spiritual inspiration, within the context of their all-female community, can be seen as symbolic of the group's equation of female unconscious mental processes with the word or will of God.

Individuality and the Collective

Individualistic in nature, dreams allowed each Commonwealth mem-ber to assert both her influence upon the other members and her own role as a source of divine inspiration. The Shakers apparently understood the individualistic quality of dream inspiration, as well as the threat of such personal visions to communal consensus and control. Therefore, they preferred visible spirit messages and gifts to dreams as signs of divine inspiration.[35] Dream interpretation did not fragment consensus in the Commonwealth, however, because of McWhirter's insistence on dream interpretation as a group activity. She explained that group members decided together "which dreams were wise, which contained leadings for them to follow."[36] Therefore, what began as an expression of individual spiritual communication was transformed into a skill of communal life that fostered both group cohesion and collective independence from outside society.

In an interview of the 1880s, McWhirter described one example of group action that was based on the collective interpretation of an individual's dream. She explained that the group was inspired to petition the governor of Texas because of a dream. Sister Nelson had dreamed of traveling to Ireland as a way to assist another sister who had been confined to the asylum in Austin for refusing her husband's insurance money. The Sanctificationists knew that the inmate was not crazy; she was merely demonstrating the group's dedication to autonomy and economic independence. On the basis of Nelson's dream, which the women finally interpreted as a directive to appeal to Governor Ireland of Texas, McWhirter was successful in obtaining the inmate's release.[37]

A Sisterhood of the Mind

The sisters' reliance upon dreams for guidance offers another example of the group's specifically female identity, even as they pursued traditionally masculine economic goals. As a component of that female identity, the belief in the collective importance of dreams also facilitated Commonwealth sisterhood on a deep, unconscious level. By predicating much of their decision making upon their intuitions and dreams, the women embraced their female identities and transformed them into a "first cause." That is, in their experience, spiritual, intuitive, unconscious inspiration preceded rational decision making. Therefore, female-identified attributes and skills preceded male-identified attributes and skills.

A contemporary observer, A. L. Bennett, suggested the power of this web of symbolism when he explained Sanctificationist success, despite rather strong opposition in Belton, as a sign that "you could not fight a Woman, and you could not fight Religion."[38] Women and religion appeared to him, and presumably to others, to share qualities more powerful than argument: neither woman nor religion could be challenged on rational terms alone. His comment also implies that forces exempt from rational control frequently prevail by other than rational means.

In the Commonwealth system, the power of woman's spiritual receptivity is supported by her cultural status in the secular domains of the community. Female spiritual authority underlies female control in economic and social life. It also contributes to a kind of sisterhood of the unconscious by supplementing the women's rationally based bonds with an intuitive, spiritual, but firmly female, connection. These qualities combine to make the Commonwealth system a strong model of the symbolic potential of celibacy for female cultural status.

FEMALE SPIRITUAL POWER AND SPIRITUAL INSPIRATION

The paths to female spiritual empowerment evident in the Shaker, Koreshan, and Sanctificationist texts under consideration in this book rely in varying ways upon traditional female qualities—such as sensitivity, purity, piety, intuition, and even irrationality. The transformation of those qualities into signs of special female powers of receptivity to divine messages links the symbolism of the celibate female and God or the spirit world. This link can, in turn, enhance female power in the symbolic (if not actual) structure of secular communal life. The Sanctificationist and Shaker systems of the late nineteenth century are the best examples of that interaction. In those two systems, female spiritual powers—both in communication and in spiritual redemption and rebirth—are supported by a transposition of female symbolism from the natural to the cultural realm. The Koreshan system is less successful in this process because the spiritual mother necessarily shares her role in theocrasis with a male. Further, the Koreshan celibate female remains more closely associated with reproductive work that lacks explicit analogues in productive labor.

Even without support in other cultural sectors, however, celibate female powers of spiritual perception enhance female cultural status because of the Christian symbolic system itself. In that system, particularly as it was interpreted by these three groups, spiritual power is inherently cultural power.

NOTES

1. Ronald Knox, quoted in I. M. Lewis, *Ecstatic Religions: An Anthropological Study of Spirit Possession and Shamanism* (Middlesex, England: Penguin Books, 1971), p. 31.

2. Lewis, *Ecstatic Religions*, p. 31. Lewis has argued that ecstatic religious practices can serve to empower disempowered groups. He has identified both peripheral and central ecstatic groups in which believers have been possessed by spirits that first afflict them in illness and then produce a cure. Consistent with the experience of the communards under consideration here, spiritual possession in many religions has frequently been a female experience. Spiritually possessed persons have often convinced those in power that large sums of money or expensive

gifts must be given to the possessed person in order to assuage the spirits. In oblique recognition of the injustices under which the disempowered live, those in power have often complied with the wishes of the spirits.

3. O[liver] C. Hampton, "Relation of Intellect and Emotion," *The Shaker Manifesto* 10 (October 1880): 218.

4. Daniel Fraser, "Materialism," *The Shaker* 1 (November 1871): 85.

5. Frederick W. Evans, "Shakerism," *The Shaker Manifesto* 9 (May 1879): 106.

6. John Lyon, "Considerations of Religious Doctrine," Enfield, N. H., 1844, in Robeley E. Whitson, *Shaker Theological Sources* (Bethlehem, Conn.: United Institute, 1969), pp. 29-30.

7. Two examples are the Edward D. Andrews Shaker Collection, Winterthur Library, Winterthur, Del., and the Shaker Collection in the Library of Congress Manuscript Collection, Washington, D.C. Several writers, particularly Frederick Evans, were careful to distinguish Shaker spirituality from the popular forms of spiritualism of the day. Evans defined the Shaker view as a belief in "spiritual manifestations, the immortality of the human soul, the intercommunication between the visible and invisible worlds," as opposed to the cheap visions and prophesies of "nominal Christians." Frederick W. Evans, "Religion and Spiritualism: A State without a Church," *The Shaker* 1 (March 1871): 20.

8. Edward D. Andrews, *The People Called Shakers* (New York: Dover Publications, 1963), p. 142.

9. For a detailed description of Shaker spiritual gifts, see Andrews, *People Called Shakers*, pp. 141-43 and Marjorie Procter-Smith, *Women in Shaker Community and Worship: A Feminist Analysis of the Uses of Religious Symbolism*, vol. 16, Studies in Women and Religion (Lewiston, N.Y.: Edwin Mellen Press, 1985), pp. 174-219.

10. Andrews, *People Called Shakers*, p. 155.

11. Hampton, "Relation of Intellect and Emotion," p. 218.

12. Chauncey Edward Sears, *Shakers: Duality of the Deity; Or, God as Father and Mother...* (Rochester, N.Y.: Daily Democrat Steam Printing House, 1867), p. 7; William Leonard, *A Disclosure on the Order and Propriety of Divine Inspiration and Revelation, Showing the Necessity Thereof, in All Ages, to Know the Will of God. Also, a Discourse on the Second Appearing of Christ, in and through the Order of the Female. And a Discourse on the Propriety and Necessity of a United Inheritance in All Things, in Order to Support a True Christian Community....* (Harvard, Mass.: United Society, 1853), p. 64.

13. Evans, "Shakerism," p. 106.

14. Ibid.; J. M. Washburn, "The Male and Female Principles in Deity," *The Manifesto* 19 (October 1889): 227.

15. Hampton, "Relation of Intellect and Emotion," pp. 217-18.

16. The historian Lawrence Foster has suggested that the formation periods of utopian groups, into which category Mother's Work might be said to fall, are liminal in character. It is this liminality that explains such phenomena as the early, frenzied worship practices of the Shakers, according to Foster. Lawrence Foster, *Religion and Sexuality: Three American Communal Experiments of the Nineteenth Century* (New York: Oxford University Press, 1981), pp. 8-9. While it is true that Shaker spiritual labors diminished over time, thus lending credence to the theory of transitional liminality, it can also be argued that the characteristics of spiritual communication and nonrational modes of thought continued in other guises throughout the Shaker experience and were, therefore, not simply liminal qualities.

17. Calvin Green and Seth Y. Wells, *A Brief Exposition of the Established Principles and Regulations of the United Society of Believers Called Shakers,* quoted in Andrews, *People Called Shakers,* p. 141.

18. Procter-Smith, *Women in Shaker Community and Worship,* pp. 199-200.

19. Calvin Green, *Biographic Memoir of Calvin Green,* ms. copy in two volumes (Sabbathday Lake Library Manuscript, n.d.), in Whitson, *Shaker Theological Sources,* p. 27.

20. Timothy Dwight, quoted in Andrews, *People Called Shakers,* p. 144.

21. Andrews, *People Called Shakers,* p. 144.

22. Edward D. Andrews and Faith Andrews, *Visions of the Heavenly Sphere: A Study in Shaker Religious Art* (Charlottesville: University Press of Virginia, 1969), pp. 62, 109-10. Only two drawings of the almost two hundred that survive were done by a man, and they are really quite different in purpose and design than those of the women.

23. The term comes from the title of Andrews and Andrews, *Visions of the Heavenly Sphere: A Study in Shaker Religious Art.* I discuss this interpretation of the gift drawings in an article, "As a Sign That All May Understand: Shaker Gift Drawings and Female Spiritual Power," *Winterthur Portfolio* (Spring 1989): 68-104.

24. Rhoda Blake, *The Autobiography of Rhoda Blake, 1864-1892* (New Lebanon), pp. 44, 71. Shaker Collection, Library of Congress Manuscript Collection, Washington, D.C. Men may also have worked to perfect their spiritual powers, but the expressions of that effort contain little association with male gender identity, as in Blake's image of the "Daughter."

25. Eldress Anna White to Laura Holloway Langford, Mt. Lebanon, N.Y., November 14, 1904, Andrews Shaker Collection, Winterthur Library, Winterthur, Del.

26. Eldress Bertha Lindsay, interview, Canterbury, N.H., July 30, 1983. Admittedly, the scarcity of male members after the 1920s distorts recent evidence about this or any other gender-specific behavior (although not gender-specific theory) of the Shakers.

27. The spirits realized the potential impact of their messages on living believers, and they instructed instruments to guard against the misuse of their roles. See Andrews, *People Called Shakers*, pp. 174-75. These warnings provide an indication of the power of such messages and revelations and suggest the importance of women's participation in them.

28. Koresh [Cyrus R. Teed], *The Illumination of Koresh. Marvelous Experience of the Great Alchemist Thirty Years Ago, at Utica, N.Y.* (n.p., [1900]), p. 12.

29. Alice Fox Miller, "Woman's Part in Evolution," from *The Athena, The Flaming Sword* 3 (April 23, 1892): 9.

30. Koresh [Cyrus R. Teed], *Reincarnation; Or, the Resurrection of the Dead*, 2d ed. (Chicago: Guiding Star Publishing House, 1892), pp. 9-11.

31. Koresh, *Reincarnation*, pp. 31-5, 25.

32. Koresh, *Illumination of Koresh*, pp. 13-14.

33. Martha McWhirter, "McWhirter's Answers to Interrogatories in B. W. Haymond v. Ada Haymond, #3037, in the District Court of Bell County, Texas, 17 October 1887," interrogatory no. 21.

34. Ibid.

35. Diane Sasson, writing about Shaker autobiographical narratives, has reported that individuals did occasionally receive inspiration for conversion to Shakerism in dreams. Diane Sasson, *The Shaker Spiritual Narrative* (Knoxville: University of Tennessee Press, 1983), p. 16. There is little evidence that guidance from dreams continued beyond conversion, however. Further, Shaker elders monitored the "appropriateness" of individual visions and gifts and countermanded those they felt were inappropriate to community purposes.

36. Eleanor James, "The Sanctificationists of Belton," *The American West* 2 (Summer 1965): 72.

37. McWhirter, Haymond v. Haymond, interrogatory no. 21.

38. A. L. Bennett, "The Sanctified Sisters," *The Sunny Slopes of Long Ago*, Publications of the Texas Folklore Society, no. 33 (1966): 139.

· 6 ·

CONCLUSION

> Through dual, hierarchical oppositions. Superior/Inferior.
> Myths, legends, book, Philosophical system. Everywhere (where)
> ordering intervenes, where a law organizes what is thinkable
> by oppositions (dual, irreconcilable; or sublatable, dialectical).
> And all these pairs of oppositions are *couples*. Does that mean
> something? Is the fact that Logocentrism subjects thought—
> all concepts, codes and values—to a binary system, related to
> "the" couple, man/woman?[1]

Although the speculations of modern French feminists, such as those of Hélène Cixous and Catherine Clément above, are separated by almost a century from the period under consideration, their concerns might have made perfect sense to nineteenth-century believers of the Shaker, Koreshan, and Sanctificationist communities. The choice made by believers in those groups of the symbolic system of celibacy implies above all a refusal to accept the primal heterosexual couple, conceived in terms of irreconcilable opposition and intransigent hierarchy, as the controlling metaphor of their thinking, or of their lives. They saw celibacy as a pivotal symbol of spiritual union and equality, both between the sexes and between other falsely stratified dualities in sexual culture. Their choice violates the usual understanding of sexual intercourse as a sign of union between male and female because, in varying ways, believers in the three groups perceived divisiveness and hierarchy within that traditional sign of union. They envisioned a more genuine form of unity and equality within its symbolic converse.

At the conclusion of this discussion of celibacy's symbolic effects upon female cultural status, it is necessary to recall the larger metaphorical implications of both heterosexual intercourse and celibacy. In addition to summarizing the meaning of celibacy for late-nineteenth-century believers in the three groups, this chapter will review

186

the dramatic implications of the key symbol of celibacy for the conceptualization of personal, economic, and spiritual relationships. Differences between celibate symbolism and the symbolism of heterosexual American culture will be analyzed in this chapter, and the relevance of celibate symbolism will be considered for such modern feminist issues as female reproductive freedom, the role of that freedom in women's economic and familial lives, the relationship between sex and power in today's society, and the new interest in chastity as a feminist statement.

The Symbolic Challenge of Celibacy: Then

> Among the marks of [the Commonwealth's] growth are households divided and families broken up. It has excited the deepest of human passions to culmination in violence.[2]

> August 27th, 1810. "The great mob of 1810" come, search the houses and ask all if they are content to live here, promising that protection should be given to all those who wished to leave. But there were none who said they were discontented [among the Shakers] and the mob dispersed.[3]

> Celibacy is the corner stone of the kingdom of righteousness. Equality of the sexes is based on the law of justice, and in the College of Life and Communal Home, woman has an equal share in all places of honor and trust.[4]

A symbolic view of the cultural systems of the Shakers, Koreshans, and Sanctificationists, based on late-nineteenth-century documents, reveals that they understood celibacy as more than the equivalent of sexual abstinence. Rather, in their systems celibacy signifies cultural changes that reach far beyond the interpersonal, sexual behaviors of those who embrace it. To the extent that sex and reproduction are basic symbols of the familial, religious, and economic systems of American culture, then celibacy, as the logical symbolic reversal of heterosexual intercourse, can serve as an alternative symbolic foundation for alternative cultural institutions in all domains. The third quotation above exemplifies that reversal by suggesting the Koreshan understanding of celibacy as the "corner stone" of cultural reform, including the expansion of women's rights.

The choice of celibacy, and the new cultural structures it inspired in the societies under discussion, sometimes created hostility and inspired violent reactions from outsiders. As suggested by the first two quotations, the Shakers and Sanctificationists were especially vulnerable to such hostility, which frequently focused on the groups' violation of various cultural norms. The most distressing of such violations was the commitment to celibacy. Hostile and violent reactions to the elimination of sexuality suggest its importance to mainstream notions of cultural organization.

Celibate Unity and Equality

Although the significance of celibacy goes beyond the transformation of the male-female relationship, such a transformation is a primary result of celibacy, particularly as it contributes to the redefinition of gender identities. The allegedly unifying symbol of heterosexual intercourse in American culture is legitimated by the symbolic opposition of the two sexes and of their respective symbolic associations. Thus, heterosexual intercourse creates opposed gender identities on the path to physical union. In fact, heterosexual attraction is allegedly predicated upon such opposition. Symbolically opposed gender differences also produce gender hierarchy because the two sexes are associated with the stratified domains of home and work. Those domains, in turn, represent the stratified realms of nature and culture.

Celibacy, on the other hand, by eliminating sexual and reproductive relationships, eliminates an important premise for the opposition of the sexes. Therefore, although celibacy physically separates men and women, it can actually promote the symbolic unity of the sexes. Texts of the three groups identify a spiritual bond as the source of celibate union. That bond transcends requirements of physical separation mandated by celibacy—whether between the sexes, as in Shaker communities, or among same-sex believers, as in the Commonwealth—and renders co-believers more alike than different on a symbolic level. Within each system, other symbolic realms traditionally opposed and stratified, such as home and work, nature and culture, are also unified. With symbolic unity as a goal, distinctions that promote separation do not necessarily produce stratification.

Although the three groups share a belief in the symbolically and spiritually unifying characteristics of celibacy, they approach the concept of unity in celibacy from different perspectives. Shaker texts emphasize unity and equality in the context of gender difference and even of complementary gender roles. Echoing many of their mainstream counterparts, writers insisted that complementary gender roles and characteristics are compatible with the concept of equality. Unlike their mainstream counterparts, however, Shakers had a symbolic premise to reinforce that claim. They explained that, as co-believers in the millennial church on earth and as aspirants to the unified spiritual plane above, celibate Shaker males and females are equal in God's eyes, united as brother and sister. The models for this unity in difference are the gender identities within God and Christ, in which male and female are distinct yet equal, balanced and spiritually united.

Symbolic gender associations in Shaker belief, as well as the physiological characteristics of the sexes, represent variations among threads in a single fabric rather than the distinctions of separate bolts of cloth. Differences in gender symbolism, or even in roles, do not require irreconcilable opposition among God's true children. Shaker social ideals also reinforce the commitment to equality in difference. Equal representation of the sexes in the Shaker governance structure and the gender-balanced system of work in Shaker communities are secular examples of the spiritual model of sexual unity and equality.

In the cultural systems of the Koreshans and Sanctificationists, concepts of sexual difference are minimized, and celibacy facilitates unity and equality by promoting the similarity or interdependence of gender symbolism. Koreshans advocated the separation of the sexes primarily to facilitate celibacy and to separate believers from outsiders (a central principle of communal unity). Koresh emphasized sexual difference primarily in the context of spiritual reproduction and redemption, wherein the female role achieves temporary superiority over the male role. That superiority has mixed results for the symbolic status of the celibate female. In other contexts in the Koreshan system, sex-specific characteristics are slated to disappear in the biune being. In fact, celibate unity is taken quite literally in Koreshanity. Eventually, celibacy will produce an hermaphroditic human being. In various ways, however, the concept of the biune being acquires masculine connotations, and femaleness is ultimately subsumed by the maleness of the Koreshan ideal.

Likewise, the Sanctificationists promoted the separation of celibate

believers from noncelibate outsiders, and they established some physical and conceptual barriers against an intimate form of unity among
themselves. Those barriers may have been designed to prevent intimacy that might be construed as sexual in nature. Emphasis on
separation need not, however, promote opposition among believers
on a symbolic level. The Shaker case illustrates that difference and
separation do not necessarily create opposed conceptual categories.
At the same time, feminist theorists have consistently argued that
goals of unity and equality need not promote identity among persons
or between the sexes, as they tend to do in Koreshanity. The Sanctificationist ideal of gender unity represents a position of celibate
unity somewhere between those of the other groups. Sanctificationist
gender unity exists in the context both of individual difference—
among the female believers—and of a limited understanding of
sexual difference.

Sanctificationist celibacy promotes symbolic and spiritual unity
among believers, but it does not prevent physical or even emotional
distance among them. At the same time, Sanctificationist celibacy
erases most symbolic differences between male and female, but it
censors male qualities, such as lust and dominance, that contradict
community ideals. The sisters freely embraced symbolism of both
sexes in the creation of their androgynous model. Because of their
insistence on celibacy, however, and because of male weaknesses in
that regard, that model acquires primarily female associations. In
short, the Sanctificationist commitment to celibacy symbolizes a
particular strength of the female sex that empowers women to embrace positive male symbolism, such as exchange-value labor and
spiritual authority, and to reject negative male qualities. The commitment to celibacy as a female strength also protects the model
being from assuming a male identity.

Female Symbolic Status

To the extent that symbolic gender differences were articulated by
believers in these groups, any hierarchy connected with those differences tends to reverse the mainstream system of gender prestige.
Based upon their perception of women's greater suffering in heterosexual culture, the Shakers and Koreshans more often bestowed
spiritual status upon the celibate female than upon the male. That

status consists of a stronger link with divine power, through spiritual communication, and a greater share of redemptive power, through women's historical dissociation from the twin sins of lust and dominance. Therefore, the celibate woman in these two systems can be seen as a symbolic reversal of Eve: the first in sin becomes the first in redemption. Even after denouncing sin, males in both systems were frequently characterized as intractably tainted by their history of lust and dominance. Writers in both groups frequently criticized traditional male symbolism, making the traditional male appear self-aggrandizing, aggressively competitive, pugnacious, and domineering. Shaker writers in particular identified female characteristics as necessary to the advancement of the entire society.

The celibate female's symbolic association with traditional female characteristics may appear perilously close to the mainstream's emphasis on some of those same characteristics. A woman's identification with female qualities in the mainstream tends to relegate her to culturally devalued domains and to rob her of personal, political, and economic power. That this devaluation does not occur in the communal systems can be attributed to the symbolism of celibacy. In the context of celibacy, traditional female characteristics are elevated in status from the natural to the cultural and spiritual/cultural domains. Because celibacy redefines the family, female associations with family or home do not limit woman or exclude her from cultural life. Likewise, in all three systems, female qualities make of woman a spiritual being for whom reproductive powers do not signify cultural exclusion. The symbolic transformation of female symbolism by celibacy suggests that female oppression is primarily a matter of social organization and culturally assigned meanings, rather than of intrinsic female characteristics or behaviors.

The Symbolism of the Celibate Family

Because the nuclear family system is one potent source of female oppression in mainstream culture, the impact of celibacy on that system is of particular interest. In contrast to the nuclear family, the celibate family promotes the symbolic unity and equality of its members. In stressing the voluntary association of family members, for example, celibate symbolism combines rational and performance-based standards for relationships, thus incorporating values from the work/public/male domain into the family/home/domestic/female domain. Examples of this merger of domains can be found in the criteria prescribed and described in various texts for the formation of genuine gospel relations among the Shakers and in membership criteria for the Commonwealth. In both cases, blood relationships of any description that were brought into the communities were transformed into sibling relationships, and the intimacy associated with blood relationships in mainstream culture was modified to suit the sibling model. In Shaker texts particularly, the love of family members is connected with the performance of good works. Shakers who did not continue to meet group criteria over time were ejected from the group. Those who did not wish to follow group norms were free to sever their Shaker ties.

Koreshan membership criteria are less formal, but there is no evidence of coercion or of involuntary association among group members. Presumably, the rule of celibacy was considered a criterion for both initial and continuing membership. Koreshans showed less concern with promoting thoroughly voluntary relationships than did the other groups, however, by ignoring the implications of their plans for spiritual reproduction. The newly created biune beings were, apparently, expected to remain in the group, just as "natural" progeny are expected to remain in their birth families. Yet voluntary Koreshan relationships obviously superseded existing blood ties, as in the other groups, and focused upon group rather than upon personal relations.

To varying degrees, then, all three groups associated family life with voluntarism, membership criteria, performance standards, and a sibling model of relationships. Therefore, group organization contrasts with the symbolism of the nuclear family, where the need for sex imposes a system of involuntary, passionate relationships conceptualized and practiced separately from the work or cultural domain.

When symbolism from the mainstream nuclear family does appear in the celibate family systems, it is generally redefined or modified. The Shakers and Sanctificationists, for example, borrowed the image of a sibling relationship from the nuclear family in their model for the celibate family. In their systems, however, the primary value of that model is its egalitarian nature—a close but nonsexual bond— rather than its identity as a blood (involuntary, emotional) relationship. The celibate systems contribute to social equity by extending the implications of mutual interest and affection in the sibling bond beyond the family to the society at large. Conversely, egalitarian social values prevent sibling rivalry — so frequently seen in the nuclear family in the context of a competitive society — within the celibate family. To be a brother or sister in these groups is to be an economic and spiritual partner with all others in the community. Competition serves no purpose. In addition, by promoting the brother-sister or sister-sister relationship over the husband-wife relationship, celibate families contribute to an increase in female status. Therefore, these three communities qualify as cultures that privilege kinship over marital ties. As discussed in chapter 1, such cultures tend to assign women greater prestige than do cultures, such as American and European societies, that privilege marital over kinship ties.[5] An example of this increase in female prestige can be found in the generalized redemptive powers assigned to celibate females in these groups. When female characteristics are identified as beneficial to men as well as to women, then genuine female cultural status has been achieved.

Doubt about the possibility of nonsexual intimacy among the brothers and sisters of the celibate family created some of the controversy that surrounded the celibate communities. Accustomed to sexual relationships among adult males and females who were not actually relatives, some contemporaries of the Shakers and Sanctificationists protested living arrangements that appeared to involve illicit sex. Ex-husbands stormed the Commonwealth in Belton, for example, and Shaker neighbors tried to "free" people presumably being held against their wills in apparent bondage, including sexual bondage. Several apostates also accused the Shakers of perverted behavior. During their long history, some members left the communities because they could not ignore the call of the flesh. Occasionally, drop-outs hastened to tie "the galling cords of wedlock" upon their departures.[6] For those who stayed, however, celibacy did not create perversion, despite the sometimes bitter allegations of secret sexual rituals. Evidence suggests that while sexual energies may have infused certain Shaker practices, most such accusations were, at best, overly imaginative interpretations of Shaker ritual and, at worst, completely fabricated.[7]

In their suspicions of sexual impropriety in the celibate family, skeptical contemporaries overlooked the strength of alternative symbolic foundations for celibate interpersonal relationships. Replacing the bonds of passion and blood are consciously shared and voluntary spiritual values. Even in the Koreshan case, in which body and spirit are merged so that Koreshan spiritual unity also entails a kind of intrapersonal unity, the goal is spiritual rather than physical union among persons. The ideal is voluntary, rational commitment to a common religious value system, rather than irrational, reproductive accident.

Celibate Unity of Home and Work

One key to the significance of the symbolic change in the celibate family—and in female gender identity—is its merging of symbolism from the home and work domains. The communal families described by believers in these three groups are not removed from the economic activities that sustain them, as they tend to be in mainstream American culture. In the communal work arrangements favored by the Shakers, Koreshans, and Sanctificationists, "relatives" become co-workers and are, therefore, subject to performance standards. Domestic work performed in the "home" is transformed into productive work that is essential to group economic survival. In Shaker and Sanctificationist texts particularly, female domestic work emerges as the foundation of the groups' exchange-value labor. In fact, the expansion of domestic skills into the public/work domain provided a major portion of group income.

At a deeper level, the merging of symbolism from the home and work domains in the celibate systems echoes the redefinition of gender symbolism implicit in the key symbol of celibacy. In heterosexual symbolism, the separation, differentiation, and opposition of male and female gender identities that legitimate sexual intercourse are paralleled by the separation, differentiation, and opposition of the domains of home and work. In the mainstream, work and family (home) are regarded as separate domains, dominated by opposed symbols (love and money, respectively) and populated by women and men who are also regarded as symbolic opposites. In the celibate systems, unifications of gender symbolism inevitably accompany the symbolic merger of home and work.

The goal of gender unity within the celibate systems does not require the identity of the sexes, however, although the Koreshans come close to this effect. When differences between the roles and identities of males and females are included in celibate ideals, the fundamental unity of the celibate group allows such differences to be conceptualized as variations within a unified economic domain.

For the Shakers, the merger of home and work in a single domain involves the economic interdependence of gender traits. It seems likely that Shaker men valued the talents of their sisters, even though different from their own, because Shaker principles emphasized the economic interdependence of the work of the two sexes. Although like the Shakers, the Koreshans apparently favored the concept of sex roles, unlike the Shakers, they did not link such roles symbolically to the principle of economic interdependence between the sexes. Therefore, the Koreshan system lacks a symbolic basis for the transformation of female symbolism from the natural to the cultural realm. Without such a basis, the unity of the sexes in an androgyne merges female symbolism into a cultural/male world without an accompanying merger of males into a domestic/female world.

In the Commonwealth, on the other hand, the merger of male and female gender symbolism parallels the blending of home and work symbolism. Evidence suggests that each woman, like the community as a whole, symbolized the interdependence of male and female qualities and the parallel interdependence of the home and work domains. Through their support of women's rights and their conscious attempts to support other members of their sex, however, the merger favors the female, and the blended home/work domain takes on female rather than male overtones.

In conceptualizing the merger of the home and work domains, the celibate systems also reverse the mainstream taboo against mixing love with money. Mainstream culture associates that mixture with prostitution and, in order to prevent such perversion, banishes money from the domain of marital sex. Like their mainstream counterparts, the celibates, particularly the Shakers, were horrified by all forms of sexual prostitution wherever they found it, including in traditional marriage. Their definition of prostitution varies from that of the mainstream, however. In their view, sex, not money, is the culprit. Therefore, they chose to exclude sex, rather than money, from the family domain. The sanctified sisters also demonstrated such a choice in demanding their share of marital property. Realizing that their devotion to love, sex, and reproduction had abrogated their economic rights in the family domain, the women acted to incorporate economic justice within the marriage relationship after they had eliminated sex from it.

Because of their eagerness to achieve economic justice and well-being in the celibate family, believers in all groups rejected the idea of women's traditional performance of unpaid and unrewarded labor in the home. Many writers identified the economic dependence produced by such a system as a key factor in female oppression and subordination, as well as in the promotion of male dominance, in mainstream American life.

Believers in all groups also criticized the implications of the nuclear family for the society at large. Many regarded that family form as an institution supportive of self-interest (rather than the common good), of private ownership of property (to the detriment of the unpropertied), as well as of male dominance throughout the culture. In addition, some believers saw an unhealthy alliance between the family and capitalistic economic values. In their view, nuclear families in capitalism serve the interests of the wage earner and his employer, but not necessarily those of the family unit. Many Shakers recognized, for example, that the quality of family life suffered from its subordination to the organizational mores of industrialized capitalism. Some writers also recognized that continued participation in the family structure would only perpetuate the class system by encouraging people to protect private property and its "legitimate" inheritance.

Evidence in all groups further suggests that the symbolic merger of work and family in a celibate system transforms the relationship between the family and economics by uniting the interests of employer and employee, producer and consumer, worker and family member, male and female, as well as by unifying the economic interests of all family members. Within the celibate family, there are no distinctions (and therefore no hierarchies) between wage earners and dependents. As God's children, rather than as merely human progeny, celibate family members share equally in both the physical and the spiritual property of the community. The ideal of unified inheritance was articulated by Shaker writers and suggested by the Commonwealth constitution, which prohibits one sister's gain at the expense of another.

The various mergers and reversals in the systems of the celibate groups are significant as alternatives to mainstream symbolism rather than to actual practices. Many mainstream women, of course, violated cultural prescriptions and earned wages—sometimes for work performed at home. It is clear, however, that female labor force participation did not necessarily eliminate a woman's symbolic associations with the family/domestic domain. The nineteenth-century female wage earner partook of the domestic and feminine symbolism of her unemployed counterparts. Female associations with home and family were so strong, in fact, that they affected the status of the women in the labor force. As symbolic anomalies, working women were frequently relegated to menial jobs in inhumane environments for inadequate pay.

The Spiritual Unity of Nature and Culture

The celibate female achieves perhaps the highest status in the three communal systems in the religious domain. Shaker texts from the late nineteenth century offer two examples of such status. First, the celibate female achieves spiritual equality with her brothers. As denizens of a just, egalitarian New Earth and as equal aspirants to the New Heaven above, both males and females rise above the petty, human-made divisions between nature and culture that plague secular society and stratify the sexes.

Second, the celibate Shaker female is associated with Mother Ann and with the female qualities of God. Writers often expressed that association through the metaphor of spiritual motherhood, which implies both redemptive powers and a special role in spiritual communication. The Shaker spiritual mother is uniquely female because her talents evolve from her metaphorical reproductive capacity, but she is not tied to reproductive activities. Thus she gains status from her gender identity, and theoretically at least, her special powers qualify her for important roles in Shaker life.

The metaphor of spiritual motherhood elevates the status of female gender identity because it unifies natural and cultural symbolism. This merger further mitigates the domestic roles of Shaker women. Their chores become cultural in the Shaker system for two reasons: they are connected with workplace symbolism, and they are associated with supracultural spiritual labors and the cleansing

197

of sin. (Whether such symbolic transformation eliminated the drudgery of housework is, of course, another question. Much Shaker work was drudgery, however, including that performed by the men.)

The Koreshans present a similar model of enhanced female spiritual status. Koreshans shared the Shaker concern with women's rights, both in their own community and in American society. They also substituted divine standards of gender identity for human prescriptions, which they believed were inevitably tainted by the curse of Adam. Like many Shakers, Koreshan writers invoked spiritual motherhood as a metaphor for the spiritual powers of the celibate female. They, too, recognized the celibate female's powers of spiritual receptivity. Such attributes enhance the symbolic status of the celibate female in the Koreshan system and mitigate somewhat the failure of other parts of Koreshanity to transform female gender identity from the natural to the cultural domain.

Koreshan spiritual motherhood is not as enhancing of female status as the Shaker version of the metaphor, however, for several reasons. First, most references to female spiritual powers emphasize a physical form of spiritual reproduction which, unlike the Shaker version of the metaphor, ties it to the natural realm. Further, Koreshan spiritual motherhood has fewer analogues in other powers or roles for women in the Koreshan community than does the Shaker metaphor. In fact, the most important parallel in the Koreshan system for spiritual motherhood is Koresh's own power of theocrasis—a female quality in male shape. The association of spiritual motherhood with a specifically female form of spiritual receptivity does suggest a transcendent, "cultural" female power, but that power is diminished for the human female by its connection with Koresh.

The Sanctificationists did associate femaleness with spiritual power, but not through a metaphor of spiritual motherhood. Female traits other than motherhood, such as intuition and receptivity to spiritual communication, form the basis of the Sanctificationist religious domain. In fact, the exercise of the female unconscious in dreams constitutes religious power in the group's system. Because dreams were considered divinely inspired, having and interpreting them became spiritual acts. Believers' dreams and interpretative powers were sanctified by their commitment to celibacy, and because it is a female trait in the Commonwealth system, celibacy itself symbolizes a specifically female form of spiritual power. The women's freedom and independence in the economic and social world resulted from that spiritual power, as divine inspiration became the basis of social action. Therefore, Sanctificationist spiritual power both created female cultural power and enhanced female cultural status.

The Importance of a Female Divine Model

Overall, the symbolic link between celibate woman and a specifically female God plays a supportive rather than a necessary role in the symbolic elevation of the female in the celibate systems. This conclusion is supported by the differences among the three groups. For example, both the Shakers and the Koreshans identified the celibate female with female qualities in God or Christ, but only the Shaker system entails significant elevation in female status as a result of that identification. The Sanctificationists, on the other hand, made no overt symbolic connection between the celibate woman and a female divine power. Yet their system successfully bridges the traditional symbolic split between nature and culture, reduces woman's confinement to the symbolism of the natural realm, and elevates female cultural status.

A female Deity or divine power becomes important to the symbolic status of the human female in a given cultural system through her representation in earthly terms. The Shakers translated divine female qualities into forms that were significant to the human celibate female. Ann Lee symbolizes celibate woman's redemptive and spiritual powers in the Shaker system. Koreshan views of the female Deity and the Messiah, on the other hand, come from Koresh. His visions of the motherhood of God and of the femaleness of Jesus are the dominant images. The Koreshan woman was offered no exclusive identification with divine female qualities as long as Koresh was their representative on earth. The Koreshan woman shared in Mother God's essences only for highly theoretical reproductive purposes which, ironically, threatened ultimately to deprive her of her female identity. No self-enhancement was predicted from a woman's participation in the process of spiritual reproduction. Therefore, the Koreshan Mother God does not emerge in the texts as a model for the Koreshan celibate female to follow or as a force to be internalized and developed into a specifically female form of secular power.

The Sanctificationists did achieve a specifically female form of spiritual and secular power, however, without a specifically female divine model. The sisters themselves internalized divine power and became its female representative on earth. Thus, their own qualities — their celibacy as well as their dreams and intuitions—signify their connection, as females, to divine powers.

The Religious Commitment to Celibacy

In many ways, the symbolic systems of the Shakers, Koreshans, and Sanctificationists merely signify the transformation of secular culture into spiritual culture, a process shared by many other groups of the past and present. As Christian systems, the three communities certainly shared in the symbolism of the religion itself, which mandates the spiritual transcendence of the mere material relation of blood. Christianity implies a spiritual commitment to God and Jesus that is sometimes understood as a second, spiritual (rather than physical) birth. The communal systems in this study are distinguished from most mainstream religious sects, however, by their varying levels of acceptance of female gender symbolism into their view of spiritual transcendence and rebirth. Mainstream Christians rarely attribute the spiritual rebirth process to female reproductive powers in either God or humans. The Shakers and the Koreshans, however, did attribute spiritual rebirth to the female who, as a celibate, embodies divine powers of spiritual birth-giving. Sanctificationists believed themselves, as celibate females, to be spiritually reborn in sanctification; beyond that they deemphasized the role of God or Jesus, concentrating instead on the role of their own unconscious minds in maintaining their sanctified status.

The celibates also identified female symbolism with the elimination of male dominance in mainstream family life. In addition to encouraging female economic dependence, the family was accused by celibate writers of perpetuating a subordinate religious role for women. To such writers, mainstream Christianity appeared to preserve the family system at the expense of women's spiritual growth. Christian sects typically supported female domestic roles that reduced female status in worship. In the view of many mainstream Christians, a woman proved her religious piety through her devotion to her family and her subordination to her husband in religious matters. Even those women inspired to practice sexual purity or sexual abstinence on religious grounds tended to form their religious identities in domestic terms. For many Protestant women, the suppression of sexuality was inspired by their wish to devote themselves more completely to their homes.[8]

The Shakers, Koreshans, and Sanctificationists, on the other hand, preferred to eliminate the family rather than to shackle woman with duties that deprived her of her rightful relationship to God. The groups' unconventional views of gender and gender relations, particularly within the dual-sex Godhead, were explained in Shaker and Koreshan texts as signs of religiously motivated social justice. True Christianity requires sexual equality in all spheres of life, they explained, thereby reversing the role of woman's piety in the determination of her social status.

The cultural transformations envisioned and, to some extent, effected by the celibates suggest the use of religious principles as a metaphor for both social and individual change. Celibacy links believers with spirituality and divine reason. Ideally, the religious commitment transforms sexual desire from its identity as a drive or compulsion to a new identity as human energy that can be controlled and redirected along a spiritual path. Celibacy lifts its adherents from their "natural" state and carries them into a "cultural" realm beyond human definitions. Celibacy inspires not the oppositions of human culture, but rather the unities of divinity, including the unity of the sexes. Celibacy enables Christians to approach God and God's design for humanity because celibacy eliminates the curse, symbolized by the sexual system, that prevents human beings from achieving that design.

Female versus Male Celibacy

It is not within the province of this study to explore the varying psychological motivations of the two sexes for joining celibate communities.[9] It is clear, however, that celibacy can have different symbolic effects on traditional male and female gender identities. Celibacy offers both sexes an opportunity to temper their symbolic gender identities with traits associated with the other sex and, thereby, to become more balanced human beings. Therefore, men and women can share the goal of androgyny through celibacy. Because male reproductive and sexual attributes place no limits on male social status, however, men have less reason than women to wish to alter their reproductive roles through celibacy. In its link with economic security, celibacy also impacts both sexes identically, because the need for food and shelter is identical for them both. Men's ability to meet that need independently has not, however, been identical to women's. Therefore, women may have been more willing, historically, to sacrifice their sexuality for economic reasons. By the same token, men may be more motivated to join celibate communities at times of high unemployment, such as after the Civil War, or of other social crises, whereas women's economic motivations for joining such groups remains as constant as the social norm of female economic dependence in marriage.

Evidence of celibacy's greater significance to women can be found in the groups' membership statistics. Women typically outnumbered men in the dual-sex communities and constituted virtually the entire membership in the Commonwealth. Women comprised 72 percent of the Shaker population by 1900. There were almost no male Shakers by 1920; in fact, the dearth of males influenced the group's decision to stop admitting new members at that time.[10] In addition to their greater economic need for community, some women may have been attracted to the groups because of celibacy's promise of freedom from reproductive restrictions (both symbolically and actually) and from the dangers of pregnancy and childbirth.[11] Perhaps those factors help explain why Shaker women in the primary childbearing age group of twenty to forty-four outnumbered men two to one (as opposed to the ratio of three to two in other age groups) in nineteenth-century Shaker communities. In one village, in fact, the ratio in the childbearing age group was three women to every man.[12] Many Shaker converts were mothers with small children.[13] Many women with young children also joined the Sanctificationists.

The dominance of women in the populations of these celibate communities may also reflect differences in male and female expectations in and from marriage. Nineteenth-century marriage may well have been more discouraging to women than to men. In addition to its economic consequences for women, the custom of male domination in marriage also resulted in a certain amount of wife abuse, as it does today.[14] Considering the burdens of child-rearing, excessive male sexual demands, and the violence suffered by some married women of the period, marriage may have been a prime motivator for a woman's choice of a celibate life. The depletion of the male population by mid-nineteenth-century wars may also have been a factor in women's greater attraction to the celibate life. Without marriage, women with no independent means had fewer alternatives than did their male counterparts.

Summary

Although they vary somewhat, the celibate systems of all three groups challenge the mainstream symbolic separation of nature and culture that has played such an important role in the subordination and oppression of women. The distinctions and degrees of success among the systems illustrate important caveats in this reversal of a symbolic norm. For the celibate woman to be promoted in cultural prestige, her female characteristics must be defined in cultural, as opposed to natural, terms. Danger lurks in efforts that privilege traditional female traits—such as intuition, piety, and birth-giving—without also emphasizing their cultural rather than their natural implications. On the other hand, depriving woman of a specifically female identity entails different dangers. The Koreshan system minimizes the importance of gender identity, and in the process a male prototype threatens to subsume the identities of both sexes. This phenomenon echoes the experience of those early Christian female celibates who sacrificed their female identities in order to achieve status in their religious system.[15]

The retention of a specifically female gender identity, particularly when accompanied by sex roles, has an admittedly discouraging history of lowering female cultural status. Critics of the Shakers point out that sex roles probably contributed to the failure of sexual equality in Shaker communal practice during certain periods of the group's history. In symbolic terms, however, such a failure does not necessarily detract from the ideal—a concept of sexual difference that promotes female status by linking woman with honored spiritual and redemptive powers of a Mother God. In contrast to the mainstream concept of separate spheres, the Shaker ideal of sexual difference is not meant to reinforce a system of sexual hierarchy.

A further benefit of maintaining distinct gender identities is the promotion of group solidarity and sisterhood among women. This effect is most evident among the Sanctificationists. Evidence also suggests that female solidarity was a feature of Shakerism at various periods.

If these three groups can be seen as a representative sample of the symbolic effects of celibacy on female status, then, on the whole, the maintenance of female gender identity appears salient. Gender distinction permits women to value those aspects of their socialization and experience—including intuition, familial fealty, domestic skills, and nurturance—which they already enjoy and may believe to be beneficial for themselves and for humanity in general.[16]

Although the wish to retain symbolic sex differences may seem somewhat ironic because gender distinction so often produces sexist forms of gender separation, opposition, and hierarchy, its alternative may be worse. Merging gender symbolism in an androgynous model and rejecting traditionally female traits can result in the loss of femaleness altogether. Male characteristics tend to be privileged when no effort is made to preserve femaleness. Gender difference provides a basis upon which woman can shape her cultural power. Gender difference, coupled with respect from both sexes for qualities females have developed, can result in the feminization of a culture gone mad with excessive male influence.

THE SYMBOLIC CHALLENGE OF CELIBACY: NOW

Equality means physical wholeness, virginity—for the woman, equality requires not ever having been reduced to that object of sensuality in order to be used as a tool of men's desire and satiation in sex. What is lost for the woman when she becomes a sexual object . . . is not recoverable.[17]

Although the concepts of celibacy and of cultural structure suggested by the three groups in this study are, in some sense, locked into the nineteenth and early twentieth centuries, they do raise some provocative issues for modern feminism, whether defined as the achievement of equal rights for women or the total reconstruction of American personal and political life. The relevance of the celibate structures of the Shakers, Koreshans, and Sanctificationists may not, however, be found in a literal application of their key symbol. In a cultural context that permits birth control without sexual abstinence and recognizes the value of sex for personal pleasure and relational

TABLE 2. SYMBOLIC UNITIES IN CELIBACY

1. *Female-Male Symbolic Opposition (Sexual Bond)*
becomes
brother/sister egalitarian relationship (nonsexual bond);
spiritual gender unity and equality; and
merging of male and female characteristics in androgyne.

2. *Home (Family)-Work Symbolic Opposition*
becomes
domestic workshop (use- and exchange-value labor combined);
communal ownership of property;
voluntary, objective, but loving relationship criteria;
love/money combination (economic security, not prostitution);
merging of tangible and intangible rewards;
combination of public and private goals and activities.

3. *Religion (Spiritual) v. Family (Blood) Symbolic Opposition*
becomes
spiritual reproduction, spiritual motherhood,* and
spiritual, communal family.

4. *Nature-Culture Symbolic Opposition*
becomes
divine nature=highest form of human culture; and
spiritual perception as evidence of human connection with divine.*

5. *Celibate Symbolic Omissions from Sexual System*
blood;
passion (but not love);
involuntary relationships; and
competition.

* Symbols of female spiritual power.

enhancement, celibacy may no longer be the same transformative key symbol as it was in earlier times. Even though the dramatic effects of celibacy upon female status in the three groups have become clear, they may not support Andrea Dworkin's opinion that only a virginal female can achieve equality with men. In fact, the overemphasis on a single symbol, without reference to the entire cultural system in which it exists, should inspire great caution. After all, celibacy has just as often been used for misogynistic purposes as for purposes of female liberation (Table 2).

Parallel Problems

Many modern feminists would certainly agree with Dworkin, however, that the social roles surrounding female sexuality and reproduction remain problematic for women's achievement of independence and autonomy, as well as for their full participation in the
nondomestic, cultural domain. Like many of the celibates, today's
feminists argue that "body and politic are joined through acts of
the most public and most intimate oppression." They further explain
that female sexual pleasure in modern society remains tied to patriarchal relationships between power and sexuality and that such
relationships will not be easily altered.[18] The most extreme, like
Dworkin, argue that the physical act of intercourse is inevitably an
act that degrades woman because it involves man's physical possession of her body. Regardless of changes in social conditions, Dworkin
argues, the question remains "whether intercourse itself can [ever]
be an expression of sexual equality."[19]

In general, most contemporary feminists also agree that despite
vast changes since the nineteenth century, women continue to suffer
for their participation in heterosexual relations and reproduction.
Women are still responsible and pay disproportionately for sexual
liaisons both inside and outside of marriage. Extra- and pre-marital
sexual liaisons can diminish a woman's social status if exposed,
whereas a man's status can remain unaltered or can even be enhanced
by the same activity. Both within and outside of marriage, motherhood exacts sacrifices of a modern woman's time and identity and
limits her participation in public activities, including those necessary
for a child's support. Fathers are still perceived to be the child's
legitimating parent, while mothers remain primarily responsible for
childcare. Few social structures exist to support or reward mothers
in the fulfillment of their role. Women who mother well are seen
as behaving naturally; therefore, their performance receives no recognition. In fact, a woman's dutiful performance of reproductive
and domestic roles probably earns her less respect in today's society
than it did in the nineteenth century. Although the glories of motherhood are routinely extolled in American society, a woman is rarely
regarded as an expert on political or social questions because of the
skills she has developed in human relations, developmental processes,
or survival through motherhood and home management. Even more

rarely is a grandmother accorded the rank of elder stateswoman based on her maternal and domestic experiences.

It is also clear that although the twentieth century has brought advances in female control over sexuality and reproduction, the ultimate and final right of women to such control has not yet been achieved. Because that right is not guaranteed, celibacy may appear a logical step toward female control of birth and sexual experiences. Certainly, modern women have something to learn from the politics of the celibate communities as they argue for abortion rights and safer, more effective birth control technology. For example, the views of the nineteenth-century celibates on various social questions, including women's rights, tended to be liberal, causing social conservatives to find celibacy objectionable because of its association with objectionable political views. Likewise, those who oppose abortion rights and the freedom to practice birth control in today's society tend also to oppose other related issues, such as the modification of the traditional nuclear family structure and the enhancement of women's roles in organized religious, economic, and political life. This parallel continuum of issues suggests that female control over reproduction—whether it takes the form of sexual abstinence or of abortion rights—has historically implied an increase in female social, religious, and political power. Conversely, the denial of female reproductive and sexual control has historically accompanied a wish to limit female power in other cultural domains.

Contemporary feminists also agree that woman's continued association with domestic responsibilities reduces the status and cultural identification of even her nondomestic, paid work. The demands of nuclear family life, coupled with employers' assumptions about female values and abilities, create barriers for women's achievement of prestigious and lucrative careers. The resulting job segregation affects the employment opportunities and incomes of childless women as well as single mothers. In female job ghettoes, the pay scales reflect, among other things, the low esteem in which woman's work—wherever it is performed—continues to be held.

As in the nineteenth century, workplace gender hierarchies continue today to influence the status of women in the family, even if both partners are employed. Partly because of inequitable pay scales, the man's job is generally regarded as primary. Family members typically organize their lives around its demands rather than those of the woman's less prestigious and less profitable job. Because the symbolism of female gender identity has not kept pace with social realities, that identity continues to resemble its nineteenth-century counterpart.

Like the celibates, many modern feminists have also addressed the over-sexualization of male-female relationships. The sibling metaphor for all such relationships in the celibate families was designed to counteract this hazard by eliminating sex as an option that might threaten socially useful male-female interaction and friendship. Despite social changes over the last ninety years, including greater variety in relationships among men and women, the potential for sexual content remains a threat in today's male-female relationships. In contemporary professional life, for example, the spectre of sex—with its intrigue and its potential to undermine rationality—may reduce men's acceptance of women in decision-making positions involving high levels of authority and responsibility.

The issue of sexual harassment in the workplace can be seen as an example of this continued threat and of the intransigence of traditional gender identities in a new age. This form of sexual exploitation, like rape and incest, is generally defined as an abuse of power through sex. Sexual harassment ordinarily involves a male harasser and a female victim, the logical result of socialization norms that define man as the opposite of woman and find masculinity untenable in a world that blurs gender-role distinctions by allowing women to earn as much money or wield as much power as men do. Inevitably, sex becomes a weapon in male resistance to female audacity in crossing the boundaries men have drawn.

Modern feminists have also debated the value of female separatism, another echo from the experience of the nineteenth-century celibates. Modern ideas of separatism and nineteenth-century celibacy share in the rejection of both male sexuality and male prescriptions for female sexuality in women's lives. Both, therefore, eliminate an important premise for male power over women. The parallel between separatism and celibacy may not be as clear as it appears, however. Although the Sanctificationists were essentially a single-sex community, separatism was never a stated goal of the group. The Shakers and Koreshans assiduously avoided becoming single-sex groups, believing that God's ideal Creation requires both males and females. All three groups preferred the idea of reforming men by eliminating male lust and dominance to the idea of ignoring them and hoping they would go away. The groups' rejection of all forms of sex also distinguishes them from today's separatists, who tend to seek an alternative, lesbian sexuality as the least oppressive, most caring form of sex for women.

Another connection between the celibate groups and modern feminism can be found in shared attitudes toward organized religion. In modern American culture, feminists, like the celibates, frequently challenge or reject traditional religions that oppose their goals and devise more supportive alternatives. To that end, feminist men and women have reformed liturgy, theology, and ritual, at one end of the spectrum, and have revived Goddess religions and witchcraft, on the other. Today's women ministers and rabbis provide the earthly model of female spiritual power so central to the most liberating of the celibate communal theories. Just as religion offered an important loophole through which nineteenth-century Protestant women, both celibate and married, entered and influenced the public domain, religion today offers some feminists a potent source of female power, provided they can find femaleness within it. Today's believers also strive to emphasize within existing religions the potential for human liberation that applies equally to men and women.

As in the past, some traditional religious sects continue to use their cultural power to restrict women. Arguments against women clergy reflect ongoing opposition to female spiritual power within religious institutions. Some groups continue to oppose the incorporation of women and their natural symbolic significance into society's most transcendent cultural/spiritual domain. For those who argue that women cannot represent God or Jesus, the spectre of female reproductive physiology and its association with the debased and sinful flesh frequently looms large.

Few feminists have adopted the precise concept of female redemptive power conceptualized by the celibates in this study, however. That concept emphasizes the role of Christianity in restoring Creation to God's original plan of sexual equality. Unlike the celibate idealists, few modern feminist reformers address the irony of a Christianity that perpetuates the curse of Eden by its continued oppression of women and demand female leadership or other reparations for women's past suffering.

Still ongoing is the question raised by the celibate systems about the possibility of achieving any kind of feminist goals—from sexual equality, to the establishment of female autonomy and cultural respectability, to the restructuring of oppressive social institutions—in the context of gender differentiation. The debate centers on the question of pursuing feminist goals by abandoning female symbolic associations and demanding a recognition that men and women are ontologically identical or, conversely, by embracing positive traditional female traits and elevating their status within the culture. As previously discussed, the latter course was chosen by those groups most successful in transforming female symbolism from the natural to the cultural realm. Their choice risks the perpetuation of the low cultural status attributed to women in the sexist culture that spawned such traits. Yet, abandoning female symbolism altogether risks losing socially valuable and personally fulfilling female characteristics to the traditionally more highly valued male symbolic set.

Contemporary feminists also worry that the denial of female traditions—although they originate in patriarchal culture—disparages the very sex they wish to honor. Recent feminist work on the importance of female subcultures—among frontierswomen, single women, biological sisters, and even married women—suggests that there may be much to gain both personally and socially from maintaining traditional female skills, strengths, and experiences, including those that come with mothering. On the other hand, many despair that without a social revolution, any support for an intrinsic form of femaleness may perpetuate woman's lowly cultural status.

Parallel Solutions?

If, as I have suggested above, contemporary feminism faces many of the same problems, symbolized in some of the same terms, that confronted celibate Shaker, Koreshan, and Sanctificationist believers, is it inevitable that chastity, sexual abstinence, virginity, or celibacy are the proper response to those problems? Given the centrality of female sexuality to modern feminist analyses of many kinds, is celibacy really the answer? Although the symbolic system of heterosexual intercourse remains stacked against women, can celibacy symbolize the same level of cultural revision and the same potential for enhancing female cultural status today as it did in an earlier era?

In contrast to Andrea Dworkin, who rejects heterosexual intercourse (but not, apparently, homosexuality) as the *sine qua non* of female oppression, I am inclined not to take the celibacy mandate literally, for several reasons. First, although heterosexual intercourse in today's culture symbolizes gender opposition, hierarchy, and separation, as it did in the past, its meaning has changed somewhat in the modern world. Heterosexual relations have been separated from reproduction by birth control technology and abortion rights, for example, and therefore the symbolism of reproduction may no longer be identical to the symbolism of sexuality. Heterosexual relations also now symbolize, in part, sexual pleasure for both men and women. Although her discussion is powerful, Dworkin's condemnation of intercourse ignores this newer symbolism. She takes an ahistorical view in her analysis and cites literary examples from several centuries to argue a modern point. She also ignores the possibility of female pleasure in heterosexual relations and characterizes intercourse as a one-sided affair in which men feel pleasure (often from humiliating their partners) and women grit their teeth. Female sexual pleasure is neither limited to nor inevitable in heterosexual relations, of course, but it does occur.

Second, I have argued throughout this book that the problems created by heterosexual intercourse and reproduction are problems of cultural symbolism rather than of nature. The celibates rejected sexuality because of its associations with opposition, hierarchy, and oppression, as well as with sin. Although they remained somewhat fixated on its relationship to sin, they demonstrated through their understanding of celibacy itself that sexuality as a concept is subject to cultural transformation. In their case, it was transformed into spiritual and social energy. In that context, celibacy depends on and utilizes sexuality rather than eliminates it.

In short, the symbolism of sex and its reversal by the symbolism of celibacy is the critical message of the celibate communities. Plucking their solution from their context and transplanting it in the modern world might create a sacred icon from a symbol. History offers too many examples of misogynistic disavowals of intercourse for modern feminists to feel sanguine about the automatic effects of any isolated practice, or symbol, on the solution of complex cultural problems. The modern context must be taken into account, including the development of the symbolic process, and the symbolism must not be mistaken for the real.

Dworkin herself shows some confusion on the latter point. At times she argues that heterosexual intercourse is inherently, naturally oppressive for women, that it is rape, that it is an imperialist act no matter what the feelings or circumstances of the partners. At other times, she identifies the problem not with intercourse but with the distribution of goods and power in society at large. Women are "poorer than men in money, and so we have to barter sex or sell it outright . . . we are poorer than men in psychological well-being because for us self-esteem depends on the approval—frequently expressed through sexual desire—of those who have and exercise power over us," she writes.[20] In this analysis, sex does not cause inequity; it reflects and perpetuates inequities already in place. Why not eliminate the poverty and the psychological oppression rather than the sex?

Many contemporary feminist theorists identify sex as a cultural construct even more explicitly than the celibates did. Some, particularly the French, consider sexual desire itself to be the product of institutionalized forms of power that reside outside of the bedroom.[21] In defining sexuality as a strand in the cultural web that includes not only opposition in gender symbolism but also the private ownership model of family and property, competitive work values, and other negative social characteristics, the celibate systems presage and echo such interpretations. The celibate arguments parallel modern concepts of sexuality as a psychological force, activity, and value system created by culture and thereby subject to cultural changes. The Shakers, Koreshans, and Sanctificationists rejected sex because they perceived its involvement with oppressive and hierarchical modes of family, work, and religion, but their own success at transforming those modes underscores their belief in social mutability rather than in fixed social forms with necessary relationships to sexuality. In addition, both the Koreshans and the Shakers expressed belief in sex itself as a mutable symbol. Writers in both groups discussed sex before the Fall as a symbol of God's original plan for Creation. Lust and sin ruined sex; without the introduction of those evils, they might not have condemned it.

The assumption by Dworkin and others that sex without intercourse has inherent virtue also contradicts the celibate arguments. The celibates rejected all forms of sexual behavior; they did not privilege or even recognize autoeroticism or homosexuality. To be consistent with the celibates, modern feminists wishing to disavow intercourse in order to promote lesbian relations, for example, must analyze cultural influences on that type of sexuality, too. The celibate message insists that culture and sex are intertwined. Nothing can be presumed "natural" or purely individual. Even the person engaging in sex is a cultural product.

Finally, celibacy works as a transformational symbol in the Shaker, Koreshan, and Sanctificationist systems only because believers were also committed to changes in all social domains. Celibacy alone does not produce increased female status or sexual equality. In fact, the history of celibate utopian communities presented in the Introduction indicates that celibacy seldom produces such results. Celibacy increases female status and produces sexual equality only when it is combined with communistic familial and work arrangements, the recognition of female spiritual power, and a commitment to women's rights. The critical symbolic transformation effected by celibacy in the three communal systems results from the merging of domains that are generally separated and stratified in mainstream culture. Through that merging, the separation and stratification of nature and culture are eliminated and a new realm—in which male and female are symbolically unified and equalized and in which female qualities become special spiritual strengths—is created. Included in that transformation is the destruction of certain symbolic truisms: woman equals sin, man equals cultural power, God equals male power writ large, difference equals opposition, intercourse equals the only union of men and women, success equals winning a competitive economic game. The whole complex of new associations must occur in order for celibacy to work. A prescription to eliminate intercourse is, by itself, too simple.

Given the role of heterosexual relations in female sexual pleasure, given the separation of those relations from involuntary motherhood, given the value of voluntary motherhood for modern women, and given the deep meanings of celibacy for the three groups discussed in this book, a choice to accept literally the symbolic solution of the celibates may ultimately be inappropriate. A better choice is to allow their beliefs to suggest "modern" symbolic possibilities. In a sense, today's woman has already embraced new symbols that share in the symbolic reversals of the celibate systems. One is an increased association of woman with paid work. By demanding and, to a limited extent, achieving status in the labor force, today's woman is already transforming female symbolism from the natural to the cultural realm. Another symbolic change is the increased association of men with their identities as nurturing fathers. By supporting male participation in child-rearing and domestic labor, today's Americans are beginning to blur, if not merge, the edges of "traditional" male and female gender identities. A third change, already discussed, is the decreased association of sexually active woman with reproduction through birth control technology and abortion rights. These changes represent the cultural revolution entailed in the celibate systems, even though they exist in a context of sexual activity.

A final symbolic catalyst is feminist activism. By advocating changes in female gender identity, feminism represents the merger and revision of symbolic domains that celibacy symbolized in the nineteenth century. Feminism's articulations of the deep structures of society and of human behavior may eventually contribute to the resymbolization of sexual intercourse. As men and women gain social and economic equality, sex may become what the Shakers and Koreshans believed it was intended to be—a symbol of mutuality and the celebration of human life by physically different human beings, a sign of the ontological sameness underlying sexual difference. New meaning can be given to the symbolism of intercourse. Entry need not represent bodily violation. Food entering the body is not seen as such. Difference need not represent opposition, as the Shakers realized. In short, heterosexual intercourse has no inherent symbolic import. Symbolism is a human creation; humans can change it.

Having defended the possibility of transforming heterosexual symbolism for a feminist future, I hasten to admit that Andrea Dworkin is quite right to point out that misogyny and intercourse have too often been symbolic partners. Changes in heterosexual symbolism must entail new visions of the relationship between sexuality and power. The celibate systems can be seen as guideposts: sex is not merely a physical act, and celibacy is not merely abstinence from that act; the meanings of each are subject to interpretation. The Shakers, Koreshans, and Sanctificationists transformed sexual politics through celibacy. A deep reading of their experiments suggests that sexual politics might be transformed the other way round, by starting with the politics underlying the sex.

NOTES

1. Hélène Cixous and Catherine Clément, "Sorties: Out and Out: Attacks/Ways Out/Forays," *The Newly Born Woman,* trans. Betsy Wing, vol. 24, Theory and History of Literature (Minneapolis: University of Minnesota Press, 1986), p. 64.

2. George Pierce Garrison, "A Woman's Community in Texas," *The Charities Review* 3 (November 1893):28.

3. Entry in Abigail Clark's journal, 1805-1900, Union Village, Ohio. Shaker Manuscript Collection, Library of Congress, Washington, D.C.

4. Frederick W. Evans?, "A Synopsis of Discourses Delivered by Dr. Cyrus Teed of the Koreshan Unity, on Dec. 11th and 13th, at Mt. Lebanon, N.Y.," *The Manifesto* 22 (March 1892): 66.

5. Sherry Ortner and Harriet Whitehead, "Introduction: Accounting for Sexual Meanings," in *Sexual Meanings: The Cultural Construction of Gender and Sexuality,* ed. Sherry B. Ortner and Harriet Whitehead (Cambridge, Eng.: Cambridge University Press, 1981), pp. 14-21.

6. Priscilla J. Brewer, *Shaker Communities, Shaker Lives* (Hanover, N.H.: University Press of New England, 1986), p. 140.

7. See, for example, the accusations answered by Richard McNemar in *The Other Side of the Question* (Cincinnati: Looker, Reynolds, 1819), pp. 130ff. See also the anti-Shaker testimony of Mary (Marshall) Dyer in *The Rise and Progress of the Serpent from the Garden of Eden to the Present Day: With a Disclosure of Shakerism* (Concord, N.H., 1847).

8. Sheila M. Rothman, *Woman's Proper Place: A History of Changing Ideals and Practices, 1870 to the Present* (New York: Basic Books, 1978), pp. 81-84.

9. For a discussion of some reasons that people of both sexes may have joined the Shakers, including a description of Shaker efforts at conversion, see Brewer, *Shaker Communities,* pp. 85-90, 113-14, 150-56.

10. William Sims Bainbridge, "Shaker Demographics," *Journal for the Scientific Study of Religion* 21 (1982): 360. Bainbridge suggests that the sexual imbalance among the Shakers may have been intentional—more girls may have been recruited because they could be counted on to stay in the communities longer than boys would.

11. Carl N. Degler, *At Odds: Women and the Family in America from the Revolution to the Present* (New York: Oxford University Press, 1980), p. 60.

12. D'Ann Campbell, "Women's Life in Utopia: The Shaker Experiment in Sexual Equality Reappraised—1810 to 1860," *New England Quarterly* 51 (March 1978): 29n.

13. Bainbridge, "Shaker Demographics," p. 363.

14. Barbara Eastman, "Feminism and the Contemporary Family," in *A Heritage of Her Own,* ed. Nancy F. Cott and Elizabeth H. Pleck (New York: Simon and Schuster, 1979), pp. 560-61. Carl Degler has attributed the phenomenal rise in divorce in the nineteenth century partially to the response of women to unsatisfactory marriages. He found that 63 percent of divorces between 1872 and 1876 were granted on grounds that imply misbehavior by husbands, including cruelty to wives. He has concluded that perhaps half of those grounds referred to physical abuse. Degler, *At Odds,* pp. 168-70.

15. Jo Ann McNamara, *A New Song: Celibate Women in the First Three Christian Centuries* (New York: Haworth Press, 1983), pp. 109-10. Rosemary Ruether has identified other consequences of the choice of celibacy or virginity by women in the early centuries of Christianity. The assumption of virginity (even late in life) was seen as a means for restoring fallen, carnal woman to a spiritual state. Such an antidote had the effect of increasing the church's overall contempt for female physiology and sinful female "nature" (as defined by church fathers). Also, even though celibate women, especially in the fourth century, experienced the liberating effects of becoming pseudo males (nonsexual females), some church fathers, such as Augustine and Jerome, refused to accept the virility of the celibate woman. They continued to insist that female subordination was natural, even for nonsexual women. Rosemary R. Ruether, "Misogynism and Virginal Feminism in the Fathers of the Church," in *Religion and Sexism,* ed. Rosemary R. Ruether (New York: Simon and Schuster, 1974), pp. 158-60.

16. These ideas have been offered by Sara Ruddick, Carol Gilligan, and others in recent texts. For a summary of such views, see Jean Bethke Elshtain, "Feminist Discourse and Its Discontents: Language, Power and Meaning," *Signs* 7 (Spring 1982): 603-21, especially pp. 620-21.

17. Andrea Dworkin, *Intercourse* (New York: Free Press, 1987), p. 16.

18. Michèle Aina Barale, "Body Politic/Body Pleasured: Feminism's Theories of Sexuality, A Review Essay," *Frontiers* 9 (1986): 81-82.

19. Dworkin, *Intercourse,* p. 127.

20. Ibid.

21. Barale, "Body Politic," pp. 85-86.

INDEX

Abortion rights, 207, 211
Adam and Eve: Koreshans on, 58–59;
Shakers on, 48, 50, 54, 58, 131–33
Adoption, of orphans by Shakers, 87, 89
Adultery, 51, 58
Agnosticism, 62
Alchemy, association of celibacy with,
94–95, 143–44
Aletheia, The, 17
Alfred (Maine) Shaker community,
longevity in, 81
Allen, Catherine, 136–37, 140, 146
Amana (Iowa) colony, 7
American Eagle, 12
Anderson, Martha, 50–51, 52, 55
Andrews, Edward, 91, 175
Andrews, W. Watson, 52–53, 77–78, 86,
130, 133
Androgyny: benefits of, for women, 75;
Sanctificationists on unity of, 75, 102
Anthropology: gender symbolism in,
24–25; sexual symbolism in, 25–32
Atheism, 62
Atonement, Shakerism on, 80
*Autobiography of Rhoda Blake,
1864–92,* 175
Autoeroticism, 213
Avarice, 41; in the work domain, 55
Avery, Giles, 17, 77, 81, 84, 86

Baptism: Koreshans on, 97–98; Sanctifica-
tionists on, 67; Shakers on, 78, 87
Barlow, Joseph, 106
Beecher, Catharine, 35, 110
Belton Investment Company, 110
Belton (Texas) Sanctificationist commu-
nity, 110, 151, 152, 156, 193
Benedict, Ruth, 6

Bennett, A. L., 181
Bible: Koreshans on, 143, 158; Sanctificationists on, 63, 67, 104; Shakers on,
57, 77–78, 127, 128–31, 132–33, 158
Birth control, 34, 204, 207, 211
Bisexual God, 11; Koreshan view of, 10,
102, 143–44, 177–78; Sanctificationist
view on, 102; and sexual equality,
127–32; Shakers on, 10, 76, 82, 94,
127–32, 159*n*1
Biune Genus, 96–97
Biunity in God and Christ, Koreshans
on, 60, 75, 94, 96–98, 100, 142–45,
148–49, 189, 192
Blake, Rhoda, 175–76
Blinn, Henry, 16, 130, 131, 132, 134–35,
137
Blood, as dominant natural symbol, 26,
33–34
Borden, Lucie Page, 18, 96, 145, 146
*Brief Exposition of the Established Prin-
ciples of the United Society of Believ-
ers, Called Shakers,* 17
Briggs, Nicholas, 53, 54
"Broom, The," ii, 8
Bullard, Harriet, 138
Bussell, William, 129, 130
Byrdsall, Annie, 176

Calvinism, 157; male dominance in, 36;
and marriage, 34
Canterbury (New Hampshire) Shaker
community, 9, 16
Canterell, Eunice, 87
Capitalism: American system of work in,
37; association of heterosexual intercourse with, 3; avarice, lust, and intemperance as outcomes of, 41;

217

A Note on the Author

SALLY L. KITCH is an associate professor of women's studies at Wichita State University. She is also director of the Center for Women's Studies, and she has recently been director of the Master of Arts in Liberal Studies program, both at W.S.U. Previous publications include articles on feminist literary criticism and analysis, as well as the analysis of women's cultural status in the nineteenth and twentieth centuries. She is currently at work on a book about the Sanctificationists, which will be based on their recently uncovered private correspondence. She has degrees from Cornell University, the University of Chicago, and Emory University, where she was a Danforth Foundation Fellow.

DATE DUE

The Library Store   #47-0106